Menachem Robinson

The Absolute Truth

The Solution to All Your Problems - Guaranteed in Writing!

Hakodesh Press

Imprint

Any brand names and product names mentioned in this book are subject to trademark, brand or patent protection and are trademarks or registered trademarks of their respective holders. The use of brand names, product names, common names, trade names, product descriptions etc. even without a particular marking in this work is in no way to be construed to mean that such names may be regarded as unrestricted in respect of trademark and brand protection legislation and could thus be used by anyone.

Cover image: www.ingimage.com

Publisher:
Hakodesh Press
is a trademark of
International Book Market Service Ltd., member of OmniScriptum Publishing Group
17 Meldrum Street, Beau Bassin 71504, Mauritius

Printed at: see last page
ISBN: 978-3-639-79415-1

Copyright © Menachem Robinson
Copyright © 2015 International Book Market Service Ltd., member of OmniScriptum Publishing Group

Contents

1

4

PREFACE

The intent of this book is to serve a twofold purpose. One is to relate the story of what happened in my life that led me from a state of total confusion and despair to a life of success, peace of mind and happiness. This is not just to tell my story, but to reveal what may be very familiar situations in your life, and what can be done to rectify your life. Since I consider myself a common individual with very ordinary needs and desires, you may find yourself relating to my previous situation and, hopefully, curious as to how I made changes. It may sound very familiar. As an added benefit, I hope to save you much time in resolving some of life's problems by telling you what I have discovered over decades of probing that has led me and my loved ones to the complete state of peace and tranquility that we enjoy now.

The second purpose is to provide you with the actual sources and examples that led me to some very startling conclusions about life and the world we live in. By trade I am an engineer and always have looked for the logical answers to everything (always asking many questions). I've always had a deep interest in science, but have been disturbed by the conflicts of science and religion. Why are the mysteries of life so allusive that we must go through life without answers? Who is correct in the analysis of this universe, the scientist or the theologist? Through careful investigation I have found answers. Answers, that are not only logical, but completely substantiated by evidence. I do not claim to have all the answers to life's mysteries, but feel confident that I have found the true source for the information. As I continue to probe and answer my questions of life, I feel it important to share my discoveries with others so they can achieve the same joy and peace of mind in having answers. Although I have many fascinating facts to relate, I will not tell you everything that I uncovered, for that would take many volumes (more like thousands, considering one source available to me is presently at 71,000 volumes and increasing rapidly – I will mention this source later. Even where I worship every day I am with thousands of volumes). The most important purpose that I wish to accomplish is to give sources for you to further investigate areas that are of interest to you. I also hope to give you complete confidence that these sources convey the absolute truth about life. I highly recommend that you write down questions that you may have as you read this book. Whether prompted by what you read in this book or just something that comes to mind, I have become a firm believer that the answer exists and should not be ignored – one must only look in the right place.

I wrote this book for my fellow Jews because the conflict that I needed to resolve in my life was centered on finding the truth about Judaism. As a result the message that I wish to convey is pertinent to Jews, but also can be of great benefit to righteous non-Jews. As you will see in my story, I had trouble finding direction in life, with much conflicting information. I also noticed that most people have this problem. I hope with the help of Hashem that by telling my dilemma and where it led me, I can shorten your search for direction.

You may notice in the last paragraph a reference to "Hashem". Out of respect for our Creator, throughout the book I will use Hashem, which is Hebrew for "The Name" as a reference to Him.

You may wonder why I called this book The Absolute Truth. Throughout the book I will make statements or present evidence that should not be read so rapidly that the true meaning is missed. I find most people read quickly and rarely stop to think or analyze what they have read. I suggest that you not read this book, but try to internalize the information. I am suggesting that you stop, perhaps re-read what was just put forth and think more deeply about what you have just read – especially if you are hearing something for the first time (or finding the information totally disagrees with what you have heard).

You may want to reread a subject under two different circumstances. One may be when I discuss an experience that I had that may sound very familiar. I don't believe that my search for the truth is so uncommon. I would like you to think about your experiences and how they may parallel what I went through. The other time for rereading will serve the purpose of giving you chills and making you realize that there is a mysterious, unexplainable aspect to life. As an example, I have been told by friends and relatives "If I could witness a miracle, such as the parting of the Red Sea (which was actually the Sea of Reeds), or a burning bush that was not being consumed, I would have a completely different outlook on Judaism and the existence of Hashem." The fact is all of us have experienced miracles in our lives, but have ignored them without giving them a second thought. I will tell you about miracles that you have witnessed and others that you will be able to experience as you read this book, but you must think about them. If you give them careful analysis, you will conclude that what I am saying seems impossible and may even defy logic. If you investigate, and not just take my word for it, you will be amazed at the validity, and find yourself bewildered at the mystical discovery that you have experienced. As I made such unexplainable discoveries, it gave me a completely new outlook on life by giving me confidence that I have found the absolute truth.

I recommend an additional concept that you should follow when reading this book. Read the book in order of the chapters. If your curiosity causes you to jump ahead looking for delicious tidbits, you will lose continuity and miss many important points. This will cause some of these tidbits to be meaningless.

I must convey one additional note prior to your reading this book. As I will discuss at the onset of this book, I set forth years ago on a quest for the truth. What I have discovered to be the absolute truth about this world and this life is not always easy to accept in fact very unbelievable and sometimes very uncomfortable. I'm not a Rabbi, I don't have to soft-soap concepts that are difficult or impossible to grasp. As an engineer I deal in absolutes. My goal is to disclose concrete evidence of the truth that I could not write about if my findings were clouded with emotions. I do not work on gut feelings, only truths that are supported by substantial proof including empirical data. My intension in writing this book was not to tell you what you want to hear, but to tell about subjects the way they are. You may find some of my answers to questions very disturbing. I don't apologize, but request that you thoroughly research the subject yourself. If you are in total disagreement with what you read, check it out, don't just complain. If your disagreement leads you to investigate, I have succeeded in the mission of this book. An open minded approach is to your benefit. Get angry with me if you want. You can even call me names (but not to my face), but let your anger cause you to want to prove me wrong. Your investigation may bring to you the startling revelations that have come to my life and the lives of my family. Either way, enjoy the adventure. Just remember one concept throughout the book: "If you don't agree with the truth and reality of this world, it doesn't go away." You must fully understand what the reality is; and, you too will have peace of mind. I'll give you one hint that you won't believe, but I'll show you the unshakable evidence. Hint: "All the truth is good news and for our benefit."

MY STORY

I grew up in Philadelphia, Pennsylvania, USA in a typical middle class Jewish family. I spent eight years going to Hebrew school in the afternoons after regular public school. I was an average student, bored and always anxious to get home. My Hebrew education consisted of Aleph – Bet (learning Hebrew), prayers, traditions and holidays. Nothing too exiting, but I didn't know any better, so I went. As I got into my teens it became more of a social affair – a way to be with my Jewish buddies and even meet Jewish girls. Never was there talk of mystical subjects, prophecies or proof of Hashem. The subjects that I studied rarely seem to have any significance in my life. They were cut and dry (very dry) and to be taken mostly on faith. You might want to do a self-evaluation of your life at this point; because, this may sound very familiar to you.

About the time I started college, I became aware of the fact that much was missing. This is the time in our lives when we start to ask deeper questions about the mysteries of life and the universe around us. I studied other faith systems to see what they had to offer and found even fewer answers to my questions. Basic questions such as: Is there a Supreme Creator and, if so, why is He so allusive to us? Who wrote scriptures and what is its purpose, since I really don't understand it anyway? What is the purpose of life; and, why must it include so much suffering? What happens when we die? Is there an eternal life, as we have heard about? Why do scriptures seem sexist; was it written by men for men? Etc, etc, etc.

Even more frustrating was that the sources available for my search for truth didn't seem to be substantial, leaving me with little confidence in my findings. I concluded that everyone has theories, but nobody knows what it's all about. The problem that greatly added to my skepticism was that all the so-called experts completely disagree. I've had conversations with individuals who grew up with the same confusion, and found that many of them had even fewer answers. One good example is the question: Who wrote the Torah? When I asked an Orthodox Rabbi, he answered emphatically "Hashem." The Conservative Rabbi answered that it was written over many years by many great scholars, but inspired by Hashem. The Reform Rabbi told me to believe whatever makes me feel closer to Judaism and Hashem. If you talk to a science minded secular Jew, he'll tell you that the Torah, and even the rest of the Bible, is a bunch of great allegorical stories, but you have to turn to science to understand reality. Then there is the question of what does the Torah even mean. Why read it if I don't have a grasp of its meaning? I've also been told that the Torah and all its laws are antiquated, not for today – that makes Judaism seem old fashion and not pertinent to today's modern life.

By the time I was in my forties I became quite the skeptic, wanting to know the truth, but believing that I've only received bad answers all my life. What was even more disturbing was that if the truth were told to me, I was so skeptical that I wouldn't believe it, or I couldn't even recognize it. I trusted no one. I was deciding truth through my own logic, my own life's experiences – what else was there? The basis for these decisions was strictly "what made me feel comfortable," whether or not the answers could be substantiated by evidence.

Besides my college studies in Engineering, I found myself diversifying and taking many psychology and sociology courses. I am only 15 credit hours short of a psychology degree (which I will never complete since I am retired). I have always found the human psyche a fascinating subject. One particular concept that I was aware of in trying to discern the truth about everything was something called "cognitive dissonance". We human beings have a problem when we become aware of two distinct answers to a question or two solutions to a problem, which are diametrically opposite to each other. We satisfy this problem by taking the path of least resistance. As long as the solution seems comfortable, no matter how far from reality it may be, we justify our behavior and convince ourselves that "wrong" is "right."

Perhaps the best example that I can give is "smoking". For more than sixty years we have heard the medical proof of the dangers of smoking. We have years of statistics telling us of as many as a half a million deaths a years in the U.S. of A. alone from smoke related ailments. Yet, statistics show that we have approximately a million new smokers a year. Are these people crazy? Is the peer pressure of teenagers so great as to override the danger involved? Is the advertising so persuasive to sway us to a life of sickness and possibly early death (painful death as I have witnessed)? Is watching our parents and friends smoke so reassuring that nothing will happen to us? The answer to all these questions is: with cognitive dissonance we can justify it all. It becomes easy to throw out the statistics, based on an exorbitant number of studies of many millions of people, when we can make the statement "I knew a guy that smoked all his life and lived to be 90 years old. I also know someone who never smoked and died at age 20 (of course the person being mentioned died in an automobile accident, but we can ignore that for our purpose)."

I knew that for me to approach any question about life, I would need a very open mind. My skeptical nature should not prevent me from seeing the absolute truth, but should be to an advantage in sifting out the effects of cognitive dissonance, which at this stage in my life. I was suffering a severe case.

I should mention that cognitive dissonance is actual a gift from Hashem and includes a very positive element. It helps us get over the death of a loved one. If we continued to feel the great pain for years to follow, we could not continue in life so easily. I am not saying that we don't continue to miss our loved ones, I am saying that cognitive dissonance allows acceptance and diminishes our grief.

Another example is childbirth. The pain of labor and delivery (as I have been told) is as such that many women at the time say "I am not doing this again!" Cognitive dissonance brings us into the joy of having a new life in our midst, and the desire to have another. If not, the world population would be tremendously smaller.

As an engineer I was involved for decades in Research and Development. What I did for a living is to perform research projects using techniques of science and logic. In an organized approach I basically answer questions and solve problems. In 1991 I came up with an interesting idea. Why not use these same methodical techniques to solve the riddles of life? By organizing my approach in a most scientific way, could I solve all of life's problems and find answer to the deepest questions? The thought may seem comical; but, the direction that it sent me was a path of serious discovery and positive results.

A series of events occurred that changed my life forever. I started to meet people and found myself in certain places at certain times that would all result in me finally organizing my thoughts and discovering substantial evidence of the truth. This series of events in itself was so coincidental, almost miraculous, that I became certain that it was Divinely inspired (but we'll go into that later).

I found that much more is known about our physical existence and the existence of a spiritual world than I could have imagined. What will be important to you as I disclose my discoveries is that you pay attention to the sources I used to get my

11

questions answered, not just the information itself. Once I had gained confidence in the sources, the information became totally valid and easy to accept. From then on I was able to ask further questions of the deepest nature and have complete confidence that I was learning the truth. I mention this because there is a warning that occasionally comes with the truth. Although it is mostly very pleasant, the truth sometimes can be very frightening. Being the skeptic that I was, my human nature did not allow me to always accept what I was hearing or reading, even though I had absolute proof of its validity (more cognitive dissonance). I did go through some tough times of being pulled between my skeptical past and my confident future. I finally came to grips with the fact that I was very closed minded and only could believe whatever felt comfortable through my own logic. Once I got over the fear of hearing the truth and realizing what it meant to me, I was able to accept it and actually feel comfortable. Fortunately my curiosity prevailed and my eyes were opened. The truth not only became very comfortable, but very beneficial.

I mention this because if your search for truth in life, up to now, has put you into a similar category, I hope that you can avoid the anguish of years of discovery that I experienced and come to grips with reality much quicker. My goal as I put forth this information is to save you time and effort, but you must approach the information with certain concepts in mind.

Instead of me telling you to try to forget what you believe as answers to questions, I suggest that you compare your belief with what I've have found to be truth. You must do the comparison by studying the source of the information. If your source is not reputable, or even merely your own logic (with which you are comfortable), admit it and then compare it to my source. You will find my information to have unshakable evidence. I therefore ask you to read my information, but not to take my word for it. Investigate! You will come to the same conclusions that I have. If nothing else be aware that the nature of skeptics is to just ignore the truth rather than investigate.

Most Jews, including me, thought answers weren't even available. This would cause us not to investigate or to give up quickly. There are many unhappy people who are confused and can't find answers and unfortunately go astray in life. As I go into the information, put down the barriers. Open the mind and instead of outright disagreement, stop and do some serious research. Remember to think about what evidence you have (or don't have) that led to your present belief, and compare it to answers that I put forth based on my extensive investigation – thousands of hours of research. I have incredible evidence; don't sell it short. No matter how ingrained in your mind is your system of values in life, question whether it is true according to proper sources, or just comfortable for you based on your own life's experiences. Even if you are up in your years and feel that your value system has served you for many years; evaluate. You may be on a road to destruction and suffering and not know it (many are and I'll tell you why later). Just pay close attention to what you think reality is versus what I am stating. A comparison of the two may prove them not to be the same or even close.

Another concept to keep in mind is that as an engineer with a scientific background, my approach to this was from a very subjective viewpoint. In the past I sometimes felt very turned off at lectures by Rabbis that I believed to be biased, in some cases brainwashed by their education. I believed these speakers to have a very narrow viewpoint of the subject and I found myself quickly rejecting information rather than investigating. I often approached the subject from the opposite direction. I was stubborn with an "I don't buy it" attitude, even though I had no evidence to refute their information.

You, also, should not justify incorrect information on emotions or your sense of logic just because it is comfortable. As I said (and stress strongly), not having to face the truth and accepting it, doesn't make it go away. Before you dispute a source of information which is backed up with concrete evidence, you should get evidence yourself to back up your objection. In other words precede with as open an attitude as possible. If you reject the truth you have done yourself a tremendous injustice because you still have to live with it.

One additional fact about me is that I am a retired US Army Officer. I bring this up to let you know that one of the greatest traits that I have developed over decades is discipline. Doing tasks in my career, which were very uncomfortable but necessary, even for purposes of survival, benefitted me greatly. I learned how to accept the uncomfortable. Another advantage was my career allowed me (and most of the time, family) to travel to 20 different countries and 39 states in the US. I even lived in five US states and eventually on three different continents. The important aspect of this was that my observation of people living the truth, or not living the truth, was not limited to one area of the world and was even multi-cultural.

MY RESEARCH

When I began this effort to search for substantial truthful sources to answer my questions, I found an immediate roadblock. I realized that every source that I read was written by a person. This was not comforting considering they all had the same human frailties as me. They have emotions; they use logic which is based on the experiences of their five senses; and they have the desire to be comfortable with the truth. How can I be certain that I am reading the truth when I am leery about the author? How does one separate fact from opinion?

Then one day in 1991, through the most unlikely source, I heard the most incredible news. On the national evening news the commentator talked about some Rabbis in Israel who put the entire Torah, letter for letter, into the computer. It had been known by many of our great sages for hundreds (or thousands) of years that there are hidden messages in the Torah. These messages are encoded into the Torah and reveal information that no person could have known over 3327 years ago when the Torah was put to parchment. The news program didn't elaborate with an abundance of specific information, but the news intrigued me, especially when he mentioned that it is believed that all of history was written in the Torah before it happened. With this I did a reality check. If there is much information in the Torah that no person, I repeat NO PERSON, could have known, then Who wrote the Torah? Was this the proof that I needed that the Torah, as the Orthodox Jews have always said, was letter for letter from a Divine Source? If these hidden messages were legitimate, then could the Torah be the source of absolute truth? Was Hashem Himself giving us absolute proof that the Torah came from Him and, if so, what did this mean to my research? Additionally, what did all of scriptures have to offer – the rest of the Bible, the Oral Torah (known as the Talmud), the Zohar (the mystical explanation of the Torah), commentary from Rabbis over thousands of years, etc, etc, etc?

My investigation really began in earnest at this point since I found a possible source that I could rely on. I must admit, however, that although I was excited about the possibilities of discovery, my skeptical nature was prevalent and still left me with much doubt.

Since I was approaching this investigation with the best of research and analytical techniques that I have used for decades, I setup a list of criteria by which to gauge the Torah as a possible source of truth:

1. There could be no mistakes. If there were statements in the Torah that were absolutely false, the credibility would be lost; and, I wouldn't need to look at the Torah any further. This includes conflicting statements from one part of the Torah to another. Since I have heard theories about multiple authors, finding conflicting statements could verify multiple authors.

2. I have been told that there are many prophecies in the Torah. Have any of them come true? Prophesies are predictions of the future. We have had the Torah for 3327 years (as of this writing), have any of the future predictions come true? What type of track record could be set by comparing over 3300 years of history with the Torah's information?This is where my investigation expanded with the research to all of Jewish scriptures. The book of the Prophets, for example, should have some correlation to history. Once again, if the events of history didn't correlate with Jewish scriptures, credibility would be lost.

3. Are there any facts in the Torah that no human being of that time could have known? If so, what is the probability of the author making lucky guesses? Was the information specific or so general that it is statistically insignificant?

4. What does the Torah tell us? I've looked at it all my life and really didn't understand its purpose or its meaning. It would serve me little purpose to gain full credibility that the Torah is a source of absolute truth and then find myself not understanding its deepest messages. I knew that I couldn't rely on my own very uneducated interpretation. Important and truthful answers to our questions are often missed because we think we know what we are reading and completely miss the point. Note: I also had to consider the language difference, since scriptures were handed down in Hebrew (was there much information lost with the English translation?)

5. Could I perform a statistical and mathematical evaluation of the Torah information? Is the hidden and not so hidden information found in the text significant or merely random? Was there an abundance of information or just some accidental facts that could also be explained by coincidence? What was the nature by which the Torah holds this information? Is it very interpretive or so precise that its miraculous nature is obvious?

6. Why is the information in the Torah? What purpose does it serve?

7. Were there other phenomena that could give credibility to the truth? Besides the written text, what is the validity of individuals who predict the future, or have very mystical events happen in their lives, that can only be explained as metaphysical or ontological?

With my premise for beginning the research having been established, my next step was to learn more about these mysterious hidden codes, prophecies and any other unexplainable aspects of this thing called Torah (and the rest of Jewish scriptures).

It wasn't too long after hearing the news broadcast that I received my first taste of hidden messages in the Torah. Today there are many books written and many videos made on the subject; but, in 1991 it was difficult to gather information. Through a series of strange events, I had become a member of a particular Synagogue that just happened to have a Rabbi who just happened to come across a lecture by a Rabbi from New York. The subject just happened to be "Coded Messages in the Torah." Soon after watching that video tape, I just happened to be invited to Monsey, New York (an observant Torah community) for a weekend. I heard more about the hidden messages, but just happened to come across someone who suggested a Discovery Weekend Seminar given by an organization called Aish Hatorah. I attended the Discovery Weekend (and highly recommend it for every Jew) and by some coincidence they gave a class on the hidden messages. I mentioned previously that my finding the truth seemed to be destined by Hashem, but this series of "just happened" events was far from over. The point I wish to make is that my confidence in what I had found went beyond mere coincidence. I became aware that I was being led step-by-step to the most miraculous and convincing evidence that "the truth" was attainable. I should add that the codes were only the beginning. I started to discover other ways that information was coded in the Torah and all of Jewish scriptures. How many ways are there? How much info is there (that no human could have known)? Let's find out.

PART 1 - What Are The Sources Of Absolute Truth?

Very simply, the main source that I use is the word of G-d (I only used the G name to make sure you were totally with me – back to calling Him "Hashem"). What? Before I lose you, let me give you details that will astound you and give you complete confidence in what I am saying.

Let us start with the most miraculous text in the world – the five books of Moses, the Torah. It says in the book of Exodus that Hashem dictated the Torah to Moses on Mount Sinai one letter at a time. Hashem actually showed Moses the letters in a fiery display. What we have is 304,805 letters (not one more or less) that was handed down 3327 years ago (as of this writing). The Torah is our handbook of life as well as the blueprint of creation. We have verified over the past 30 years what has been known for thousands of years that "everything is in the Torah" – I mean everything. By putting the Torah into the computer, we have been able to analysis that the Torah contains hidden codes and messages. Everything that happens in the world can be found in the Torah with astounding detail. By reading every second letter, third letter, etc or going up in the alphabet or down in the alphabet, through letter substitution (folding the alphabet different ways), new spaces between the string of letters, etc, etc, etc we see a new body of text with all new information.

Two questions beg asking: how many coded messages are there and how many methods of coding exist. The coded information includes every detail about every person that has ever lived, every animal, plant, tree, blade of grass, rock, insect, every star, galaxy, planet in the universe, etc, etc, etc. In other words, if something exists, it is in the Torah. What you are wearing today, what you had for breakfast, every word that you said today is in there. All of science (the correct answers and even all the incorrect answers that still plague scientists), mathematics, medical knowledge, law, trivia, etc, etc, etc it in the Torah. What are you thinking? "That is impossible!!!!" Now you are catching on.

Next question: What is the purpose of the Torah and why does it include everything?

I am glad you asked. As mentioned above, Hashem gave us the Torah as a handbook of life. It is all the instructions we need on how to survive and thrive for eternity. For a Jew there are 613 commandments that guide our every action in life. When followed properly, we achieve total success and happiness in this world and beyond (more detail of this is forthcoming). Non-Jews have a total of 7 commandments to adhere to. Why the big difference between Jew and non-Jew is also a subject forthcoming.

Note: The absolute truth about everything is known. I didn't say that it is comprehensible by human beings. Since I will convince you that all comes from a Source of Infinite Intelligence, I will tell you truths that I know without a doubt, but do not totally understand. Let's begin with one.

On a much deeper level, the Torah serves a very fascinating purpose. Hashem is consistent. We see, as an example that in every cell in any living organism there is a computerized DNA code. If I said that the body is described in every cell in the organism, it would be an accurate statement. But, a more accurate statement is that the body actually grows in accordance with the blueprint that is the genetic code. If I make the statement that everything in the universe is found with complete detail in the Torah, it is an accurate statement. But, a more accurate and completely correct statement is that **"the 304,805 letters of the Torah is the genetic code of the universe and everything that is in it."** In other words, we are living out the script that is Torah. If it isn't in the Torah, it doesn't exist!

You may ask: Doesn't that eliminate free will (you do ask good questions)? Not at all! Hashem, who is not in this allusion of time that He provided for us (I will expound on that statement in a later chapter), saw in advance every thought that we would have, every word that we would say and every free will decision that we would make. Including everything that we do, Hashem scripted the genetic pattern of our existence.

It is like describing in great detail to someone everything that will happen in a video that you have already seen. It doesn't mean that you have decided what the individuals in the video will say; you have a copy and were able to give a complete description to someone else before they watched the event in the video.

Before I can really get into the meat of the topic and the purpose of this book (what all this truth means to us and how we need to react, prepare and even use the information to our benefit), I need to "wow" you with the fact that Hashem gave us information, thousands of years ago in writing, about everything in this world that has happened, is happening and will happen. The biggest problem that

I have is that it is an overwhelming amount of information that is known. My dilemma: how do I very concisely write it in a book? I personally have about 600 books (in English, not including the Hebrew books) that are mostly concerned with this topic. There is an organization that sells a hard drive compendium of Hebrew books that have been written over thousands of years. They cover scriptures and all the commentaries written in support of what is known, or more appropriately put, what Hashem has told us about everything. That hard drive is now over 71,000 Judaic books of information. Hopefully, you see my problem. Don't think for one second when I give examples of miraculous phenomenon that Hashem has told us that they are the only examples. I could show you 71,000 books of information and not cover it all (that organization is Otzar HaHochma and the number keeps increasing regularly).

1.1 More about Torah Codes

One of my favorite subjects is the hidden codes that are found in the Torah. Why? Being an Engineer, I have always been a skeptic, who wanted proof about everything before saying that this is the absolute truth (there's my favorite expression again). Even though I have been studying Torah and scriptures for about 66 years, it was only 23 years ago that my life really changed because of Torah. In the 1980's when the personal computer came into vogue, there were Rabbis who put the Torah into the computer to sift out coded messages. It has been known for thousands of years that the Torah contains hidden information about everything in its letter structure; but, until the PC came along, it was difficult to decipher. When I started to see what Rabbis, mathematicians and statisticians were finding in the Torah, my curiosity was peeked to the point that I had to get the software used for code finding and check it out for myself. The result of finding this information changed my life. The question about Who wrote the Torah had been solved once and for all.

There were many skeptics and still are today who say "give me any text and I will find accidental random words in it." What I have found over the years was that the individual, who says such a statement, has not studied the Torah codes. Anyone who has looked into the codes, seriously, is totally convinced of its validity. One reason is (as I have mentioned already) the number of bits of coded information in the Torah that no human beings could have known, is infinite. If you think that is impossible, you are starting to catch on to my amazement with the subject. It is so overwhelming that I found no way to avoid the Torah and its message. I became a Torah Jew knowing that the Torah truly

19

was the handbook of life and the only true source of information to guide me and my family through life.

So, what did I actually see that changed me forever? I'm glad you asked since I detected that you too were very curious and maybe even skeptical. I started to see that everything that was happening in the world can be found encoded in the Torah. A real eye-opener was when three mathematicians did a controlled experiment that was so impressive, so profound that it was written up in the August 1994 addition of Statistical Science magazine. Their experiment was to subjectively prove or disprove the statistical validity of coded information in the Torah and to demonstrate that it was not due to random happenstance. The curious among you may view a copy of the full report on line:

http://projecteuclid.org/DPubS?verb=Display&version=1.0&service=UI&
handle=euclid.ss/1177010393&page=record

The study basically asked "if everything is encoded in the Torah, we should be able to put the full names of the most famous Rabbis in history into the computer and find these individuals." The find was to be researched by using Equidistant Letter Sequences, ELS. More simply, ELS is the skipping of letters to detect encoded information. Instead of every letter, maybe every other or every third letter, etc. They came up with a list of 66 names based on write-ups of these individuals in an encyclopedia Judaic. The probability of finding all these names (completely spelled out) was extremely low but would be a good indication of it being in the Torah intentionally. Needless to say, they found all their names (only looking in the Book of Genesis), and miraculously next to each of the names they found their date of death. In later experiments, more recently performed, using much more sophisticated computer hardware and software (doing many more permutations of the experiment), they found their date of birth, date of death, place of birth and more. All this information in text that was written thousands of years before these Rabbis were born. The final conclusion in this secular magazine was:

We conclude that the proximity of ELS's with related meanings in the Book of Genesis is not due to chance.

Before I give you some real cool examples of Torah codes, I want to tell you my personal experience in realizing how difficult it is to encode such information and still have readable text. In the 1990's I was involved with outreach efforts, trying to introduce my fellow Jew to the wonderful world of Judaism. One of the tools that I used, coming from Hashem, was the Torah codes. It was prophesied that in the end of days there would be a big return of the Jewish world to Torah Judaism. The movement is called the Ba'al Teshuvah movement. A working cohort of mine, ask me one day "why do you think Hashem gave us the personal computer at this time in history?" Since the PC allowed many to witness and marvel at the coded messages in the entire Bible, Hashem gave us this tool to prepare us for the time of redemption and Messiah. Thank you, Hashem.

Because I was so fascinated and so involved, I was asked to go to synagogues, schools, Sabbath retreats, etc to lecture on the subject. Since most people at the time were not familiar with the ELS concept, I constructed a simple example in English to demonstrate. My slide said:

I am happy to be in your class to tell you a story.

I told the audience that within this statement was a secret code.

I am Happy to bE in your cLass to teLl you a stOry.

Starting with the H in happy and counting every 8 letters they saw my secret message:

HELLO

This silly example took me about a half hour to construct; but, it gave me great appreciation of codes that were shown to me.

As an example, if we look at the narrative about the Garden of Eden in Genesis 2:7 to 3:3, we find encoded within this short paragraph the names of 25 species of trees that were in the garden (as described in the Talmud). I am convinced when I see something like this that if we were to connect every computer in the world to construct one big supercomputer; and, we attached all the brains of everyone alive today (super brain), we still could not write a Torah.

Another example was discovered by Rabbi Michoel Ber Weismandel, a prominent 20th century Jew, without the use of a computer. As was stated by the

Vilna Goan (another prominent Rabbi who lived 250 years ago), every person is alluded to in the Torah. When the Vilna Gaon was challenged to find a reference to Rabbi Moses ben Maimon, the Rambam, he pointed to the verse in Exodus 11:9 that shows the acrostic RaMBaM is the first letters of each word in the phrase "My marvels may be multiplied in the land of Egypt." The Rambam was also with the name "Moses" and also was great in the land of Egypt in the 12th century. This is the only place in Torah that you will find the four Hebrew letters of Rambam as the first letter of four consecutive words. Rabbi Weismandel was curious to see if the Rambam's most famous work, the Mishneh Torah, was encoded in the text below his name. The fourteen-volume Mishneh Torah still carries canonical authority as a codification of Talmudic law – giving great insight into the 613 commandments that are in the Torah. He saw that by starting with the first Hebrew letter mem, מ and counting every 50 letters (a significant number in the Torah) the word Mishneh appeared. He continued down the paragraph quite a distance and found Torah towards the bottom of the text – additionally with a letter separation of 50 letters. But, why was there such a distance between the two words? When he counted the letters separating the first letter of Mishneh to the first letter of Torah, he saw a separation of 613 letters between them. What a coincidence? To add to the code, the Rambam's date of birth just happens to be in the middle of the paragraph. Cool – huh? (And statistically significant).

Another code that I like quite a bit deals with the Magilah that we read on the holiday of Purim. Magilas Esther appears in the Torah one time. It starts in a verse that just happens to have the word Esther in it (the only place in the Torah) and has a letter separation 12,110 letters (the word Magilah is in Genesis and Esther is in Exodus). What is so exciting about finding Magilas Esther with an ELS of 12,110? That just happens to be the number of letters in the Magilah. Wow, what a coincidence? You can't make this stuff up.

Two more codes of interest to me. My last name Robinson has eight letters in Hebrew. The name is encoded once in the entire 24 books of the Jewish Bible. It has a letter separation of over 19 thousand letters and includes the names of every relative that I have with that name, starting with my paternal grandfather, Abraham. So my last name starts just before the first time Abraham is mentioned and it goes to just beyond the name Betzalel, which happens to be the name of my oldest grandson. All the names of the rest of the family are within that one finding in the Torah. What a coincidence?

I have a friend with whom I went to high school that is not observant, but was interested in all my involved Torah effort. I told him about finding my name in the Torah and, of course, he asked if I can look for his name. It's a little involved but there are verses that are commensurate with everyone's birthday. If you go to the Portion of the week that we read during the week you were born, and, being seven Aliyahs, seven men that are called to the Torah to give a blessing, each Aliyah representing a day of the week, go to the day you were born and read those verses. It actually tells you what your mission is in this world. I looked at one particular verse of the day of my friend's birth that described my friend. Within the verse I found his first name, his last name and crossing over the word was his middle name. What a coincidence?

Since I personally have about a dozen books with codes, scores of printouts, over the years, of events happening in the world that are encoded (of course everything that has ever happened is in the Torah) and even a large number of slides that I used in lectures, I could go on for weeks and not show you everything. Just be totally aware of Who wrote the Torah, and that everything and everybody that ever lived, lives now or will live, is in the Torah. Not just names but every detail of every moment in one's life. What you had for lunch (if you are reading this after lunch), what socks I am wearing today, who you talked to and what you said – there is nothing missing. As I have already mentioned, the Torah is the Genetic code for the entire universe and all of history – there is nothing missing. By the way, there is no such thing as coincidence – everything is destined.

In the Torah there are other phenomena in the coding, not just the skipping of letters. The number that separates the letters of the coded message as an example is usually a significant number, such as 7, a number that appears many times in Judaism. The number of days of creation, the number of days in Passover and Succos (as is stated in the Torah), the number of days we honor a bride and groom or sit Shiva for the departed, etc. We also find multiples of significant numbers such as 7 times 7. 49 is the number of days we count the Omer (signifying the time we left Egypt to when we received the Torah at Mt. Sinai). We saw that in the Rambam code which used 50 and 613.

Another interesting phenomenon is that many coded messages relate to the paragraph within which it appears, either giving more information about the paragraph or telling about something that will happen in the future that relates to the theme of the paragraph. This becomes even more astounding since there are often many messages pertaining to the subject in the same area of text (the more messages the higher the probability of them not being random). In other cases the message is spread throughout the entire Torah. This is significant since the transmission of the Torah from Mt. Sinai to the present would have to be flawless, or this type of message could not have occurred, one letter off and the code disappears. We already saw this demonstrated in the Megilas Esther code that had a letter separation of 12110 letters.

There are fascinating messages to be read directly without skipping any letters. These usually appear by taking words or even full sentences and removing the spaces between the words. By putting spaces in other places within the same text, the string of letters now says something completely different, usually pertaining to the original sentence.

The Torah was given to Moses as letters only. The vowels in the Hebrew language, which appear as symbols beneath these letters, do not appear in the Torah. By changing the vowels one can find an abundance of additional meanings to the text. These differences can change a seemingly insignificant message into a profound lesson in life. There are a tremendous number of hidden and not so hidden messages that appear using this concept of changing vowels.

As I give additional examples of each we can start to see the deeper significance of the message. All these additional phenomena enhance the possibility of the coded messages being legitimate and not just a random occurrence. This will become more obvious as we review examples of hidden messages.

One additional note to keep in mind as you read these messages. As mentioned earlier, you can experience something miraculous as you read. If you apply logic to these messages, you will discover that it is virtually impossible for them to be in the text unless put there on purpose. The only explanation that can be offered for their existence is that some Being had the ability to see all of the future in tremendous detail and had the absolute brilliance to be able to encode all this information in written text. In addition this was all encoded in legible text. We define a miracle as an occurrence that is totally unexplainable and perhaps even violating the laws of physics (or just defying logic) – events being told to us before they occur. With this in mind think carefully about the information that I am presenting and enjoy the miraculous nature of what you are reading.

What does the Torah say about Chanukah? Since Chanukah occurred over 1100 years after Moses received the Torah, it is not covered in the Torah (even though there are passages that allude to Chanukah). In code, however, the list of messages is extensive. Within a small area of text we find the words Chanukah, Judah, candles, eight days, Hasmonean, Mattathias, flask of oil, menorah and 25th of Kislev. All detailed words pertaining to Chanukah. Where in the Torah do we find this collection of words? The portion Mikeitz which is the portion of the Torah that is almost always read on the Shabbos that falls on Chanukah. Once again logic would tell us that this is not accidental, not random and, in the vernacular of many who hear about it, "spooky."

I'd like to mention how I have always been intrigued at how people are fascinated with Nostradamus. His vague predictions of the future in the form of quatrains mystify people. They are so vague that you can interpret them anyway you want in an effort to give them validity. The truth is he offers little. I believe my favorite is that he mentions the name Hister and everyone took this to mean hitler (I prefer not to capitalize hitler's name purely out of disrespect), only off by one letter. Wow! If you check history, you will find that Hister was an ancient name for the Danube River, and that is to what Nostradamus was referring. He didn't know a thing about hitler and probably wasn't even predicting such an individual. It was the Nostradamus enthusiasts (including hitler himself) that made up the almost believable connection. The Torah, however, does mention hitler and even spells it correctly.

In the Portion Noah in Genesis where there is a discussion of the evil inclination, we find numerous coded messages pertaining to World War II. The list is even more incredible than the list found for Chanukah (even though I believe the list for Chanukah to be even longer, I only covered those that I have personally seen). In one small area of text we find hitler the slaughterer, nazi, Germany, Berlin, swastika, eichmann, Auchschwitz, slaughter house, Zyclon B (the gas used in the chambers), one third of the nation (approximate portion of the Jewish population murdered), destroyed, in the hands of the SS, death trains (cattle cars), etc. This list is probably not complete for each time I go to another lecture on the subject I hear about additional messages found. Could great scholars (human beings) have written this in the Torah over 3300 years ago or are we convinced yet of the source of Torah?

Not convinced, let's talk about the Gulf War. In a portion in Genesis that just happens to be discussing war we find Saddam Hussein, Bagdad, Scuds, Russian missiles, the 3rd of Shevat (the day the ground war occurred), and Schwartzkoff. Schwartzkoff? Yes, the General is in the Torah!

How about some modern diseases. In Genesis where Jacob is trying to obtain the birthright from his father Isaac. Isaac is blind so Jacob pretends to be his brother Esau who is the older brother. Encoded in this text is Diabetes, blindness, Pancreas and Insulin.

Even more astounding, guess what we find in the story of Sodom and Gomorra? AIDS! We also find HIV, in the virus, out of Africa, from monkeys, in the blood, and death. The obvious question that comes up each time: "Is the cure for Aids in there?" If there is a cure, it is in there even though I have been told that the words "no cure" appear in the proximity of the other information. Although I have mentioned that we generally don't find coded information before the fact, I heard about the "no cure" code in the mid 1990's. To date, there are medications and procedures that are considered preventative and/or termed as "helping to cause relief," but no actual cure has been found – one that can eradicate the virus once contracted.

The purpose of these coded messages is not for us to have advanced information, but to realize the total validity of the Torah (there are more profound reasons that will be discussed later). Therefore cures to diseases should not be sought. Since Hashem gives us information when He feels we are ready, we wouldn't find these details until it is time. One way to insure this is that the information wouldn't be understood. If I said to you in the mid 1980's that Schwartzkopf is in the Torah, you would have said "What is a Schwartzkopf?"

There are instances where advanced information was found. One was the famous words "Yitzchok Rabin will be assassinated." This was found approximately one year before it occurred. The message was given to Prime Minister Rabin who answered "Don't bother me with such information." It was destined to happen, according to the Torah code found, and it happened. The details about the time, date, place, assassin, etc, were not discovered until after the event took place.

Why can this not be a warning? The Torah is the script for all of history, as I have already mentioned, the genetic code. We are living out the script – the way the Torah tells it, is the way it will or has happened. Can we change the future? Definitely, but the Torah will tell it as such. In other words, it might say how something was to happen, how it was changed and how it happened.

I have been asked, as an example, if the Torah tells me every detail of my life, such as: what am I going to do tomorrow? Or even more curious a question: "What is my date of death?" I answer with a statement: "Please, go over to that microscope, look at the cell and read me off the DNA pattern – specifically tell me the color of the eyes of the person from which it came?" When you are dealing with a source of infinite intelligence, the concepts are beyond our comprehension. Because, the answers to such questions are only known by the Infinite Intelligence; and, it gives us very definite verification of the Torah not possibly being written by human beings.

The messages discussed so far give examples of codes that demonstrate importance of significant numbers, such as the coded messages about RAMBAM or the 66 sages with Yahrzeit. These show that the coded messages are not random. The code of 25 trees in the Garden of Eden demonstrates pertinence to the paragraph. The list for Chanukah is the pertinence to Torah portion. The lists of historical events such as WWII and Gulf War show absolute accuracy about events that happen thousands of years after it writing. The diseases absolutely confirm that NO PERSON COULD HAVE WRITTEN THE TORAH. There are an endless number of coded messages about all of history, such as the American and French Revolutions, the Dreyfus Trial, assassinations and the Holocaust.

An interesting Rabbi who searches for current events as they happen is Rabbi Matisyahu Glazerson, shlita. He has a website with an abundance of information. He has written many books that I highly recommend. One of the best services he offers is his videos that appear on YouTube. As events happen in the world, Rav Glazerson finds the details in the Torah. Recently, there was the news of the lost Malaysian Airline flight. Rav Glazerson found many details about the event in the Torah as it was big news in the media. Yet, here again, is another rare example of a detail being seen before the fact. When the plane was still considered missing, Rav Glazerson found encoded that the plane went down in the ocean. It was a rare situation where we heard about the tragic end before the world was informed. It once again demonstrates that no human being could have encoded this information thousands of years before it occurred.

There are many other messages that go through the Torah with large letter skips. These coded messages prove single authorship, not many authors over time. Why? If one letter of the Torah is incorrect, the code doesn't work.

The Psalms were written about four hundred years after the Torah was received. The word for Psalms in Hebrew is Tehilim, consisting of five Hebrew letters. The Psalms, as the Torah, consists of five books (containing the 150 Psalms). Think about this carefully, it is a little more involved than the previous codes mentioned. If you count the number of letters in each book of Psalms and then use that number of letters to count in each book of the Torah, you will come to the five letters that spell Tehilim. As an example the first book of Tehilim has X number of letters. If you count from the beginning of Genesis X letters you will come to a Tav, which is the first letter of the word Tehilim. The same for the second through fifth books, and the letter count. This demonstrates that the Torah was dictated to Moses on Mount Sinai, letter for letter, and if one letter is off, a coded message as this would not work.

Let's assume that you have been doing a personal assessment as I have been describing some of the many miracles of the Torah. You at this point should be either convinced, or at least, less skeptical about the Torah being Divinely created. If nothing else I hope you're a little more curious as to what all this means. Even if you do believe that there is validity to the Torah being from Hashem and being total truth, there are many other questions that you may have (I know I did).

So far I have only discussed information that is coded by letters separation. When I started my research about 24 years ago I was astounded to find many other ways that hidden information can be found. Here is a list that I started to create when I was doing the initial research:

- Codes – every letter of the 304,508 letters are involved in many coded messages by letter separation – every second letter, every third letter, etc.
- Prophecy – throughout scriptures every letter, every combination of letters, every word, every verse.
- Repetition of words with a significant count – a word may be repeated 7 times, as an example, within a paragraph or Torah portion.

- Gematria, numerology. Words, versus, etc that are related have the same numerical value. Example: there are 613 commandments "in Torah" – the expression "in Torah" has a numerical value of 613. One of my favorite is the "23rd day of Teves in the year 5760" which was 1 January 2000. The Hebrew date has a numerical value of 2000.
- Lashon Hakodesh – shapes of letters, relationship between letters, every letter has multiple meanings, number of letters in a verse.
- Number of verses in each portion that we read every week has significance to the portion of the Torah.
- Number of the verse vs. a year in history. Every verse in the Torah hints to what happened the year that it represents. Example: the 5708th verse (1948) talks of us returning to Hashem – being brought back from where you were dispersed (return to Israel).
- No vowels, every letter, every word and group of letters (including full verses) have multiple meanings just by placing different vowels beneath the letters (the Torah does not have vowels).
- Remove spaces between words and regroup words into new sentences.
- The chant that is sung when reading the Torah. Each chant and combinations of chants have deeper meaning and even prophecy.
- AT-BASH Folding the Hebrew alphabet in half to substitute letters – giving new meaning. Example would be if I took English and substituted an A with a Z, a B with a Y, etc.
- AL-BAM Cutting the Hebrew alphabet in half and doing letter substitution
- ACHBI Another folding of the alphabet
- AVIK-BECHER Another folding of the alphabet
- ACHAS-BETA Another folding of the alphabet
- AT-BACH Another folding of the alphabet
- Next letter up. Substituting as an example in English an A with a B, a B with a C
- Next letter down. Substituting as an example in English a B with an A, a C with a B
- First or second or etc letter in consecutive words. We saw this in the RAMBAM code which the four Hebrew letters spelling Rambam were the first letter of four consecutive words.

- Everything that happens in the world. Every person, animal, plant, rock, etc. is covered in great detail.
- All of science and mathematics can be found encoded.
- Each of the types of code I just mentioned can have a book or books written about the subject (and most do have such books).

The next question. Did I capture all the ways that hidden and not-so-hidden information is encoded in scriptures? Not even a drop in the bucket. According to certain Rabbis that I have asked this very question, there are 600,000 ways that information is encoded. There are many mathematical progressions, algorithms, combinations of methods, etc, etc, etc, delineating methods of encoding. Once again, we are discussing a subject that is beyond human comprehension and definitely beyond human capability.

The next question. What is the total number of hidden messages and not-so-hidden messages in the Torah and all of scriptures that no human being could have known? The number is "INFINITE." You may ask: How can that be? If it sounds impossible that there is no human being or group of human beings that could have created such a text, you have just answered your own question. Only an Omnipresent, Omnipotent Deity with Infinite Intelligence could encode everything that ever was, is and will be in something we call "Torah." Anyone who believes that the Torah was written by a bunch of old men has not studied the Torah.

1.2 How Accurate is the Torah?

The great success of Jewish tradition is the meticulous transmission of the Torah text. But, actually how accurate is it?

How do we know that the Torah we have today is the same text given on Mount Sinai?

The Torah was originally dictated from Hashem to Moses, letter for letter. From there, the Midrash (Devarim Rabba 9:4) tells us:

Before his death, Moses wrote 13 Torah Scrolls. Twelve of these were distributed to each of the 12 Tribes. The 13th was placed in the Ark of the Covenant (with the Tablets). If anyone would come and attempt to rewrite or falsify the Torah, the one in the Ark would "testify" against him. (Likewise, if he had access to the scroll in the Ark and tried to falsify it, the distributed copies would "testify" against him.)

How were the new scrolls verified? An authentic "proof text" was always kept in the Holy Temple in Jerusalem, against which all other scrolls would be checked. Following the destruction of the Second Temple in 68 CE, the Sages would periodically perform global checks to weed out any scribal errors.

1.2.1 Writing a Torah scroll

To eliminate any chance of human error, the Talmud enumerates more than 20 factors mandatory for a Torah scroll to be considered "kosher." This is the Torah's built-in security system. Should any one of these factors be lacking, it does not possess the sanctity of a Torah scroll, and is not to be used for a public Torah reading.

The meticulous process of hand-copying a scroll takes about 2,000 hours (a full-time job for one year). Throughout the centuries, Jewish scribes have adhered to the following guidelines:

- A Torah Scroll is disqualified if even a single letter is added.
- A Torah Scroll is disqualified if even a single letter is deleted.
- The scribe must be a learned, pious Jew, who has undergone special training and certification.
- All materials (parchment, ink and quill) must conform to strict specifications, and be prepared specifically for the purpose of writing a Torah Scroll.
- The scribe may not write even one letter into a Torah Scroll by heart. Rather, he must have a second, kosher scroll opened before him at all times.
- The scribe must pronounce every word out loud before copying it from the correct text.
- Every letter must have sufficient white space surrounding it. If one letter touched another in any spot, it invalidates the entire scroll.
- If a single letter was so marred that it cannot be read at all, or resembles another letter (whether the defect is in the writing, or is due to a hole, tear or smudge), this invalidates the entire scroll. Each

letter must be sufficiently legible so that even an ordinary schoolchild could distinguish it from other, similar letters.

- The scribe must put precise space between words, so that one word will not look like two words, or two words look like one word.
- The scribe must not alter the design of the sections, and must conform to particular line-lengths and paragraph configurations.
- A Torah Scroll in which any mistake has been found cannot be used, and a decision regarding its restoration must be made within 30 days, or it must be buried.

1.2.2 Success of the System

Maintaining the accuracy of any document as ancient and as large as the Torah is very challenging even under the best of circumstances.

But consider that throughout history, Jewish communities were subject to widespread persecutions and exile. Over the last 2,000 years, Jews have been spread to the four corners of the world, from Yemen to Poland, from Australia to Alaska.

Other historical factors make the accurate transmission of the Torah all the more difficult. For example, the destruction of the Temple 1,947 years ago saw the dissolution of the Sanhedrin, the Jewish central authority which traditionally would unify the Jewish people in case of any disagreements.

Let's investigate the facts as we have them today. If we collect the oldest Torah scrolls and compare them, we can see if any garbling exists, and if so, how much. How many letters are there in the Torah? 304,805 letters (79,847 words)

	Words	Letters
Genesis	20,512	78,064
Exodus	16,723	63,529
Leviticus	11,950	44,790
Numbers	16,368	63,530
Deuteronomy	14,294	54,892
Total	79,847	304,805

Letters in the Torah (according to the alphabet)

	Letters		Letters
א	27,057	ל	21,570
ב	16,344	מ	25,078
ג	2,109	נ	14,107
ד	7,032	ס	1,833
ה	28,052	ע	11,244
ו	30,509	פ	4,805
ז	2,198	צ	4,052
ח	7,187	ק	4,694
ט	1,802	ר	18,109
י	31,522	ש	15,592
כ	11,960	ת	17,949

Total   304,805

If you were to guess, how many letters of these 304,805 are in question?
(Most people guess anywhere from 25 to 1,000 letters.)

The fact is, that after all the problems in history, communal dislocations and persecutions, only the Yemenite Torah scrolls contain any difference from the rest of world Jewry. For hundreds of years, the Yemenite community was not part of the global checking system, and a total of nine letter-differences are found in their scrolls.

These are all spelling differences. In no case do they change the meaning of the word. For example, how would you spell the word "color"? In America, it is spelled C-O-L-O-R. But, in England, it is spelled with a "u", C-O-L-O-U-R.

Such is the nature of the few spelling differences between Torah scrolls today. The results over thousands of years are remarkable!

One additional note is that the oldest text that is available for comparison is the Dead Sea Scrolls, which is estimated to be about 2200 years old. Every letter of the Torah that was found in 1947 was exactly as we have in our modern Torahs of today.

1.2.3 Torah Compared to Other Texts

But how impressive is this compared to other similar documents, such as the Christian Bible?

First of all, which would you expect to be more successful in preserving the accuracy of a text?

You would think the Christian Bible, for several reasons. First, the Christian Bible is about 1,700 years younger than the Torah. Second, the Christians haven't gone through nearly as much exile and dislocation as the Jews. Third, Christianity has always had a central authority (the Vatican) to ensure the accuracy of their text.

What are the results? The Interpreter's Dictionary of the Bible, a book written to prove the validity of the New Testament, says:" A study of 150 Greek [manuscripts] of the Gospel of Luke has revealed more than 30,000 different readings... It is safe to say that there is not one sentence in the New Testament in which the [manuscript] is wholly uniform."

Other scholars report there are some 200,000 variants in the existing manuscripts of the New Testament, representing about 400 variant readings which cause doubt about textual meaning; 50 of these are of great significance.

The Torah has nine spelling variants—with absolutely no effect on the meaning of the words. The Christian Bible has over 200,000 variants and in 400 instances the variants change the meaning of the text.

The point of course is not to denigrate Christianity. Rather, this comparison demonstrates the remarkable accuracy of the Jewish transmission of Torah.

1.2.4 The Torah and the Universe

There is a famous story in the Talmud (Eruvin 13a):

> When Rabbi Meir came to Rabbi Yishmael to learn Torah, he was asked:
> "What is your profession, my son?"
> "I am a scribe," was the reply.
>
> He said to me: "My son be careful with your work, for it is the work of
> Heaven. Should you perhaps omit one letter or add one letter — it could
> result that you destroy the entire world.
>
> Rebbe Meir remarked: "Needless to say, I do not err by omitting or
> adding (letters)... but I am even concerned for a fly — lest it come and
> alight upon the right-hand corner of a dalet ד and erase it, thereby
> rendering it a reish ר

The famed commentator Rashi (11th century France) offers examples of how the
addition or deletion of a single letter can lead to a blasphemous or heretical
reading of the Torah — i.e. a mistake that could destroy the entire world.

Maharsha (16th century Poland) explains there is a danger even if the error does
not affect the meaning of the word. This is because of a Kabbalistic tradition that
the letters of the Torah form the sacred Names of Hashem written as "black fire
upon white fire." These letters were employed by Hashem in creating the world,
and it is through them that He sustains it. The deletion of even one letter of this
sustaining force therefore threatens the existence of the world.

Carefully guarding the words of the Torah has been a Jewish priority throughout
the centuries.

Note: A big thank you for this brilliant essay from Yeshivah Aish HaTorah. I
decided that I couldn't do any better to state the importance of every single letter
in the Torah; so, I reproduced it here with some minor embellishments from me.

1.3 Another Way That Hashem Talks to Us.

The next source to be disclosed is prophecy in the Torah and the remainder of
Jewish scriptures. The remainder includes, but is not limited to, the rest of the

Bible, the Oral Torah (commonly called the Talmud), the Zohar and many others. Scriptures are replete with prophecy. In the Torah, for instance, every word, every letter, every combination of letters (thousands of ways to combine and read the letters), even the numerical value of each letter (another subject to be discussed) has profound prophetic significance. We have a long list of prophecies that we are told will happen in the time preceding the end (meaning the redemption, Messiah, 3rd Temple, etc). I have been actively involved for about twenty-four years in comparing what is happening in the world to what will happen just before this time of redemption according to scriptures. With great excitement I can report to you that **all the events have already happened over thousands of year or are happening now, with completion being imminent, and all has come true as written.** The most important concept to take from this is that all of history is in scriptures and most of history is completed with total accuracy according to the prophecy. My confidence level couldn't be higher when I say that all the events meant to happen in history, according to scriptures, is the absolute truth (I love those words). I will only give you a few of my favorite examples since, I have stated, I could write volumes on the subject and not even cover the tip of the iceberg.

One thing that I have found to be true is that my telling you of exciting items that I have experienced, especially miracles (which I could talk about for hours), is meaningless. You digging and experiencing your own discoveries is what does it for you. I hope to direct you to sources, books, videos, etc that will teach you what it's all about, B"N (bli neder means without taking a vow, without making a promise – it is considered very serious in the Eyes of Hashem to promise something and not deliver. I do not wish to be in violation and will add B"N to such statements).

For now, let me tell you some prophecies that demonstrate how Hashem talks to us and guides us. What makes these examples chilling is the detail, not generalities.

One example can be found in Isaiah 21 which talks of the prophecy of the downfall of Babylonia. Babylonia is modern day Iraq. This particular prophecy sounds a lot like the 1991 Gulf War. How so? Isaiah begins by saying that it will be like "Desert Storms". Either Isaiah called the Pentagon 2700 years ago to ask them "what are you going to call this war?" or we have a very chilling prophecy. Many more details can be seen in Isaiah and Jeremiah. What was spooky was that a Dr. Moshe Katz gave a lecture in Tel Aviv one day before the war started. He gave predictions of what was about to happen based on the prophecies he saw in the Bible. Those predictions included:

- The failure to resolve the Gulf crisis by diplomatic means.
- The first war in history to be shown on "live time."
- The coalition of nations against Iraq (Bavel).
- The-blockade of all sea routes to Iraq.
- The use of smart-bombs!
- The uncontrolled oil fires.
- The massive destruction of Iraq.
- The protection of Israel from afar.
- Israel's self-restraint under attack.
- The sealed rooms used in Israel during the war.

Dr. Katz also talked about the devastating Oslo Accord, and where it is prophesied in the Bible.

We get miraculous prophecies even from Rabbis down through the ages. Rabbi Shlomo Yitzhaki, who lived in the years 1040 to 1105, is known to us as Rashi (most of the great Rabbis throughout history are referred to by abbreviated names – either an acronym or by a book that the Rabbi wrote). Rashi wrote miraculous commentary on the entire Bible and the Oral Torah. In Ezekiel 47 we get a prophecy of waters flowing from the Temple Mount and going all the way to "Galila". The waters represent the study of Torah which will come out of Israel and spread throughout the world (the prophecy has been fulfilled). But what is Galila? Rashi explains "to America." What? A Rabbi who lived about 400 years before Amerigo Vespucci (March 9, 1454 – February 22, 1512), after whom America was named, knew about America? No way. Oh contrar – yes way. But, since Hashem put the commentary into the mind of this great Rabbi, he was able to tell us the name of a place centuries before there was such a place. I must make an additional comment about this prophecy. There are individuals who have written on the web that Rashi's statement means "to the border or frontier" and not "to America." We have several things to learn from this. One, the web consists of billions of opinions that are totally bogus and have no other basis than someone's flawed opinion. You can find any answer you want to any question by looking on the web, but not necessarily the correct one. Two, prophecy is miraculous. Hashem telling us what is going to happen thousands of years before it happens, should give one chills. If I told you that Torah study will flow all the way to the border, does that send a chill up your spine? But, telling us that Torah study will spread all the way to America, hundreds of years before there was such a place, gave me goose bumps when I first heard it. Additionally, I heard it for the first time about 19 years ago. I have since told it to about 200 Torah scholars, including some very prominent Rabbis of today. They all agree that it is no less than a miracle; and, that anyone who states that it means something else is not aware of the awesome ways of Hashem. Also, we are told in the Torah to listen to the great sages throughout history that Hashem will continue to give His word and guide us through them. No Yeshivah studies the word of Hashem without studying the Rashi, his commentary is invaluable and helps clarify the text being studied.

Another miraculous bit of information. In the Torah Hashem tells Moses that the redemption will not happen until the two giants, Sichon and Og, are destroyed. Sichon and Og were two kings who were a hindrance to the Israelites when they had to pass through their territory entering the land of Canaan. The statement is, as mentioned above, a prophecy that will take place in the future before we have the final redemption – that the two giants will be destroyed. A Rabbi Yehudah Aryeh Leib Alter (1847–1905), also known by the title of his main work, the Sfas Emes called the two giants "towers." The Talmud (Tractate Berochos) tells us that Moses, who was ten cubits tall, had a sword that was ten cubits long and that Moses could jump up ten cubits. He was able to reach a height of 30 cubits which brought him to the ankle of Og. If you multiply 30X24 (the ankle is proportioned at 1/24 the height of the body) and using the length of just under 22 inches for the length of a cubit (according to several distinguished Rabbis of modern time), we come to approximately 1350 feet. What a coincidence that that just happened to be the height of the World Trade Buildings 1 and 2. Sichon and Og represented materialism which Moses had to destroy for the Israelites to enter in a higher spiritual level. The World Trade Towers were the epitome of materialism in modern times. Hashem didn't make the towers fall, but was aware of the event when He gave us the Torah and gave us the prophesy through the event of Sichon and Og. One additional note was that Sichon was slightly taller than Og and one of the towers was with an antenna that put its overall height slightly above the other. A tremendous amount of information is found in the Bible, encoded in the Torah and described in the Zohar about 911 (Zohar parshas Balak talks about 3 walls falling, since building 7 also fell that day, the sun being blotted out by smoke and dust clouds, a palace like structure being damaged, referring to the Pentagon, etc). I actually have a book, 264 pages long, that gives extensive detail.

There are many prophecies (possibly most prophecies) that the true meaning can only be seen in the Hebrew. When the translation is read, whether in English or any other language, the Bible verses are written but the intended meaning, the true prophecy, disappears. One example is in the prophet Joel 3:3. The paragraph is talking about horror that will happen before judgment day, and how one can avoid the horror, be protected by simply doing repentance. The description in English is: "blood and fire and pillars of smoke, the sun will turn to darkness and the moon to blood (red)." It sounds devastating but it is even more so in Hebrew. The word used for pillars, when describing the smoke, is the Hebrew word for Date Palm. In other words, it is describing a column of smoke shaped like a date palm tree, more commonly known as a "mushroom cloud" shaped column of smoke – a nuclear explosion. There are several places in the Bible that clearly describe nuclear devastation, but only if you read the Hebrew, not a translated version.

This subject can go on for thousands of pages but, once again, it would have more of an impact if you discovered the information yourself. I will, however, be bringing up more exciting and mysterious findings as we go along. The most important concept to observe is that these are not generalities open for interpretation, but are replete with very specific details including dates, places and names, either read outright or encoded – but irrefutable.

1.4 Another Proof - Near Death Experience

All the proof that I sought was to verify that the words in scriptures are from Hashem and that they are totally valid. A very common question that arises is do we have proof that there is a Heaven and Hell? There are many stories of people who have actually died and come back to tell about it. We also get into the question of whether this is the real life here on Earth; or is this a very temporary existence, making our eternal existence "the real life." Even people who have had an out of body experience, without witnessing Heaven or Hell, have testified beyond a shadow of a doubt of our spiritual existence.

The most important thing about these stories is the tremendous consistency giving them total validity. If, as some Psychologists have pondered, this is dreamlike or even allusion, how is it possible for people to have such tremendous consistency and clarity in what they experienced? An impossibility that occurs is people returning with information they could not have known. The first commonly described experience is that of floating above the physical body.

Witnesses describe being aware of all of the events that happened around them even though they may be in a state of anesthetization or even in a coma. When an individual comes out of an operation and can describe every detail that occurred during the operation, it goes beyond a dream or allusive situation. Non-medical people have described the technical details of the operation, conversations that occurred by the medical team during the operation, identifying who was in the operating room, what they were wearing, details about any difficulties that arose, etc. In other words, they described totally impossible information for an individual under anesthetics.

People have gone to Heaven and met relatives that they never knew and came back to tell details of which only the family was aware – not the one who had the near death experience.

The consistent near death experience, where the individuals describe finding themselves in a place of light and great inner beauty, and then "gliding" through a dark tunnel towards a bright light. Many describe a voice speaking to them. Disabled people describe a sense of freedom from their limitations, and almost everyone mentions the loss of human fears from the mystery we call death.

I could never do justice in describing the experience as well as an individual who lived it. There are many videos on the web of individuals telling their stories and how it changed their lives.

The well-known psychiatrist, Elisabeth Kubler-Ross, has seriously investigated the matter of near death experiences for many years. "I know beyond a shadow of a doubt that life continues after physical death," says Ross, summarizing research of more than twenty years. "I am very skeptical at heart and this is why I tested every aspect of this phenomenon with rigor. I discovered, for example, that people who have lost limbs told of how their souls were whole again when they left their bodies. Moreover, people who were blind from birth described to me with incredible precision what the people in the room with their body were wearing — the jewelry they had on, and what they were doing. This is impossible! How could they have known that?"

Kubler-Ross does not feel any need or reason to convince other people of the truth of the phenomenon: "Those who are open to hear it — will hear it. And, if they close their ears, then they are in for a surprise."

Research into the realm of near-death experiences points to shared elements reported by millions of witnesses (an estimated 30 million!) from around the globe.

Back to me. One day while I was involved in our study group, we got into the subject of out of body and near death experiences. Some in the group were skeptical until a particular Rabbi walked by and overheard our conversation. He immediately exclaimed "Oh, it's real! I experienced an out of body experience during a recent operation." He told us how he watched the entire procedure while hovering over his body and was even able to relay all the details after he had recovered. He observed every individual in the room, what they were wearing and even disclosed details of conversation during the operation. The most fascinating detail he told us was that he felt more alive than when he was in his body. He knew that his spiritual experience was the real life. Being a very righteous and honest individual, the Rabbi was extremely credible in his story and convinced the skeptics in the group to believe such experiences do exist and are real.

Rabbi Dr. Akiva Tatz, a renowned Rabbi and doctor explains that this is not the real world. He gives as an example: sometimes when we sleep we have very realistic dreams. We wake up in the morning thinking – that was realistic; but, now I am back in the real world. When we come to the end of our lives and change address, we have the same sensation of "that was a very realistic experience, but now I am back in the real world." Our entire life on Earth will seem like a dream.

Another famous Rabbi verified that Hashem had curtailed the first attempted nuclear attack by Iran on Israel in 2008 (a second attack, was also miraculously curtailed in 2010). Rabbi Mordechai Eliyahu, a"h was sick in the hospital and died. After approximately twenty minutes, he came back to life and told of his experiences in Heaven. He met the eight yeshiva boys who had been killed that summer in a horrific Arab terrorist attack at Jerusalem's Merkaz HaRav Yeshiva. The sacrifice of those boys was an atonement, and the reason Hashem stopped the attack by Iran. Rabbi Eliyahu said that the boys were very happy and had a wonderful eternity that came from their sacrifice. It is estimated that this nuclear dirty bomb attack could have killed thousands it not tens of thousands of Israeli. The boys were totally aware of how Hashem honored them with the save.

There is no doubt about our experience in this life on this physical planet being an opportunity to perfect ourselves and set up an eternity so wonderful, so great it is beyond human comprehension. It is worrisome how people, using their flawed human logic, think they know better. Please, please you owe it to yourself and your loved ones to open your mind, search for the truth and take advantage of the great opportunity of a perfect future. It is a gift and a blessing from Hashem. Just remember the too late date is approaching rapidly (I will discuss all this in later chapters).

1.5 More Proof - Science versus Scriptures

As with many subjects that I have written about, I have many books that try to unravel controversies that have existed for thousands of years. One of the most controversial which is a personal favorite of mine is the subject of the correctness of science as opposed to what scriptures tell us. I have worked as an Electronics Engineer or within some other capacity in the technical realm for about 38 years. I have been surrounded with very science minded individuals of the belief that science has the answers, not scriptures. In the 57 years that I have been studying science, many major changes have come about as new information is derived. There is not too much information that I recall from my studies in the 1950's and 1960's that exists today. However, in the past 3327 years, the Torah hasn't changed one iota (actually even long before that since the Torah was actually conceived by Hashem 2000 years before the creation).

What I have discovered in decades of research is that the laws of Physics, Chemistry and Biology were created by the same One Who wrote the Torah. All of science and mathematics is in the Torah and the rest of scriptures. If science has the correct answer to a question, then there is agreement with scriptures – where there is disagreement, science hasn't caught up with reality, yet. There are some major problems with science that negates total truth being told. One is "science is a business." I hate to be harsh about it but scientists are always fighting each other for whatever grant money is available or whatever employment opportunities exist. To that end, scientists have always attempted to look worthy by coming up with new theories about the universe and the world we live in. It is important that they are correct; after all there is money and their reputation riding on it. This has caused a very dishonest approach to discovering what the reality of everything is. In many, if not most cases, scientists of all types have come up with good sounding theories (guesses) and tweaked reality to fit their theories. Take Darwin, for instance, please take Darwin. He was able to succeed because he came up with guesses that the ignorant atheist community can embrace. I'll talk more about evolution later (as my thoughts evolve on the subject).

Competition is fierce but once one develops a reputation for being a good guesser, people believe almost anything they say. Take Darwin for instance – oh, I already said that.

This cynicism has changed my approach over the years in determining what is true, and what is the effort of a desperate person trying hard to stay employed. The key to my finding the absolute truth came from discovering, on any subject, the answer to my favorite question: "What is Hashem's opinion?"

I have books covering a myriad of scientific subjects that show discoveries made by brilliant scientists over the past 20, 50, 100 years and then seeing that the subjects have been known for thousands of years by our great sages. There are volumes written proving that scriptures have all the right answers and that scientists are catching up.

I'm reminded of the story of the guy that gets a new computer. This is probably about the tenth upgrade he has purchased, after all he has been a computer whiz for decades. He takes it home, takes it out of the box, sets it up, downloads his software package and even though he is not familiar with all the new bells and whistles, after about an hour or two he is getting this thing hummin'. After all he is experienced and knows all about this stuff. Then there is the individual who buys the same computer, looks at the operators manual and within 15 minutes sets it up and gets it hummin'. What's the big difference? One guy is a scientist who by trial and error eventual gains some truth (maybe). The other is the Torah scholar who opens the handbook of the universe to see the detailed instructions from the Manufacturer of the universe. Of course, one is interested in truth the other one already thinks he knows it all – after all he has experience and an opinion based on his experience.

I would like to give you some examples of subjects that we can compare. When we see what scientists have accidently discovered and then see what the Creator of science verifies as the correct answer, it does not take long to gain confidence in the Real Source.

A good way to start is by showing numbers (quantitative analysis) that scientists have discovered in modern times, but then show more accurate readings that Moses was told on Mount Sinai. The age of the universe, as an example, is perhaps the most misunderstood.

The important thing to grasp from this subject is that until the 1980's and probably even the 1990's the most prevalent theory about the universe was the Steady State Theory. It was not until the Hubble Space Telescope was able to see and verify the background radiation of the big bang that scientist officially changed their thinking from the "universe has always been here" to "there was a beginning." In the 1960's when I personally was studying theories of the universe, science was totally opposed to the idea that there even was a beginning as the Torah states. But now, there is no conflict. Wow! The Torah was correct after all and it took many millions of dollars and a space telescope to change the minds of scientists – they just didn't want to open the owner's manual of the universe.

1.5.1 The Age Of The Universe

So, what is the age of the universe? I am glad you asked. By far the age of the universe is the most controversial argument brought to my attention, especially from fellow engineers and scientists. After all, everyone knows that the Torah begins with the six 24 hour days of creation, while science knows that the universe is about 14 billion years old.

The kabbalist (mystical Rabbi) whose studies of the creation account in Genesis are the most precise and authoritative was Nechunya ben HaKanah. Among other matters in which he was expert, Nechunya specifically asserted that the 42-lettered name of Hashem, that is encoded in the text of creation, allowed one to deduce from the creation account the correct age of the universe. Because in his day this kind of information was considered religiously sensitive (as it is today), Nechunya's own explanation of the numbers involved was somewhat sketchy. But another kabbalist who followed closely in Nechunya's footsteps -- Rabbi

Yitzhak deMin Acco – laid out the calculations precisely. These make it doubly clear that the calculations of the "starting date" for the first new moon and of the "primordial year" (which values both Nechunya and deMin Acco used) were to be understood *literally* only insofar as the numbers produce accurate results. NOTE: I have also seen reference to each day of the creation being a Shemitah cycle as we are in now but referring to the 6000 years of history and 1000 years of Shabbat. Each day being 7000 years give us the same 42,000 years derived from the 42 lettered name (6X7000).

Thus, Nechunya claimed that if you properly understand how to use the 42-lettered name, Genesis provides for a period of time between the origin of the universe and the creation of man, namely 42,000 "Divine Years." But a "Divine Year" isn't 365.25 of our days; it's 365,250 of our years (a day in Heaven is 1000 years on Earth, from the Psalms). Therefore, we calculate that between the origin of the universe and the creation of man there transpired 42,000 X 365,250 years. In other words, says Nechunya, Genesis tells us that the universe came into existence *15.34 billion years ago.*

The information that the kabbalists use was derived from sources in the Zohar (the mystical explanation to the Torah).

Science is presently at 13.7 billion years which means they are getting close. From several books that I have on the subject and this Wikipedia write-up:

> The age of the universe is the time elapsed since the Big Bang. The best current estimate of the age of the universe is **13.75 ± 0.11 billion years** (4.339×10^{17} seconds) within the Lambda-CDM concordance model. The uncertainty range of 0.11 billion years has been obtained by the agreement of a number of scientific research projects, such as microwave background radiation measurements by the Wilkinson Microwave Anisotropy Probe and other probes. Measurements of the cosmic background radiation give the cooling time of the universe since the Big Bang, and measurements of the expansion rate of the universe can be used to calculate its approximate age by extrapolating backwards in time.

Using the effects of Einstein's relativity one concludes that the six 24 hour days of the creation took 15.75 billion years, which is .41 billion years different from the Zohar (from Dr. Gerald Schroeder's book, Genesis and the Big Bang). A very detailed answer is needed, but I will try to explain in a nutshell.

The effects of General relativity are due to gravitational pull. The effects of Special relativity are due to velocity. If one could be at the big bang which was the entire universe in a pinpoint (you see the gravity of the situation) and expanded out at close to the speed of light, you would experience such a tremendous slowing of time that the calculations come out to be as follows:

- The first of the 24 hour Biblical days, as viewed from the "beginning of time perspective" would last 8 billion years as viewed by our present relative time.
- The second 24 hour day would slow down and only take 4 billion years.
- The third 24 hour day also would be half of the previous day, 2 billion years.
- The fourth 24 hour day — one billion years.
- The fifth 24 hour day — one-half billion years.
- The sixth 24 hour day — one-quarter billion years.

When you add up the Six Days, you get the age of the universe at 15 and 3/4 billion years.

Yes the final answer is that the universe took exactly six 24 hour days to create and those six days took 15.34 billion years (I didn't say the answer would be easy to understand).

By the way, concerning the age of the world, both Torah and science seem to agree, it is about 4.5 billion years, according to scientific research. The Torah states that on the fourth day of creation the luminaries were put in place, meaning our solar system was established. This interpolates well with the 15.34 billion years as derived from the Zohar, meaning that 4.5 billion years ago would have occurred on the fourth day. This does not fit into the Einstein model, but that is of little consequence since we are comparing modern scientific calculations to the Torah answer.

This was not a simple, nor a cut and dry answer, but I guarantee the Torah has all the answers, not science.

The Rabbis have passed down all the information through the millennia with the commentary of many Rabbi's (Rashi, Rambam, Ramban, Arizal, Ramchal, etc, etc, etc). Like the Torah, all Jewish scriptures and commentary meticulously have been transmitted from Hashem through Moses and all the prophets to us thousands of years later. It is the most reliable body of text in the world. When you get into the depth of Torah, the answers are beyond human comprehension – after all it comes from an Infinite Source of Intelligence.

Books that I recommend that will explain where in scriptures one can find answers to scientific discoveries and other mystical subjects are (there are many others):

- The Coming Revolution and all the other books and videos by Rabbi Zamir Cohen (originally written in Hebrew but translated into several languages including English)
- Mysteries of the Creation by Rabbi Dovid Brown
- Books and videos by Dr. Gerald Schroeder
- Books and videos by Rabbi Dr. Akiva Tatz (my favorite is Worldmask)
- Books and videos by Rabbi Pinchas Winston
- Books and videos by Rabbi Matisyahu Glazerson
- Books and videos by Rabbi Ezriel Tauber
- Books and videos by Rabbi David Aaron
- Books and audio tapes by Rabbi Avigdor Miller
- Videos by Rabbi Yosef Mizrachi
- Books by Rabbi Aryeh Kaplan
- Many others (the problem with recommending is that you leave out excellent books and lectures that are well worth the time. I have only mentioned some of my favorites).

1.5.2 Another Scientific Discovery

As recently as the late 1990's, there was a popular belief that the universe was expanding and would reach a point of equilibrium where gravity would start to collapse the universe. This would be called the Big Crunch. After all, if the universe started with a big bang, it should end with a big crunch. They also believed that this scenario may have happened countless times – a big bang then crunch followed by another bang, crunch, bang, crunch, etc, etc, etc.

Well, this idea disagreed with the Torah, since we know that in the beginning Hashem created a universe that would be here forever. So what was the big revelation of the late 1990's? The universe is expanding at an accelerated rate – meaning it won't slow down, reach equilibrium and eventually crunch. That was one small step for man, one giant leap for the Torah. Go get um Torah – correct again. This was in the international news in December of 1998. I love seeing such startling headlines in the news, especially when it means that scientist, once again, had to acquiesce to what the Torah has told us for thousands of years.

1.5.3 Another Number To Ponder.

How many stars are in the universe? Science calculates anywhere from a few to hundreds of sextillion stars. They overdid it since the Talmud tells one how to calculate the number and it comes to only 1.06434 quintillion. Science is obviously drawing straws since I have reviewed various methods of calculation that they use and found them to be very strange and inaccurate. The only thought is maybe they are including TV and movie stars – there are many of them. One thing they did get correct. The Talmud gives the calculations by stating that space is divided into 12 sectors each being represented by a constellation (the Zodiac which is of Jewish origin). Behind each constellation are divisions and subdivisions and more. By multiplying all that is behind each constellation we get the total for the universe.

Science in 2003 discovered that the universe is shaped like a soccer ball with 12 spherical pentagons tiled together on a sphere. This divides the universe into 12 sectors with all the stars being behind them. Where did I hear that one before? Once again science caught up to Jewish scriptures. I love it.

1.5.4 Disclaimer, Or Is It?

You may think that I am pointing out comparisons that I have no way of knowing the real numbers. Even though if the Torah is correct about everything else, I gain tremendous confidence in what Hashem is telling us. But, let's give another example of something we do have as an accurate measurement. Since the first commandment, of the 613 that are in the Torah, is to celebrate Rosh Chodesh, the head of the new month, it was imperative that the Torah tells us a way to calculate the average length of the lunar month. If we don't know exactly when the new moon appears, we cannot accurately know when to celebrate.

NASA in the 1960's went to the moon. Because their spacecraft was to head to a moon over several days that was continuing in orbit around the Earth, NASA needed to accurately calculate the exact position of the moon and in turn the length of the lunar month. They spent millions of dollars on what was at the time the most sophisticated method of measuring. They came up with a calculation that was 6 millionth of a month different from what the Talmud (Rosh HaShanah 25a) has as a calculation (which was told to Moses on Mount Sinai and put down in the Talmud thousands of years ago).

What is even more exiting is that in the 1990's NASA sent a satellite to the moon and needed to recalculate the length of the lunar month. State of the art measuring methods had improved greatly and gave NASA a calculation that was within 2 tens of a second from the Talmud calculation. Science obviously is getting much closer to what the Talmud calculated for nothing (a much better price – as a taxpayer I object to NASA wasting my money). Once again, trial and error versus opening the handbook of the universe.

Another cute scientific fact comes from the requirement in the Torah for men to wear a prayer shawl, a Tallis, with fringes on it. Actually we are required to wear a four cornered garment that has the fringes on it all the time (except while sleeping). The more important item for our purpose here is that the fringes are white, but in the time of the Temple, there was one blue thread, called Tekhelet, that was in the fringes. Tekhelet is one of the colors mentioned in the Torah, traditionally associated with a shade of blue. There is a Biblical commandment to tie a thread of Tekhelet around the Tzitzit (fringes) of cornered garments. In addition, Tekhelet is required in the garments of the High Priest, as well as for the coverings of the holy vessels. So what is the problem? We anticipate the Third Temple possibly this year, which means returning to the tradition of wearing Tekhelet. The Talmud describes Tekhelet as coming from a sea-creature called a Chilazon. The formula to make the dye for Tekhelet is being researched in Israel in an effort to meet the requirement. But are we sure of the exact color, the exact shade of blue? From artifacts during archeological digs, we have found samples that give us the shade of blue. When a spectrum analysis was performed on Tekhelet we discovered the actual frequency and wavelength that we need for the proper shade of blue. Every color can be designated by the peak measurement of wavelength for that color's frequency. What was the wavelength for Tekhelet? Are you ready for this? It is 613 nanometers (billionth of a meter). You can't make this stuff up.

I recently saw a website from a Jew in Jerusalem named David Avraham. He has the most fascinating information about Hashem's explicit Name in terms of its mathematic and geometric reflections. The website is the Sapphire Magen David and can be seen at:

http://sapphiremagendavid.blogspot.co.il/?m=0

One subject that put a big smile on my face was talking about the two tablets of the Ten Commandments that Moses brought down from Mount Sinai. These tablets were very miraculous as it is. They actually weighed quite a bit, since they were made of solid sapphire and were much bigger than the C, B, DeMille version. The size of each tablet was 6x6x3 handbreadths, which is approximately 22 by 22 by 11 inches. The Ark of the Covenant which carried the two sets of tablets (the first that were broken and the second that Moses brought down from Mount Sinai) plus the Torah and other items, were estimated to weigh about 8 tons, about 16,000 lbs. One of the miracles was that the individuals who transported the Ark did not actually carry it, but the Ark carried them. Even Moses was not able to lift the tablets because of the weight, but that tablets floated as long as the letters were on them. When Moses came down with the first set, and saw the Golden Calf, the letters ascended from the tablets. Moses did not break the tablets, but actually dropped them because they were now of full weight, which he could not hold. Even the letters themselves were miraculous since they were carved out from front to back. Even though one could see that the letters were hollowed out from front to back, if you saw the letters from the rear of the tablet, it was not backwards, but miraculously appeared as they did in the front. There are letters that have a center portion that actually floated within the letter. The letter Samech as an example is like a circle within a circle, ס. The center circle floated and wasn't attached to the outer circle of the letter.

One last miraculous fact about the tablets that is in concert with our subject of science (this I saw on David Avraham's blog). The actual measurements in handbreadths came to 108 square handbreadths per tablet (216 for a set of tablets). The four tablets that were made (first and second set) totaled 432 square handbreadths. The square of that number 432x432=186,624 is the speed of light. The diminished speed through a *'false vacuum'* (which is currently measured at 186,282 miles per second) is a relatively scant 342 miles per second slower). You will also find that the radius of the sun is a function of the number 216, which is the cosmic/mathematic 'root' of 432,000 (the measure of its radius of the sun in miles). David's blog also covers the idea of the extent to which Hashem's Names "rules" over everything, and specifically how its letters give rise to the physical universe and even the history of mankind.

One last caveat to the information in scriptures. After Rosh Chodesh each month we say a blessing of the moon's reappearance after about 3 days of the moon getting larger. One of the blessings says "Just as I leap toward you and cannot touch you, so may all my enemies be unable to touch me with evil intent." It's a beautiful thought, but I once heard a story that the wording was changed. At one time, the verse read "just as it is impossible for me to touch you" (the moon that is)... About 250 years ago, the Vilna Gaon who knew the Talmud by heart, made the change offering insight from the Talmud. He said that we someday will travel outside the Earth and will go to the moon. The impossibility of touching the moon was removed. How did he surmise such a conclusion? The Talmud talks about flying towers that will allow people to fly. The Vilna Gaon's genius expanded the concept of flying towers to mean flight on Earth and beyond. There is nothing missing from scriptures.

This is an endless topic that as long as someone can suggest a new idea scientific or otherwise, information can be found on the subject in scriptures. Letting us know that the great sages and Rabbis of thousands of years ago were aware of what our modern day scientist has discovered and has yet to discover, gives great validity to scriptures and absolute validation to the Source of the information.

1.6 Darwin Nonsense

150 years ago Chuck Darwin wrote a book about his THEORY that Hashem doesn't exist and that everything is here, including all living things, by accident. You may not think that was his actual purpose but knowing his colleagues that supported his effort and the popularity that he would gain from such an undertaking, I believe it was his foremost motive. He came up with such wonderful expressions as natural selection, meaning that nature has some way to just, out of necessity, design itself. With the help of mutations that occur in nature, all the species of plants, animals and even human beings just happened. Chuck stated that after about 100 years of gathering fossils, scientists would be able to document the links between the species proving the evolutionary pattern. He also stated that he can explain everything except the

eye. The eye was way too complicated and sophisticated to have possibly evolved by natural selection.

Well, here it is 150 years later and the only thing that has been proven is how ignorant scientists, governments and the education system can be.

Let's review what was proposed as a theory and what actually has been proven. First of all, it is so convenient that just about none of Chuck's theory can be proven. To prove it evolved by accident instead of being created by a Source of infinite intelligence comes down to personal opinion – not scientific verification. But, let's look at what Chuck told us to observe and what the outcome really was.

He said: After about 100 years of fossil collection, we will see the connection. Well, after 150 years of fossil collection we have seen no connection. Even worse is the total lack of necessary intermediate stages that were needed to complete the picture. As an example, when did we go from cold blooded sea creatures to warm blooded land creatures? Shouldn't we find millions of years of intermediate species making the transition? Another concern: when did we go from scales and fins to skin with hair? Shouldn't we find millions of years of intermediate species making the transition? The biggest thing that was lacking was intelligence.

The entire concept of natural selection ran into a problem. Paleontologists performed statistical analysis determining how long it would take for an organism to form and start to improve or redesign itself. I am not talking about the trillions of parts to all plants, animals, insects, bacteria, humans, etc; they wanted to guestimate how long any one improvement would take. The answer was anywhere from maybe 20 billion years to never. Since the Earth is estimated to be 4.5 billion years, the whole concept of natural selection becomes unworkable. Of course, there is a Dr. Burke who theorized accelerated evolution. Most scientists believe this theory to be farfetched. I see it as a lame attempt at proving that evolution is not bogus. To me it is like saying that an individual is very unhealthy because he is sick all the time or that an individual is very poor strictly because he doesn't have any money. That explains it all.

But wait, we also have the process of mutation to enhance evolution. One problem is mutation is basically a degrading reaction. When two chemicals are mixed together and the resultant compound is a mutation, it means the reaction resulted in something less than what was available to begin with, not something enhanced. Mutation has the same effect on organisms, and could never be used to explain evolved or improved results.

An interesting event that happens every day is that new species of plants, animals, bugs, etc. are found. Biologists, botanists, mishagologists (I think I just made up a new species of scientist) scratch their heads not just because of new species, but that they don't even seem to have a forerunner from which they may have evolved. What, a new species that didn't show signs of evolution? Hashem has a sense of humor – no doubt about it.

Darwin couldn't explain the eye. Way too complicated for it being self-designed. What would have been Chuck's reaction if he knew about the cell structure, especially the computerized genetic code in the cells of every living organism? I would hope he would have abandoned his nonsensical effort realizing there could be no truth to it. In my engineering career I never saw anything simple design itself, let alone something of infinite complexity. Does anyone realize that, to this day, we still, even with our great intelligence, have not been able to create life? What the brilliant scientists have accomplished with amino acids is bearskins and knives compared to real life. We may give a farmer complete credit for making apples, but all that was done was the farmer took a seed, which came from the apple and that we are not able to create, put it in the ground and watch Hashem's miracle come to life. Out of a piece of wood comes a beautiful red, juicy, delicious apple and that happened by accident? Did you ever pay attention to an apple? It is the size of our hands; it is attractive to the eye (only on the outside where the attractiveness is needed – the inside of the skin doesn't have the colorful advertising); it is very nutritious to meet the needs of a human being – one a day keeps the doctor away. It is a very satisfying treat with just the right moisture, taste and appeal (you can even eat the peal). The variety of apples is staggering meeting all kinds of taste and cooking requirements (even though the brilliant geneticists have eliminated many species for financial gain – more brilliance). As an engineer I am so impressed with the design of a single apple. To think that this happened by accident is lunacy.

There are millions of examples of species that cannot be explained by natural selection. I remember a particular bug that I heard about years ago (I don't remember the name -- I'm not a bugologist). This bug protected itself by squirting two chemicals at its predator, which become very lethal when combined. It renders the predator non-functional (a polite way of saying he kills his enemies). The two chemicals are in individual sacks within the bug and are both dangerous to the bug itself. The bug, however, is protected by the design of the sacks. I thought about how this sophisticated system could have evolved accidentally. Maybe the bug himself went to a chemical store and purchased the two chemicals after getting advice from a PHD bug friend that he had. If I am sounding silly, you are catching on. I don't know if I could have engineered such a complicated system, let alone envisioning this happening over millions or billions of years by accident. Besides how did this species of bug survive until the final Research and Development stage had been completed and the lethal system went into operation?

One question: what about all the human-like species that have been unearthed over the past century? Do they not fall into Chuckey's theory even if we can't find a definite connection? It is brought down in scriptures that Moses was of the 1000th generation. Since there were only 26 generations from Adam to Moses, we are told that there were 974 human-like generations before Adam and Eve, but that they were not human beings – just human-like. Since science hasn't found that many prehistoric beings, it looks like the handbook of the universe has the answer again to which scientists needs to catch up. Science always seems to be lagging behind. Of course, we cheated, we read the book. All the details about the 974 generations are too extensive to be discussed here. Once again, I invite you to investigate.

It's interesting that scientists have discovered that 99% of all human DNA is common in all humans and is called mitochondrial DNA. This means that the differences that we have, hair color, eye color, height, head shape, etc are all contained in only 1% of our DNA structure. Paleontologists have concluded that all humankind has descended from one woman. Since this mitochondrial DNA is passed down through the mother and is found in every man as well, they believe also that we all have descended from one man. Paleontologists call this original couple, ready for this one, "Adam and Eve." Those scientists are so clever. There are estimates that modern behavioral humans have been around for about 10 to 50,000 years. Here again, scientists are getting close but don't have the correct number since it is definitely 5775 years since Adam and Eve were created.

You may get from all this that I have very little respect for Chuck Darwin. I would say on a scale of 1 to 10, I would give a rating of about -245. Sorry Charley (there's something fishy about that statement). I never met him personally, but I'm sure he was and still is a Hell of a guy. I know that materialistic atheists, who hang onto his nonsense, are a Hell of a group. I would stay away from them – their future is not too promising.

What did Darwin do and why did he become so popular? Darwin wrote a theory that explains everything without Hashem, even though Hashem is mentioned in the original manuscript; but, I believe, was removed in subsequent publishing. The atheists of his day made him an instant success. But why should this bogus science continue to this day, when everything said has been disproved or determined to be impossible to prove?

The basic answer is yet to be discussed. It is called Jew-hatred. The people of the world are fighting Hashem. They do not want His message and will resort to any fantasy to avoid the truth. Why do the governments of many countries including the wonderful US of A insist that everything has to be done with a separation of church and state (I guess that means synagogue and state, also)? To avoid the truth about this world, even the education system in most countries have to avoid anything that may look like Devine involvement. I think the motto of all public schools should be "Don't confuse me with the truth!!!"

The biggest reason that I know that Darwin and his nonsensical theory is not worth the paper it was printed on is that it disagrees with Torah which I know beyond a shadow of a doubt is the absolute truth. Any deviation from Torah on any point is a deviation from the truth. It is only fair to mention that there actually is an evolutionary pattern mentioned in scriptures, but under complete controlled of the Creator of everything. Any mention of by accident is heresy, and will get the individual a very unpleasant eternity. This is not a good time in history to gamble with ones eternity – our day in the Heavenly court is not too far away and that could evolve into much suffering. Stay with Hashem – stay with the truth; that is my natural selection.

1.7 Mythinformation

There are so many myths about the Bible and Judaism that I thought I would mention a few and clear the air. When I hear such statements as "I don't believe certain individuals really existed; or, I don't think that really happened (especially miracles)," I know that I am talking to someone who has not studied the truth.

Examples:

Adam and Eve (you know, the couple we just talked about). Was there really a first couple or is this just an allegorical example of the beginning of human beings? Other than the proof that the mitochondrial DNA came from a single couple, how do we know it is the couple in the Bible? In other words, what other proof do I have that the first couple was real people? If they weren't, then who is buried in their graves? I happen to live about a half hour's drive from where they are buried in Hebron in the Cave of Machpelah. Genesis 23 records the purchase by Abraham of a plot of ground in Hebron, including a burial cave, for his wife Sarah.

In a deal that foreshadows many such other Middle Eastern deals; Abraham paid an outrageous 400 shekels of silver to Ephron the Hittite. Later, along with Sarah and Abraham, Isaac, Rebecca, Jacob and Leah would be buried there. Jacob's wife Rachel is buried in Bethlehem, which happens to be about 15 minutes away.

What brought Abraham to this cave in the first place? One day when Abraham was grazing his sheep and one went astray, he found the sheep at this cave and noticed an odor emanating from the entrance. He entered to discover that within the cave was the entrance to the Garden of Eden which was the pleasant odor he was experiencing. He then realized that this is the burial cave of Adam and Eve. This is the building that was erected over the cave that is today used by thousands of visitors, especially for prayer.

There is much to be said about all this but the most important idea is the not only were Adam and Eve real people, but also the patriarchs and matriarchs. A side note is that the Garden of Eden also is real. Throughout Israel one can see the burial spots of most of the people in the Torah and even the Bible. The prophets, the Rabbis of the Talmud, the kings, etc are accounted for and not just legendary names, and definitely not mythical people.

Not too far from me are places where events occurred in the Bible.

The valley where David fought Goliath.

This panoramic view of the Elah Valley from the south is an approximate view of what the Philistine army saw as they faced the Israelites in the battle (the highway in the middle was added later). The Philistines were encamped on the south side of the valley and King Saul's forces occupied the hill on the northern side. Yes, it is a real story and they were real people.

West of this area is where Samson lived and fought. Yes, also he was real.

A controversy of the existence of the two Temples can be solved by many archeological finds. They have found so much that came from the time of the Temples. It is easier to send you to sites such as this (there are more – just Google away to your hearts content).

http://www.templeinstitute.org/archaeological_finds-2.htm

The best evidence is the fact that the Moslem Wakf has been destroying as much evidence as they can, since the Arabs don't want the truth known. They are totally aware of what was on the Temple Mount; but, it's not good for business or Arab propaganda if they can't perpetuate their myth. The biggest lie comes from the fact that Islam only dates back to the 7th century, 570 years after the 2nd Temple was destroyed. They certainly can't lay claim to the area if they didn't even exist.

I have always been fascinated by the myth that the Torah was coauthored by many and some of the myth-interpretation (there goes my spell check again) of what is said in the Torah. There are many names for Hashem. Two of the most important are L-rd and G-d (of course that is the English translation). L-rd is the name which has a connotation of mercy – G-d is the name of judgment. The beginning of the Torah only uses the name of judgment and later it switches to the name of mercy. The so-called experts therefore stated that this was due to a change in writer. They didn't consider Adam and Eve were created on the sixth day and mercy was not needed before that. In fact, since the first five days of creation were Hashem creating and judging that it was good, His name for judgment was appropriate. It's easy to make mistakes when you are a literary expert and only evaluating literary style, but not an expert in the text that you are evaluating.

Then, there are those who misinterpret words to satisfy their own agenda. The name of Hashem connoting judgment has what appears to be a plural ending. Generally in Hebrew words are made plural by adding an "im" (for a masculine word) or "ot" (for a feminine word) to the end of the word. The actual translation of the name used for judgment is "the G-d of many powers." Powers being plural gives the name a plural ending, but it is definitely only talking about One G-d. This, of course, has been used by gentile clergy and missionaries for thousands of years who claim that this is proof of the trinity concept. They say "you can see it is right in the beginning of your Torah the idea of g-ds, plural."

58

The absolute proof of them making an intentional mistake is that in Hebrew, as in many languages, the verb agrees with the subject of the sentence. Since it says "G-d created the heaven and the earth" and the verb created is in the singular form, it absolutely cannot be translated as g-ds created. Those who say it is, are greatly sinning and have completely mythed the boat.

There are no errors in the Torah. If someone finds an error, it is definitely that person's error, not Hashem's. There are so many misinterpretations especially if you have a translation in a different language. People are not aware that the King James Version of the Bible has an estimated 20,000 differences from the Hebrew Jewish Bible. Most are strictly interpretive changes but many are intentional to create prophecies that aren't valid. When text in Hebrew is translated into Greek and then into Latin and finally into English, many errors creep in due to the incompatibility of languages. But when your agenda is to purposely change the text, we are back into the sinning category. Hashem's word is sacrosanct and not to be changed in any way. He or she who does will not be happy on his or her judgment day.

Dealing with the Adam and Eve story, there is a myth that the forbidden fruit was an apple. That probably goes back to the Bible story that we heard when we were 5 years old. One reader suggested that Malum is apple in Latin and is the same word for evil. When translated from the original text it could have been misinterpreted. I am not familiar with the word but that is the sort of misunderstanding that has been handed down through the years.

So what was the fruit? We get a hint after the sin occurred. They realized they were not clothed (a polite way of saying you know what). The commentary states that they took leaves from the tree from which they ate, and the leaves that they took were fig leaves, which are bigger. Hence, they must have eaten figs.

One might ask: was the sin of eating the forbidden fruit so severe that it should cause close to six thousand years of problematic history for us needing rectification? There are two answers. One that I will mention here and the other is complicated enough to be covered with more detail later.

Hashem in his mercy is forgiving once we repent our sins, and follow-up with corrective actions. If done inadvertently, we are forgiven after repenting. Adam sinned. When Hashem asked him what he did (Hashem knew, He was testing

Adam), Adam answered "it was that woman you gave me – she made me do it." Not the best repentance; but, instead it was the first tattletale episode, known in Hebrew as Lashon Harah (an evil tong – a very severe sin). Even worse, he blamed Hashem – "You gave me that woman." If Adam had repented, and said how sorry he was and that he would work hard to avoid such sinning (and succeeded – not words, but actions), the sin would have been forgiven and the world history would have been very different. The full answer is much deeper and will be covered at a later time.

1.7.1 Next Topic:

The miraculous splitting of the Red Sea is another very misunderstood episode. First of all it is not the Red Sea but the Sea of Reeds. The story goes that in the 1800's there was a non-Jewish Bible printer who was proof reading his layout and came across the name the Reed Sea. Even though it was totally correct, he thought it was a spelling error and changed it to Red Sea. Even though we know that throughout Jewish scriptures is the name Yam Suf which means the Sea of Reeds, this printer's mistake was adapted by many other printers and became the new name of the sea (both names are valid, but not the same sea – the Red Sea is elsewhere).

Then we have the scientific explanation of why there was no miracle, but merely a fluke of nature. The so-called experts explain that there was actually a ridge in the water and that a wind came along to expose the ridge allowing the Israelites to cross. That explanation eliminated all the miracles involved and even diminished the C B DeMille version (The Ten Commandments) which was also totally inaccurate.

What were some of the miracles that everyone ignores? The main purpose of Hashem trapping the Israelites at the sea was to show them once and for all that Hashem is there and protecting them. He made it look hopeless but it was a setup. They were on a very large beach area that had mountains behind with only one entrance. That way when the Egyptians arrived they occupied the only passageway to get to the Israelites. This made it simple for Hashem to block the Egyptians with the pillar of fire. The sea did not actually split, but instead 12 separate tunnels formed – one for each tribe. They entered on completely dry land. The walls between the tribes were hard vertical surfaces yet, if the Israelites were thirsty, they could put their hands into the wall which became good drinkable water. They did not cross the sea but instead the pathways

60

became semicircular and cause them to exit the tunnels on the same side (according to the Talmud).

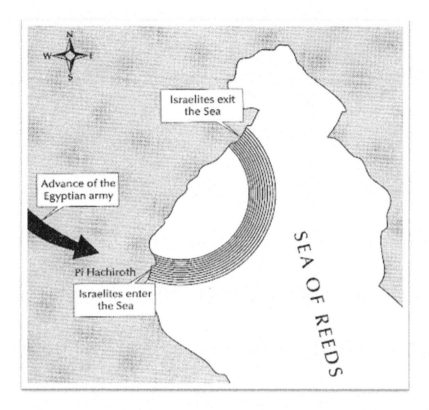

When the Egyptians entered and where completely into the sea area, the ground became soft, the horses stopped (controlled by Hashem), the chariots were mired in the mud and the sea closed. The walls of the sea remained hard surfaces not just to drown the Egyptians but to injure them as a wall falling on them. Their bodies were washed ashore for the Israelites to see since (all within the same beach area). Hashem buried the Egyptians by having the ground open and swallowing the bodies. After that day the Egyptians were seen no more and the Israelites were in total awe of the power of Hashem.

The most amazing thing is that Hashem has provided us with further proof of the event. In recent years chariot wheels have been found at the bottom of the Reed Sea.

Here are some of the many pictures:

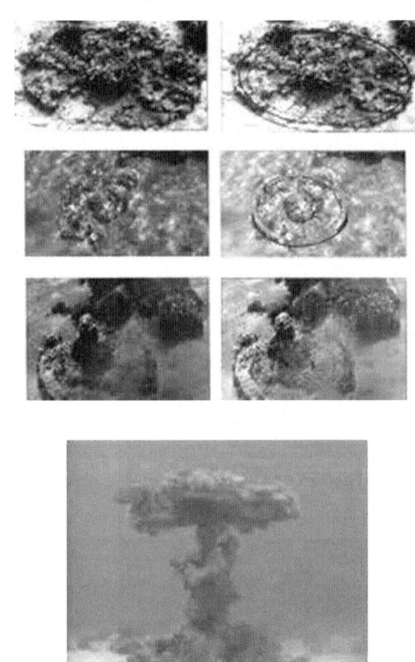

Actual coral covered chariot wheel   **Shape of wheel -- enhanced image**

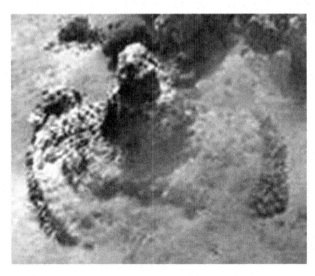

There are so many other miraculous details about the Exodus from Egypt that, once again, I could write a book. Some very curious examples to whet your appetite:

There were an estimated 2 ½ to 3 million Israelites who left Egypt and miraculously they left immediately. How long would it take for that number of people with all their belongings to leave and travel into the desert? There is more happening here than meets the eye.

They were surrounded on six sides by the clouds of glory. It is even brought down that they were in a climate controlled atmosphere and actually rode on the clouds (definitely not the movie version).

One of the factors that determine a kosher animal is that there are no physical defects or blemishes. This is both outside and inside the animal. Since the animals were used in the portable Tabernacle for offerings, they had to be perfect. One can inspect and see the external acceptability of the animal, but as is done today, the internal situation can only be determined once the animal is killed and cut up. That was not the case in the desert. Are you ready for this? The pillar of clouds that was leading them through the desert was actual an X-ray machine. They were able to place the animal in front of the cloud and see if it had internal blemishes (another scientific discovery – not in the last century, but 3327 years ago).

During the 40 years in the desert, they ate the manna that fell from Heaven every day. The manna would take on the flavor of whatever the Israelites craved. The manna also got completely absorbed in the body meaning that for forty years there was no need to go potty (once again I am trying to be polite with my words).

Our entire time in Egypt, the 40 years in the desert and beyond is so replete with miracles and unexplainable events. Many books have been written on the subject. I, once again, encourage you to investigate and be in awe of our history and how Hashem brought us to be a nation.

1.8 The Talmud

I have mentioned that the Torah consisted of the written Torah, the five books of Moses and the Oral Torah or the Talmud, which is necessary in fully understanding and in determining halachah (Jewish law). I found that Wikipedia has a very extensive and accurate write-up which gives more detail than I would cover here. Go to:

http://en.wikipedia.org/wiki/Talmud

There are several concepts that I can add which will help clarify the role of Talmud in Judaism. One misnomer is that it is strictly the opinion of the sages (of the great Rabbis). It is the Oral Torah that was passed down from Hashem to Moses and was taught during the 40 years in the Sinai desert and beyond. The discussion of the sages and the debating of the halachah is not their opinion, but is the accurate handing down of answers to just about any question that could come up about our lives, the universe and everything in it.

Important to know is that the Talmud is not the halachah (law) that we live by. It is the basis for discussion on how halachah came to be. The refinement of halachah as we know it today has occurred for thousands of years. The Shulchan Aruch and Mishnah Berurah along with much commentary of the great sages throughout history are the culmination and fine points of law that have been set down. The disagreement on any topic in the Talmud is intentional as a way of evaluating its interpretation and getting to the truth. As in a court of law, the truth is not known until all arguments are presented. It is not opinion of the Rabbis, but supporting arguments based on verses in scriptures. All is for the purpose of getting to the truth about everything. When there is much debating in the Talmud about a halachah, which is usually the case, it is generally the last presented argument that is considered the answer. However, there are certain Rabbis that we follow and others that we generally don't. There are also arguments that hold true before the Messiah comes and others that will come about after the Messiah. There are many arguments that are left open for Elijah the Prophet to settle. It is so complicated, but that is what makes it fascinating and has kept it alive for so long. If it were simple, we would have stopped studying it a long time ago. All we need to know, as a final answer, is the final codification of the halachah that we live today.

How can I be sure that the Talmud is giving me accurate information – that it truly is coming from Hashem and not the opinion of human beings? There are several ways to gage the accuracy and validity of the text. One is that the Talmud has more outright prophecy (that is more understandable) than the prophecy of the Bible. By that I mean that the Talmud requires less interpretation where the Bible is deeper in its presentation and evaluation. Another point is in the accuracy about subjects that I have already discussed. Science, mathematics, astronomy, medical, philosophy, etc are all with such detail that it could not have been the opinion of the Rabbis, but only information that Hashem could have given to Moses.

One last point of interest demonstrates how the Talmud was so misunderstood throughout history. There are many groups of people who opposed Jewish halachah if it came from the discussions of the Talmud. The say that they believe and follow the Torah as the word of Hashem, but believe the Talmud to be antiquated and only the opinion of the Rabbis, therefore making it irrelevant to our daily lives. The Sadducees, the Essenes, the Karaites, the Xtians, Muslims and even the Reform and Conservative Jews of today have all practiced rejection of the Oral Law saying that they only adhere to the written Torah. I have had the privilege of working with people of this belief. I like to give them a test – just some simple questions, such as: Do you light Shabbos candles? Do you light Chanukah candles? Do you celebrate Purim (giving shalach manos, drinking, wearing a costume, a big meal, etc), do you wear shatnez (combining wool and linen), do you mix milk and meat, do you observe ritual purity (there are actually many questions pertaining to this subject)? Everything that these people have said yes to was a custom from the Talmud. Everything they said no to or maybe partially was a definite commandment from the Torah. I know, it is not nice to trick people but the point is clear. Most Jews know very little about Judaism because they haven't studied what Judaism really entails and, more importantly, what obligations have come directly from Hashem. All obligations really come from Hashem; but, if Jews believe that they don't have to do something because some Rabbi said it thousands of years ago, they are deceived and not meeting their obligations as Jews.

Hashem has instructed us in scriptures to follow the words of the great Rabbis. Hashem has continued to give us instruction to this very day through the greats of today. Knowing who are the Poskim, which are the authoritative sources to follow, and who are not authoritative individuals to whom you should not listen is part of the education one gets in studying Torah. I found that you often can find a Rabbi who will go along with whatever you want to do. It is extremely dangerous if you live by a Rabbi's opinion that is not adhering to the Torah. The only opinion that is valid is Hashem's opinion and that can only come from the right books and the right people. It is a very difficult subject but the bottom line is always measure for measure between you and Hashem. Education is the answer.

As I had mentioned that the Torah is the genetic code for everything. That means that the events of the world and the events of our lives are not documented in the Torah, but are happening because of the Torah letter sequence – we are living out the script called Torah.

In the same way, the Talmud Rabbis are not just interpreting the answers to questions, especially halachic concerns, the answer are happening because of what they said. Hashem put into them the genetic code, so-to-speak, to cause their arguments to occur as they stated them. It is interesting that the Torah was not questioned in any way as long as there were prophets to continue Hashem's instructions. The Oral law was known by everyone and lived by everyone. After the prophets no longer existed, and the Oral Torah was put to parchment, Hashem made sure that His word was carried on by the great sages of the Talmud.

The study of Torah covers everything that exists in the universe and in life. Although we have very clear cut halachic guidance, the learning of how we got to each obligation is not so simple, but is fascinating. Hashem wants us to be partners in creation and to be involved. It makes our daily lives much more interesting than just reading and following directions. We are not a "blind faith" belief system but diggers of the truth. We are greatly encouraged to ask questions. It gives us great confidence in what we do. The truth is what our future is. Getting deeper and deeper into the study of all its details is our preparation for the future time – the time of the redemption and the Messiah (which I believe is a lot closer than we think).

1.8.1 The Oral Torah

Wait a minute, you just talked about the Talmud and now you want to talk about it again by just changing the name? Further information to clarify a very, very deep subject.

First of all it should be made clear that the Torah consists of more than the written five books of Moses. It is brought down that all the empty space on the original Torah that Moshe (I think I will start calling Moses by his real name) wrote contained the information of the Oral Torah. Whether that is literally or figuratively true is unimportant – the message is that Moshe was taught all the detailed information that was eventually written in the Talmud. To say that the information came from the Rabbis and not from Hashem is blasphemy – the Rabbis codified the information but it was handed down from Mount Sinai. It is the excuse that all the heretical groups used for thousands of years to not follow the word of Hashem. Proof of all this can only be seen by scholars of the Oral Torah, who see very quickly that what the Rabbis said could not have come from them.

The Oral Torah, the Talmud which is a very detailed and complete explanation of the laws in the Torah, was passed down orally until the time of the Roman siege. The Oral Torah faced the problem of the information being lost after the Jews were exiled from their land. To preserve the Oral Law, the sages of Babylon constructed the written Talmud that we study today. The event was miraculous and proved to be very accurate, guided by Hashem all the way. Rabbi Judah the Prince gathered Rabbis from all over who had knowledge of the Oral Torah. He found that even though they were strangers to each other, they had the exact same details handed down through their Rabbis.

This miracle could have come only from Hashem. Another great miracle is that a tremendous amount of prophecy is in the Talmud. The Rabbis disclosed details of what was coming up including that which is happening in modern times. If this were their opinion, then they seem to have had the same opinion as the prophets who received the information from Hashem. You may think "well, that is where they got their info." Fact is they came up with details that are not in prophecy and are only being disclosed in our generation. As I mentioned above, Hashem made sure that what they said happened exactly as they stated it. I have already covered some examples:

That before redemption can happen, the two giants, Sichon and Og, called two towers must be destroyed. My calculations came from the Talmud description of their height is prophetically the height of the World Trade Center towers. It is an obvious message from Hashem. How did the Rabbis know that?

The crossing of the Sea of Reeds and the miraculous detail. How did the Rabbis know that?

The number of stars in the universe and much more information about outer space that scientist have only discovered in recent years (or haven't discovered yet). How did the Rabbis know that?

The details about kosher animals, birds, fish and crawling things (details are forthcoming in a later chapter). How did the Rabbis know that?

All of science and mathematics is covered, both overtly and covertly. How did the Rabbis know that?

An extensive discussion of what is going to happen in the end of days before the coming of the Messiah (details are forthcoming in a later chapter). The accuracy of what is happening now gives one chills. How did the Rabbis know that?

An interesting discussion is in Yoma 10 which is the upcoming attack on Iran (details are forthcoming in a later chapter). How did the Rabbis know that?

I think I can go on with quite an extensive list of subjects that are covered in the Talmud that we call "de-rabbanan," from the Rabbis. One would logically question "How did the Rabbis know that?" There is only One Source of information Who sees all of time and events and can tell us about it. I rest my case.

There is another very important aspect of the Talmud that can't be ignored. The Torah tells us what the 613 commandments are, but gives us very little detail about how to meet our obligations.

Examples include:
From the Shema: "And you shall bind them for a sign upon your hand, and they shall be for frontlets between your eyes." What does that mean? My interpretation is: get a small Torah with all the commandments in it, some rope and tie it to my arm and have a much smaller copy right between my eyes – on the bridge of my nose. The Oral Law carried down all the details of the phylacteries, Tefillin that we wear today. But did that come from the Rabbis?

Let's get spookier. There are basically two types of Tefillin we wear today. Let us concentrate of what we call Rashi Tefillin. The famous commentator Rashi (1040 to 1105) gave us all the details about what was brought down and talked about in the Oral Law. So are we saying that the Tefillin we wear today is the opinion of a Rabbi from the 11th century? In 1947 with the famous find of the Dead Sea Scrolls, we found Tefillin which just happened to be exactly as Rashi described. Wait a minute! We found Tefillin that was put in a cave about 2300 years ago (about 13 centuries before Rashi was born) and we didn't even find them until the 20th century. How did they know what Rashi's opinion would be 13 centuries before he was born? The consistency of information that could have only come from Hashem becomes obvious. Let me put some more icing on the mystical cake.

While considering the spiritual effects of Tefillin, we must note the famous research of Dr. Steven Schram of the United States, an expert in the areas of acupuncture and chiropractic procedures. His article in the British Journal of Chinese Medicine showed that the points where Tefillin touches the head and the arm perfectly match the Chinese acupuncture points for increased spirituality and purified thought. He further emphasized that the very order in which Tefillin are traditionally put on, first wrapping the arm, then placing it on the head and then returning to wrap the hand, mirrors the pattern of treatment found in acupuncture and Chinese medicine. In conclusion, Schram claims to have no explanation for the fact that the millennia-old Jewish tradition, which has never had any connection with Chinese culture, employs procedures used by Chinese healing techniques. I guess the One Who created acupuncture is also the One Who commanded us to wear Tefillin.

From the Shema (a prayer that we are commended to recite twice daily): "You shall inscribe them on the doorposts of you house and upon your gates." Once again my interpretation of what the Torah is saying means that I can use a ballpoint pen or maybe crayons (I like crayons) and write this message as I have been commanded. The Oral Law carried down all the details of the Mezuzah that we use today. But did that come from the Rabbis? I think you are getting my point.

The laws of keeping kosher are what brought all this on. The fact that is does not say anywhere in the written Torah that I can't eat meat and milk together. Well as the word Tefillin and Mezuzah are not in the Torah, I guess all the details about keeping kosher need the Oral Torah information as well. Just be assured that when we received the Torah, the Jews were not educated yet on the kosher slaughtering of animals and hence the tradition to this day of having a dairy meal on Shavuot (it was delicious). We knew from day one not to mix milk and meat. I will discuss the idea of keeping kosher later, since like all the commandments, they are misunderstood and totally allusive to us.

I'm going to let you in on a little secret. The information in the Talmud isn't as miraculous as I am leading you to believe. We as a nation were at Mount Sinai, close to three million of us and we were all prophets. We heard Hashem in person. The rest of the Jewish nation also heard Hashem from Heaven. In other words, every Jew heard Hashem and spent 40 years learning His commandments. But the information wasn't just passed down through the Oral Torah; it was lived by the people on a daily basis. All our obligations about Tefillin, Mezuzah, Shabbos, Kosher, etc, etc, etc was ingrained in us from the time in the desert to when it finally was written down and codified 1800 years later. It wasn't the Rabbis that had this information, but every man, woman and child knew the details. They lived it every day. The more miraculous aspect of all this is that when we were scattered throughout the world we still kept up the tradition taught to us at Mount Sinai.

I have lived on three continents and have been in about 20 countries. Wherever I have travelled I see the exact same Torah and Oral Torah and Zohar and commentaries from the greats. No other belief system in the world can make that statement. The tremendous variations of the world's religions from country to country are testimonials to the fact that it was created by people. Only with Judaism can we see the same scriptures, customs, language, food, songs, etc whether I am in Europe, South Africa, the US, China, Australia, or if I ever travel to the moon or Mars. The only way such a miracle can happen is if the Creator of everything is the Former of the Jewish nation. All the commandments and their finest details come from Hashem. The Rabbis were the agents to bring it down through the ages. And, that is the Absolute Truth, it couldn't be anything else.

1.9 The Mystical Hebrew Letters

The ancient Kabbalistic text, *Sefer ha-Yetzirah,* discusses the spiritual significance of the Hebrew alphabet. In contrast to man-made letters, which are merely conventional, the Hebrew alphabet is considered to have been given by Hashem, and represents profound spiritual forces - in modern terms, different energies that flow through each letter. For example, the letters of Hashem's command: "Let there be light" - va 'yehi ohr actually convey and bring into being the infinite varieties of light found in creation: from the visible to the invisible, from the spiritual to the manifest. Although the Talmudic Sages disagree upon which script was used to write the Torah given at Sinai, the Kabbalists clearly state that it was the same script used today in writing a Torah scroll. This subject gets so deep that it is beyond the scope to this book; and, once again, there are many books written on the subject to satisfy your curiosity.

Everything about the letters from the shapes, the multiple meanings, the hidden meanings, the numerical value, the combinations of letters, how words are formed (to be discussed in the next section), the geometrical shapes when combined (not necessarily next to each other, but used as building blocks), the sounds of the letters (both individually and combined), the relationship to the surrounding letters in the alphabet, etc, etc, etc.

The letters are so deep, that there is no way that human beings could have created them. A study of the letters to prove my point could go on for many years and not come close to disclosing all the secrets.

The first letter in the alphabet alef, א is formed by two Hebrew letter yuds, י one to the upper right and the other to the lower left, joined by a diagonal Hebrew letter vav, ו. These represent the higher and lower waters and the firmament between them, as taught by the Arizal (Rabbi Isaac Luria of blessed memory, who received and revealed new insights into the ancient wisdom of Kabbalah). The alef, having a numerical value of 1 represents Hashem Who is One. The numerical value of the two yuds and the vav that make up the alef is 26 which is the value of Hashem's name (the very mystical name that we don't pronounce – it is very dangerous to say).

This four letter name is also the root of the expressions in Hebrew for "He was," " He is "and "He will be." This attests to the infinite essence of Hashem. Hashem always was, is and will be forever. He is infinite in time (as we know it – Hashem is not bound by the allusion of time that He gave us), He is infinite in Intelligence, Infinite in Power, Infinite in Mercy, etc, etc, etc. Hashem is everything, and it is inherent in His Name.

That particular four letter name has a tremendous amount of hidden and not so hidden information in it. One example is that if you take the last letter, the heh and break it up into a dalet and a yud, you have the word "Yehudi," which means Jew. If you stack the four letters vertically it is shaped like the human body. Interestingly enough, there is another name for Hashem that can be found on the human hand. The three letters are shaped like the three middle fingers, ש the pinky a י the ד between the thumb and the first finger. I do not wish to say these names or even spell them in the proper order – you remember the commandment not to take His name in vain.

A very simple example of letters next to each other would be the dalet followed in the alphabet by the gimel. The two letters look like this דג – Hebrew letters have many meanings by themselves. The gimel on the right can mean giva or arrogance the dalet can mean dal or poor or meager. These two letters show the concept of an arrogant rich person sticking his foot out to kick a poor person from behind. Even personality traits and relationships between people show up in the shapes of the letters.

The word for Hydrogen in Hebrew just happens to include the letters that make up the word for water. The word for water is made up of three letters, two the same and one other. It alludes to H_2O. All of Chemistry can be found the Torah with much of it being seen in the letters, including the elements. Science and mathematics, two of my favorite subjects, are completely covered in the Torah (nothing is missing), and much can be found in single letters of the Hebrew alphabet.

The value of Pi for instance is talked about in 1 Kings 7:23 and 2 Chronicles 4:2 as well as an explanation in the Talmud. The calculations are involved, but basically they use numerology of Hebrew letters to come out to the 3.1416 (carried out to 4 places, even though it is an unending number). This was needed for construction thousands of years ago. It is amazing that we find it in the Bible.

Did you know that the Star of David contains 24 letters of the Hebrew alphabet (the 22 letters plus two of the final letters)?

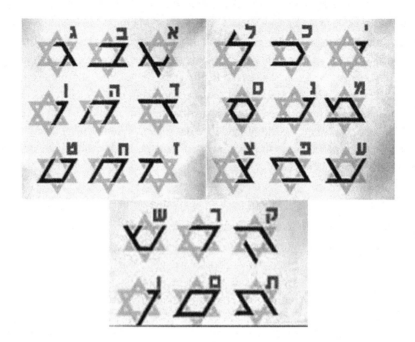

We also find that the scribes for thousands of years handed down information in the Torah by making certain letters larger. The Shema, that we are commanded to say twice a day, begins with a declaration of six words that Hashem is One. In those six words we find the last letter of the first word and the last letter of the last word to be bigger than the other letters in the Shema. Why? These letters עד are the Hebrew word for witness, evidence, testimony. We are not just making a statement that Hashem is One, but we also were a witness at Mount Sinai. We have absolute evidence and we therefore provide a testimony to His Oneness.

An interesting fact that is not read directly in the Torah is the day of the year on which Rosh Hashanah falls. We have the date specified for each of the other festival Holidays, but not the Head of the New Year – or do we? Since the days of Rosh Hashanah signify the beginning of the Creation of Adam and Eve, all we need to do is look at the first word in the Torah, Bereishis, In the Beginning. If you rearrange the Hebrew letters in that first word, you come out with Tishrei alef/bet, which just happen to be the first two days of the Hebrew month of Tishrei, which is Rosh Hashanah. Cute?

74

Another hidden bit of information (I could go on with volumes of fascinating information that is hidden in the Hebrew letters). We have a very strange two letters that appear twice in the Book of Numbers, 10:35–36. There are two verses that are delineated by inverted nuns. The scribe actually has to write these letters upside down to separate these two verses. There are several explanations in the Talmud for this phenomenon, but my favorite is in found in Sanhedrin 97b which lets us know that the letter nun, which has a numerical value of 50 sets off the 85 letters of the two verses and gives us the earliest year that the Messiah can appear on Earth. 50X85 is 4250 or the year 490CE. This is Hashem telling us that no Messiah could have shown up in the time of the Second Temple even if they thought he would come back again.

There is a brilliant write-up in the book **The Coming Revolution** by Zamir Cohen about the Hebrew letters being more than just symbols written on parchment. In his essay he talks about how it was possible at Mount Sinai to actually see the letters that Hashem had spoken as it says in the Torah (Exodus 19-20). The essay entitled "Seeing the Sounds" discusses a modern day experiment conducted by an Electro-optics Engineer. This engineer used sophisticated instruments that can transform sound waves into images to be displayed on a computer monitor. He was able to demonstrate, in tangible form, a display of the ancient Jewish understanding that the sounds of the letters actually correspond to their shape. Despite his skepticism when he began the experiment, and much to his amazement, the engineer discovered that the sound waves for seventeen out of the twenty-two letters of the Hebrew alphabet create an on-screen image very similar to the shape of the written letter itself.

The write-up is too detailed and too technical for our purpose here; but, once again, it proves that it is impossible that the mystical Hebrew letters could have been made-up by human beings.

One last note about the Hebrew letters. In our modern society we have many fonts used for the Hebrew letters in the same way as any other modern language. I am happy to say that products that we buy at our local supermarket use a fancy script, and not the shapes of the Hebrew letters as found in the Torah. It would be a Torah violation to use the holy letters as they appear from Hashem. Making the letters as perfect as possible is such exact sciences that scribes who write a Torah, Mezuzah, Tefillin, etc use computer scanning to verify the accuracy of their written letters. The computer program makes sure that the letters completely meet the tolerances as required in scriptures. Welcome to the 21st century.

1.10 Let's Have a Word

I have talked about how Hebrew is not like any other language in the world. We have discussed how mystical Hebrew letters are. I would like to follow up with some information showing how mystical Hebrew words are. One clarification that needs to be made is that I am talking the Hebrew we find in scriptures and not Modern Hebrew. They Hebrew found in Scriptures is called the holy tongue, Lashon Hakodesh.

One big difference between Lashon Hakodesh and any other language is that the letters actually describe the essence of the word. If as an example, in English if everyone in the world agreed that from this day forward we should call a shirt a chair, and a chair a shirt, it would be possible. English like most languages is a living language that new words are invented every day. By the way, that is a nice chair you're wearing today.

In Lashon Hakodesh the word describes the item. The word in Hebrew for "word" is Davar. Davar also is defined as "thing." An object and the word for that object are the same thing.

Let me give you an example that will demonstrate how the letters define the essence of a word. If I say in Hebrew "I speak" it would be "ani midabaer (אני

מדבר)." The four Hebrew letters that make the word midabear (speak) are Mem, Daled, Bet, Raish. Each letter in Hebrew has multiple meanings by themselves. The Mem often means "from"; the Daled can mean "door" (which is delet in Hebrew); the Bet means "in"; and, the Raish often means "head" (which is rosh in Hebrew). So, if you put the four letters together they say "from the door in the head." In other words, speech is described as "from the door in the head" (the mouth). All words in Scriptures are made up the same way, believe it or not. The shapes of the letters, the numerical value of each letter and the combination of letters all have significance. There are many books written that cover the mysticism of Hebrew letters and words.

Even names have deeper meaning. Adam, the first man is made up of three letters – an Alef, Daled and Mem. It is known that Adam came back again as King David and will return in the end of days as the Messiah. Hence the three letters of Adam's name represent Adam, David and Messiah.

The Talmud teaches that there are three partners needed for the creation of every human being: mother, father and Hashem. The three Hebrew letters in the name Adam have a numerical value of 45. Father in Hebrew has a numerical value of three; mother in Hebrew has a numerical value of 41. That comes to 44 which is made complete with the number one, Hashem.

What is the plural for Adam? The word does not exist in Hebrew. It is to make us aware of the fact that humanity began with but one person. That is why Jewish law warned witnesses in capital crimes to be extremely careful with their testimony, for "one who destroys even one person, it is as if he destroys an entire world; and one who saves but one person, it is as if he preserves an entire world." When we forget the singularity of every human being, that each person is irreplaceable, we take the first step of turning people into numbers, souls into ciphers. Six million victims of the Holocaust are incomprehensible, beyond human imagination. The very immensity of the number diminishes our sensitivity to the tragedy of every single soul. Anne Frank, as one counted teenager with whom we can empathize, makes the crime of the Nazis real and allows the horror to be grasped. Adam: every person is one, singular, unique, and can never be replicated.

It is interesting that even names of places today seem to have hidden meaning in the Hebrew:

- Russia is the Hebrew word for an evil person.

- Oslo, the famous accord that was set up for the destruction of Israel, means toilet bowl.

- America, I am sorry to report, can be broken down to Am Ricah – an empty nation.

- Korea, when we have a close relative pass away, we tear Kriah (rend a garment).

- Yisroel means, quite literally, "He has striven with Hashem," or "He has been saved by Hashem." The root connotes "esrah" which means "help." I had to give you one positive example.

I thought I would end with one of my favorite words – Truth. Emet, אמת has very great significance. First of all, the Talmud points out where the three Hebrew letters of the word Emet are placed in the Hebrew alphabet. The three letters happened to be the first then a middle letter and the last letter in the alphabet. The word for lie or falsehood is sheqer, שקר which are three letters together in the alphabet. The Talmud tells us that the truth is hard to find, but lies are very prevalent. Even in the Hebrew alphabet the letters of truth are spread apart and hard-to-find; but, the letters of falsehood are together and easily found. Also the three letters that make up truth have a solid foundation and can stand up by themselves. The letters for lies have a single point at the bottom and cannot stand up by themselves. The truth is unshakable – falsehood cannot stand by itself. In English we express the concept of total truth by saying that something is true "from A-Z." We find the same concept in Hebrew from Alef to Tav. Truth demands total accuracy from start to finish including every point in the middle as well.

From birth to death. That is the ultimate truth of every human being. The three letters of Emet אמת may be read in two combinations of beginning and end.

אמ- Em - Mother

מת- Met – Death

From the cradle to the grave – these are the unavoidable boundaries of our human existence. To know this truth is the first step for making the most of ourselves during the time we are granted by Hashem on this earth. Truth requires for its essence the first letter alef, the "One" standing for Hashem. Remove the initial letter in Emet and all that remains is met, the Hebrew word for death. Without Hashem there can be no truth. In its place only death and destruction remain.

That which is true is everlasting. The false and the wicked cannot prevail. Emet has a numerical value of 441. Man is a duality of both body and soul. Our flesh is mortal. It ages, decays, and withers. But that is not "the truth" of our existence. "VeHaNeFeSh," "and the soul," has a numerical value of 441. And the soul – that is the truth of our life and our immortality.

1.11 Another Proof "Miracles"

Something that has had a very strong effect on my life has been a tremendous number of miracles that I have personal witnessed. I could bore you for hours with story after story. But I know, that what happens to me, may provide very strong credibility to the existence of Hashem and the validity of scripture, but would mean very little for you.

However, I once sat through a seminar that included the topic of "miracles," and found, to my astonishment, most participants (who were almost completely secular) had their own personal stories to tell. The interesting aspect of this is that a very secular person might have a good story, but manages to convince him or herself that it was a "fluke of nature." To get individuals to accept that Hashem showed them something miraculous is very difficult even if they can't explain the phenomenon by any logical means.

To convince you that Hashem does give you a taste of the truth about His presence, would take more than personal events. The big surprise is that history, that we have all experienced, it jam-packed with miracle after miracle. We are all familiar with or at least have heard of such events, but for the most part, most of us have ignored, especially if we suspect that we are getting a taste of Hashem.

Most events that I would like to point out fit comfortably into topics that I will be discussing in upcoming chapters. I will only mention certain events, but will leave the fine details for a more appropriate discussion.

The biggest miracle of world history is probably one of the least obvious to discuss. The Jews are still here and survived history. When you consider the great empires that existed, in Egypt, Babylonia, Syria, Persia, Greece, Rome, Spain, Arabian Peninsula, Ottoman, British, Russian, Soviet, Nazi, many other countries too numerous to mention, and the fact that all of these great powers tried to wipe out the Jews, how can we ignore such a miracle. All the great powers have disappeared, but this little band of Jews, with no Army, no weapons, no protecting government body, nothing more than faith in Hashem, are still here and thriving more than ever. What makes a true miracle? The fact that Hashem told us thousands of years ago that this would occur. We are told in scriptures that "we will remain small in number, but never disappear."

Another miracle is that when the Jews return to the land it will produce again. Israel was a barren wasteland from the year 68 to 1948. It was even improperly called Palestine, which was never a sovereign nation, in other words, it has been Israel for about 3700 years with Jerusalem as its capital. When the Jewish land was reestablished in 1948 and the Jews started to return, this barren useless land miraculously changed and became the plushest farmland in the world. Because of weather, there are three harvest seasons a year in Israel. This country, the size of the state of New Jersey, exports produce to many countries in the world. How was it possible to go from a desert wasteland to a plush agricultural miracle? Hashem told us so 3327 years ago and it happened. Once again, could any human being have predicted such an event thousands of years ago? We are even told in the Torah when it will happen. Rashi, you remember him, said in the 11th century, the land producing again will be the true sign that you are in the end of days.

The tremendous number of miracles that occurred in every war, every conflict that Israel was forced into, 1948, 1956, 1967, 1973, 1982, 1991, 2006, 2010, 2012, and other conflicts and terrorist attacks, rocket, missile and mortar attacks, once again, too numerous to mention, all were successful with Devine intervention. Many of these events will be covered in more detail later including the impossible, miraculous stories that never made the news.

There are so many miracles told in the Torah that would be very haphazard to write if it hadn't come true. There are miracles about the laws of keeping Kosher, the Sabbatical years (Shemitah), 15 places that state something, followed by "until this very day," all the hidden and not so hidden messages that I have already mentioned, places and archeological references that have been found in modern times, all the events that will happen in the end of days before the time of redemption and the Messiah (a very big prediction that we can see today) etc, etc, etc. Why was this dangerous to put in the Torah? They would require a tremendous leap of faith, but even worse, a probable loss of credibility if the events didn't happen. What human been would give details about everything that is yet to happen if he couldn't see the entire future? If humans wrote the Torah, how could they guess at facts, such as every animal and fish that existed in the world and would exist forever (another miraculous detail to be discussed)?

Could a human writer predict that we would remain small in number but never disappear? This subject goes on and on, but just stop to think about the total credibility and validity of scriptures that could have only come from an Infinite Source of Intelligence with knowledge of everything that happened, is happening and will happen in this world, including the details of every one of us.

I could go on for quite a long time with examples. The important point is to know that no word, no letter in Jewish Scriptures is superfluous. The examples I have given do not represent one drop from all the oceans of the world, for the number of examples is infinite. The proof of Hashem is unshakable.

1.12 Modern Prophecy and Messages from Hashem

All the events that are to happen in the world before the redemption and introduction of the Messiah, according to scriptures, have happened (past tense) or are happening (present tense).

Do we have prophecy these days? I look at three sources for the answer. One is using Facilitated Communications, FC, which is a method that enables us to talk to individuals who are not able to converse in this physical world, but seem to be in touch with the spiritual world, Hashem. These individuals are in the categories of Autistic, severe Downs Syndrome, Comatose, etc. Second is messages that we are getting (and are coming true) from the prominent Rabbis of today, especially mystical Rabbis who also seem to be receiving messages from Hashem. Third is just, what I call, connecting the dots – an event that is in scriptures that is obviously occurring before our eyes. The third isn't new prophecy (there is no such thing) but watching prophecy that we were told thousands of years ago actually being fulfilled. Messages that come from the FC individuals or Rabbis of today are invariably prophecies that can be found in scriptures – the message clarifies the prophecy, points out that it is occurring and even tells us when to expect the event.

Let us expound on each category. I have been reading the FC messages for approximately 18 years; and, they have fulfilled the prophecy in the Talmud, tractate Bava Basra 12, that tells us: "From the day that the Holy Temple was destroyed, the power of prophecy was taken from the prophets and given to deranged people and to children. "Deranged people" has been defined as: a generic term for a mental state often described as involving a "loss of contact with reality." These are individuals who are not able to communicate. They are only physically in this world, but not mentally aware of worldly events. Yet, they seem to communicate with the spiritual realm and provide messages with deep insight of what is happening.

The more interesting aspect of the FC individuals is that they have greatly increased the number of messages in recent months. In the past we have heard many predictions, but without giving the all-important "when". There were exceptions. Galia told us years ago about the upcoming Intifada before it happened, and even predicted the day that she would leave the Earth (read the book Galia for very interesting details). Benyamin told us in 2007 that there will be a great decline in the economy with interesting details that came to fruition in 2008. He was even more specific in telling us that there will be a big explosion just before Hashanah Rabah, 5769 (2008) that will be of great concern to the world. Sure enough two days before HR, North Korea did its first underground nuclear test. He said that prediction a couple of weeks prior to it happening.

Most messages these days from Benyamin, Moishela, Menachem, Daniel, etc are encouragingly predicting the coming of the final redemption and the introduction of the Messiah. The scary part is that prior to the happy ending, as I like to call it, there will be extensive turmoil and chaos in the world. War, terrorist activity, crime, greedy leaders, ineffective governments, hatred (especially Jew-hatred), etc, etc, etc are all being predicted. Of course, we already see these things occurring, but still wonder how much more intensive it will get. What it means, why Hashem is allowing such madness and even how to survive the mayhem will be covered in upcoming chapters. The most important message to be learned from all this is "how to achieve the happiest of "happy endings." Stay tuned.

Since books have been written about the predictions of the FC individuals and the Rabbis, there is no way, once again, that I could possibly cover decades of pertinent messages from these sources. I do however wish to give you a taste of the insight that has come from Rabbis. There are many, many Rabbis that have said accurate messages, but I personally have followed certain individuals. Rav Ben Artzi, Rav Fish, Rav Shternbuch, Rav Glazerson, Rav Yitchok and many others. I should mention that this includes the greatest Rabbis of our generation, mystical Rabbis and even the most prominent individuals of the past, the Arizal Hakodesh, the Vilna Gaon, the Chofetz Chaim, etc. We are amazed and greatly encouraged that we are truly getting accurate and timely information to help us survive and thrive in the coming chaotic time.

As an example: Rav Nir Ben Artzi, shlita, has made many predictions that came to fruition shortly after, and not so shortly thereafter. The most famous prediction was the fall of the Egyptian president Morsi that the Rav mentioned two weeks before it occurred. That prediction was so astounding, it was written up by various Israeli and Arab press sources. There are countries that pay attention to Rav Ben Artzi due to his accuracy. The Rav told us of the disengagement of Gaza in 2006 and the removal of the Jews (he made that prediction five years before it happened in 2001). Also in 2001, he predicted that the next president of the US of A would be a black man (I avoid calling Obama an African American, since it has been proven that he was born in Kenya, yes African, but not an American). Obama, of course, was elected 2008, seven years after the Rav predicted the event. There are many more examples about the weather, earthquakes, planes falling and disappearing, countries in chaos, the dilemmas of the leaders of many countries and many more events that I will not go into here. These can be seen on a weekly basis on the web, a site called The Absolute Truth,

http://absolutetruth613.blogspot.co.il/ (which just happens to be my blog).

You may ask: why I believe these messages are prophetic? After all there are many Torah Jews that believe that prophecy doesn't exist these days. I always like to answer a question with another question (a very Jewish characteristic). My question is "What is Hashem's opinion?" Hashem gave us a test for prophecy in the Torah (Deuteronomy 18:15-22). They basically tell us that if an individual gives predictions of what will occur and it comes true, it was given to him by Hashem. If his predictions do not happen, it is not from Hashem and he is not a prophet.

Due to the accuracy of the messages from the FC individuals and Rabbis, I do believe they are coming from Hashem and have passed the test of Prophecy described in the Torah. The more important aspect of these messages is how they have provided me and my loved ones great benefit in life. Since they appear to be guidance from Hashem, we don't treat these messages as nice-to-know information, but words of guidance to help us through what is called the "birthpangs of Moshiach" – the difficult times before redemption of the world. It absolutely has worked; and, I thank Hashem every day for His help. Don't ignore these messages – use them to your great advantage, you will be happy you did.

Let me give one more word of encouragement regarding my connecting the dots with respect to the events happening in the world. If one pays attention (which it is probably better to stay away from) to all the craziness happening in the world, one would see all the prophecies of the end of time as we know it, happening. All the predictions about the financial situation, the attention being paid to this little country of Israel, the Jew-hatred, the evil of the governments, the evil of world leaders, the greed of the elite, the possibility of war, the terrorist activity, the weather, the social decline, etc, etc, etc, are all occurring, NOW. I am talking about a threefold comparison of (1) what is in scriptures (the Bible, the Talmud, the Zohar, the Midrash, the commentaries of our great Rabbis throughout history) to (2) what is being said by our message givers, the Rabbis and the Facilitated Communications individuals and (3) what is happening in the world. One would have to be totally out of sync with reality to not see the consistency in messages and prophecy to real world occurrences. This definitely tells me that the messages only could have originated from the One Who knows all and running the universe and that that happy ending, that all this craziness leads up to, is imminent, B"H (this is a very popular expression meaning Baruch Hashem, in essence thanking Hashem for this blessing).

1.13 Aristotle's Letter, to Alexander the Great

Aristotle: Born 384 -322 BCE. Birth: Chalcidice, Greece. Death: Chalcis, Greece. When the great philosopher Aristotle was old, he sent the following letter to his student, Alexander the Great:

"Blessed be He who opens the eyes of the blind, and shows sinners the true path. Let Him be praised in an appropriate manner; since I do not know how to praise Him for the great kindness and mercy, which He showed me. I am eternally grateful to Him, for getting me away from the foolishness to which I had devoted my life.

All my life I delved into philosophy, to explain all natural phenomena in a logical manner. I wrote many books on these subjects. Finally, in the twilight of my life, I had the opportunity to engage in a conversation with a Jewish sage. It did not take me long, to recognize his great wisdom; and he led me to understand, how great is the Torah, that was given on Mount Sinai.

He taught me the inner depth of the Torah, providing me with many brilliant insights based on its teachings. I realized how foolish I had been for not realizing, how G-d can manipulate the laws of nature; and that much of what happens in the world, is directed by G-d.

Realizing all this, I decided to devote myself to exploring the wisdom of the Torah. It did not take me long to realize, that the Torah is based on true foundations, while the axioms of philosophy are purely arbitrary.

Therefore, my dear student Alexander, if I had the power to collect all the books I have written, I would burn them. I would be embarrassed for any of them to survive. However, I realize that I do not have this power; my books have already been published, and have spread all over the world. I also realize that I will receive Divine punishment, for having written such misleading books.

Therefore, my son, Alexander, I am writing this letter to tell you, that the great majority of my theories regarding natural law, are false. While nature does exist, G-d is the L-rd of the universe, and He directs all things as He sees fit. I am telling everyone openly, that they should not waste time with my books. They should not look at them, or even touch them with their hands. It is sinful to waste time, on the false theories that I have espoused.

I feel that I have saved my soul by admitting my error; I hope that I will not be held guilty for the past, since I acted out of ignorance. But now I have revealed to the public that I was mistaken, and that my heart aches for the time I have wasted, on my foolish theories. Those who waste time on my books therefore, will deserve to be punished.

The Jewish scholar with whom I spoke, showed me the book of Proverbs (Mishley), written by King Solomon, one of the greatest geniuses of all times. The scholar showed me, that in many places, King Solomon warned against wasting time on philosophical speculation.

One such place is where he said, "Say to Wisdom, 'You are my sister,' and consider understanding your relative. That they may keep you from strange woman, from the loose woman who speaks so smoothly" (Proverbs 7:4,5).

I feel sorry for my eyes for what they have seen, and my ears for what they have heard. I feel sorry for my body, for wasting its strength on such detrimental studies.

I know that you praise me, and tell me, that I am famous all over the world because of the books I have written. People speak very highly of me. But I wish I were dead, because of the misleading books that I have spread all over the world.

People, who devote themselves to the Torah, will earn eternal life; while those who devote themselves to my books, will earn the grave. But I am prepared to accept upon myself, the punishment of them all.

I did not write to you earlier, because I was afraid that you would be angry with me, and perhaps even harm me. But now, I have made up my mind to tell you the truth. I know, that by the time you receive this letter, I will already be dead and buried, because I realize that my end is near.

I salute you with greetings of peace, Alexander of Macedon, great emperor and ruler."

Your teacher,
Aristotle

From The Torah anthology, English, (Yalkut ME'AM LO'EZ) - Volume 6, Page 154-155. Which references a book called Shalsheleth Hakabbalah.

The Jew spoken of, was Shimon HaTzaddik (Simeon the Just), who was a Cohen Godol (High Priest) during the time of the Second Temple. He is also known for his opinions which are recorded in the Mishnah, (making him a Tanna, in Rabbinic terminology).

Joseph b. Shem-Ṭob assures his reader, that he had seen it written in an old book, that Aristotle at the end of his life had become a proselyte ("Ger Tzedek").

Aristotle recants all his previous philosophic teachings, having been convinced of their incorrectness by a Jewish sage. He acknowledges as his chief error the claim that truth is to be ascertained by the reasoning faculty only; inasmuch as Divine revelation is the sole way to truth.

This "letter" is the conclusion of a book of Aristotle, "two hands thick," in which he withdraws; based on his studying with the Jew, Simeon (Shimon HaTzadik); his views with regard to the immortality of the soul, the eternity of the world, and similar tenets.

It is claimed that Aristotle derived his doctrine, directly from Judaism. Aristotle owed his philosophy to the writings of King Solomon, which were presented to him by his royal pupil Alexander; the latter having obtained them, on his conquest of Jerusalem.

1.14 Summary Statement for Part 1

The most important idea for you to keep in mind as you read on is that my presentation of the absolute truth about everything is based on decades of research with totally convincing empirical data to back up the findings. Locally I have tens of thousands of books available to me with my personal library, study halls and a library minutes from where I live. That in conjunction with tens of thousands of hour with articles, lectures, study group activity, video/audio tapes, web searches (which also taught me bogus arguments), etc, etc, etc, have given me total confidence that I have disclosed the only source of absolute truth on planet Earth (and the rest of the universe).

The sources that I have just touched upon, coded information, prophecy, near death experiences, scientific, miracles, modern prophets including the obvious fulfillment of prophecy happening in the world today and messages from Hashem (being received very frequently), are by no means the only proofs available. These areas were the most prevalent sources reviewed in my research. Since the overall statistical evaluation gives a confidence level of infinity to one (the highest confidence level possible), additional sources would only be more icing on the cake, even though there is more than enough already.

I said it before "if we could tie all the computers of the world into one gigantic mainframe, and we can tie all human brains of the world into one giant brain, we still could not write a Torah." The infinite bits of proof could have only come from an infinite Source of Intelligence. It makes the study of Torah and life itself thoroughly enjoyable. Don't miss the enjoyment – you'll love it. The answer to everything is in scriptures, especially how you and your loved ones can be totally happy and successful in this life and for all eternity!!!!!!

Hopefully, you are convinced that Hashem exists and controls everything in the universe and in our lives. It is now time to give very detailed information about the overall operation. With complete respect for Professor Steven Hawking, the next section of this book will tell you the Theory of Everything. The only difference is we will not be talking theory but absolute fact – backed by the words of the One Who created it all, including His scientific proof of its validity. The sources are nice to know, but we must dig deep into what the sources are telling us. Specifically answering: What is the purpose of this universe, this world and our lives (I believe that includes everything)?

Part 2 - What is the Purpose of this Universe, this World and our Lives?

2.1 Introduction

The world of today is a world of lies and fantasy. Very little that we see in the news is true – after all the media is for making money and not worried about informing us. Sensationalism sells, not the absolute truth. The world is so upside-down that most people of the earth are on a path to disaster. We are not only in the end of days (I will explain what that entails), but we are in the end of the end of days. It is vital to each individual on earth to know what the truth is – what the system is on this earth to survive and thrive. We must become proactive to save ourselves as individuals and to save our loved ones who depend on us for guidance. Relying on the inept leaders of today is foolhardy and dangerous.

We live under a system of measure for measure meaning that you can't blend into the crowd, but are treated and even judged as an individual. For every act that you do that is positive and good, you receive reward; and, for every wrong act or even evil act, you receive correction (or punishment). By learning the truth we will see how accurate these statements are and how each of us is affected.

The most important thing to know is we are just about out of time; and, what you do immediately will determine the quality of the rest of your life and your eternity, forever and ever and ever and ever.

The purpose of this book is to convince you of the above with unshakable evidence of the truth. The sources of information that I already have outlined are absolute and so accurate that it will not take long for me to convince you. The more important thing is for you to catch on quickly to the obligations you have and what it means to you and obligations.

Once again, there is not much time.

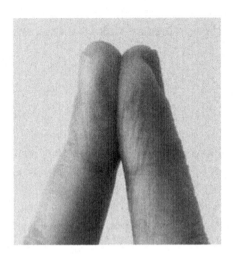

What does showing the two fingers together symbolize?

> The space between my fingers is how long life is on earth.
> The space outside of my fingers is eternity and represents our eternal life.

We work so hard to make life on earth as pleasurable and successful as can be; and, we ignore the real life which goes on after we change addresses. Yes, we do live forever and I will present evidence to that statement that is strong enough to stand up in court (especially the heavenly court). Be as skeptical as you want about the truth that I will be covering, but be aware that a day is coming soon that you will know without a doubt what the truth is. The problem is that day is what I call: "the too late date." Your opportunity to survive and thrive is now, and will be finished in the not too distant future. I am not a big fan of Elvis Presley, but what he said is the absolute truth – "it's now or never."

Before I get into the meat of the subject, you should know that I have worked diligently for a long time to find the truth and eliminate my personal opinion. All that I will cover is well documented and not my gut feeling about the reality of everything.

I began by telling you my sources of information in an effort to convince you that these sources are the only way to know the truth. I like to consider myself an extremely open minded person, with approximate 67 years of studying scriptures, 16 years of academic studies (both undergraduate and graduate) and about 57 years of studying science, psychology, sociology, etc. I probably have seen your sources of information and have validated or refuted them. Do I have the answers to everything? No, but I will continue to prove that the sources of information that I have disclosed contains the answers to everything.

I will now begin to tell you truths about yourself and the world in which you live. You will read truths that you probably have never heard, including truths that can be described, but are beyond human comprehension.

2.2 The Soul

There are many places in this book that I mentioned the spiritual aspect of the human being. It is time to define what that is. We are really spiritual beings that have been provided with physical clothing to exist in the physical world. We are here for the purpose of repair, rectification and perfecting ourselves and the world. Hashem has designed the system to be able to accomplish this task by providing the Jews with 613 commandments and non-Jews with 7 commandments. These commandments are of a physical nature requiring us to have a physical body.

Since we live forever, the only part of our existence throughout eternity that needs this body is during our visit and mission on Earth. When we finish our work here, we are able to move back to the spiritual realm; and, the body that was provided for us ceases to exist (we know it better as death). Since the soul is the actual spirit, the essence of Hashem imbued in a body, everything has a soul. I'm not just talking about animals, but everything in the universe: plants, rocks, the Earth, the moon, the stars, food, furniture – everything. We state that Hashem is One several times a day in our prayers. That means that everything is Hashem and therefore has His spirit within. I am talking concepts, once again, beyond human comprehension, but I plan to give a more meaningful description later. For now this discussion of soul will be limited to the soul within and surrounding the human being.

One proof that verifies the fact that we have a spiritual makeup comes from a scientific study that was performed over a 15 year period asking one question: "What is the mind?" A group of psychologists, neurologists and doctors probed the actual capabilities of the brain to discover that it is not the supercomputer that everyone thinks it is, but more of a router that connects the physical with the metaphysical realm (the study calls it metaphysical which is "of or relating to the transcendent or to a reality beyond what is perceptible to the senses" – the more accurate term is spiritual).

Common attributes of mind include perception, reason, imagination, memory, emotion, attention, and a capacity for communication. None of these qualities, including the processing of information from the five senses, is found in the brain nor could be incorporated in any type of computer device.

Judaism teaches that "moach shalit al halev", the mind rules the heart. Humans can approach the Divine intellectually, through learning and behaving according to the Divine Will as enveloped in the Torah, and use that deep logical understanding to elicit and guide emotional arousal during prayer. This is again not a simple computing function but a spiritual one.

Kabbalah and other mystic traditions go into greater detail into the nature of the soul. Kabbalah separates the soul into five elements or levels:

1. נפש *nephesh* (literally "living being" or animal soul), related to natural instinct

2. רוח *ruach* (literally "wind") related to emotion and morality

3. נשמה *neshamah* (literally "breath") related to intellect and the awareness of Hashem

4. חיה *chaya* (literally "life"), considered a part of Hashem

5. יחידה *yechidah* (literally "singularity"), also termed the *pintele Yid* (the "essential [inner] Jew"). This aspect is essentially one with Hashem.

The Torah tells us that the soul is given by Hashem to a person by his/her first breath, as mentioned in Genesis, "And the L-RD G-d formed man of the dust of the ground, and breathed into his nostrils the breath of life; and man became a living being." (Genesis 2:7) (Important note: Adam was created as a man/woman creature. Man is an English translation and is not what is meant in Hebrew.) Since everything has a soul, we know that even the human embryo has a soul but at the lowest level, the nephesh. Judaism relates the quality of one's soul to one's performance of the commandments. Reaching higher levels of understanding and thus closeness to Hashem becomes a function of everything (prayer, repentance, Torah study, charity, etc).

There are 613 parts to the Jewish soul, which is commensurate with the number of commandments that a Jew is obligated to fulfill. As each commandment is satisfied, that part of the soul ascends to Heaven and the correction that is needed is accomplished. What remains is what needs to be worked on. That does not mean that if I have one kosher meal I have fulfilled the commandment to keep Kosher. Hashem sees our entire life and everything that we will do even before we do it. He knows that the commandment is fulfilled because we will be keeping a strict Kosher diet for the rest of our lives, even if we start later in life. I wish to mention that the soul is not a physical item and therefore is not just confined within the body. The true nature of a soul is beyond our comprehension, but is exists in the body, outside the body and in Heaven.

There are aspects of the system that make the commandments totally achievable. There are 248 positive commandments corresponding to a person's limbs (a limb is defined in Jewish law as a bone around which there are sinews and flesh. What this means is that according Jewish law, in the human skeleton there are 248 basic components) and 365 negative commandments like the number of days in the solar year. The positive commandments are what we are obligated to do and the negative ones are those we are obligated to avoid. This means that 365 of the commandments are simple to accomplish, because we don't do them. Examples that we are all familiar with is don't steel, don't kill, don't covet, don't take Hashem's name in vain, don't make idols, etc. There are many commandments that pertain to the time of the Temple such as the obligation of the Kohain, the Priest, to perform his service. There are commandments strictly for men and others for women. There are commandments that can only be done in Israel. One of the most important aspects of Torah study is to discern what obligations pertain to each of us as individuals.

How do we accomplish the commandments that we cannot fulfill due to circumstances? There are two answers. One is Torah study. When we study in depth the details of a commandment, Hashem gives us credit for that commandment as though we had performed it completely. We cannot use this method as a way to avoid our obligations, only to accomplish those that we have no way of doing. We cannot study the laws of keeping the Sabbath holy and then violate the Sabbath. That's like cheating on a test – you will get caught.

The other method is more interesting and not so obvious. When we take on a spouse, we are said to have joined souls. The expression "marriages are made in Heaven" is very literal. We are basically a half of a soul and our soul mates (not just a cute expression) make us whole. We are required to get married and have children – it is part of the system. The commandments that are just for men or women become a team effort. In other words, when my wife (my better half – I had to say that, she reads what I write) fulfills a commandment strictly for women, my half of the soul, so to speak, gets credit for fulfillment. This is a good deal for women since men have many more obligations than women. The problem that is sometimes presented to women is that they may have to be reincarnated to help a soulmate and not need the reincarnation for themselves.

This has certain ramifications that should be mentioned. That which I am about to cover may be offensive to some of my readers, but I guarantee you that none of this is my opinion, but is the word of our Creator. He is the One that you need to resolve your differences with, not me. Similar to the subject of Jew-hatred (to be discussed), if you don't care for the message, don't take it out on the messenger. Here we go. One important fact is that the soul of a Jew is different from the soul of a non-Jew. Intermarriage is not just frowned upon, it is meaningless. Not being sanctioned in Heaven, Jews and non-Jews cannot be soulmates. If the non-Jew converts with a totally kosher conversion, then the union is workable. That means completely accepting the 613 commandments and converting because of a total love of Hashem, not the love of another person. The key to all this is that the convert completes the conversion process by immersing in the ritual bath and Hashem actually instills a new soul in the person. Just having a certificate from a Rabbi because you studied some Judaism is bogus, and does not in the eyes of Hashem make you a Jew. A Jew on the other hand by virtue of having a Jewish mother is a Jew for life. Converting to something else does not change your soul. One little note is that the strict concept of one being Jewish because one's mother is Jewish is also because of how the soul was instilled in a person prenatal. Being half Jewish makes as much sense as being partially pregnant. One is either Jewish or not. No halfsies (I think I made up a word, I hope I spelled it right).

An additional impossibility is same sex marriages. Since there are commandments from Hashem that say "a man cannot be with a man and a woman cannot be with a woman," we know emphatically that homosexuality is against Jewish law and would never provide for a soulmate union. It is easy to see that the commandments that require a union between a man and a woman can only be accomplished if that is the arrangement. As I said, your argument isn't with me but the Designer of this world and His system. Since the benefits of playing by the rules are a totally wonderful with a joyous future forever and ever, don't argue with success.

What happens if one does not accomplish all the commandments in one's lifetime? One simply gets to come back again for another try. Yes, reincarnation is a very real thing (and is very involved requiring a separate discussion).

One last word. The soul and all of its details are so complicated that my brief dissertation really does not say it all. A lifetime of study may not even give complete scholarship on the subject, but understand that Hashem gave us this system for our benefit, that is all you need to know. When we were at Mount Sinai to receive the Torah we said collectively: "Na'aseh V'Nishma" "First we will do, then we will understand." We were given the Torah because we totally accepted the commandments, did them and then spent our lives understanding and perfecting our performance. That is our goal here. Do and then, even if it is for curiosity, learn (improving is really the goal).

2.3 Reincarnation

Now that we have talked about the soul, an interesting aspect of what the soul experiences in the course of time is reincarnation, known in Hebrew as gilgul. We had mentioned that a soul that does not accomplish a completed repair or rectification in a previous life is given the opportunity to return and try again.

In Hebrew, the word *gilgul* means "cycle" and *neshamot* is the plural for "souls." Souls are seen to "cycle" through "lives" or "incarnations," being attached to different human bodies over time. Which body they associate with depends on their particular task in the physical world, spiritual levels of the bodies of predecessors and so on. The concept relates to the wider processes of history in Kabbalah, involving Cosmic Tikun (Messianic rectification), and the historical dynamic of ascending Lights and descending Vessels from generation to generation. The esoteric explanations of *gilgul* were articulated in Jewish mysticism by Rabbi Isaac Luria, known as the Arizal, in the 16th century, as part of the metaphysical purpose of Creation. The Arizal was so mystical an individual, it was said that he could look at a person and tell him who he was in a previous life.

Although reincarnation is generally into a new human body, Hashem already knows in advance how successful that soul will be. If it is known that the individual is not going to voluntarily do what is needed for rectification, Hashem will use the involuntary way of helping the soul. This may mean giving rectification by placing the soul into a non-human entity. Yes, that means that one could come back as the family pet or a plant or a rock. This is in no way favorable since the reincarnated soul is totally aware of its situation and lives a very shameful and embarrassed reincarnation. Hashem, however, knows what is best for each of us and designs our time on Earth as needed.

I have an interesting story that happened to me when visiting a cousin in the states. This cousin did not live in a Jewish neighborhood so when it came time for my afternoon prayers, I had no choice but to just go into a quiet room in her house and pray. As I began, her two dogs entered the room, sat down beside me – one on each side of me, and faced east as I was doing. When it came time to stand the two dogs stood when I sat down, they likewise sat. I knew exactly what they were and what they needed. When I told my cousin that she had two Jewish dogs that had returned from a previous life, she was hysterical and probably could never look at them in the same way again. I, of course, mentioned to the dogs after praying how happy I was that they could join me.

One more note about animals that is not so obvious. We come back to finish our correction. Sometimes this can consist of a single act of high merit that will complete the job. Hashem uses kosher animals to help us. If one were to come back, as an example, as a chicken that was bred and killed with proper Kosher procedures and wound up on an observant family's Sabbath table, one would receive with high merit his or her final correction. In other words, when people complain about sacrificing animals because that is a barbaric practice, they have no idea how beneficent an act it may be. The sacrifice of animals and birds in the Temples was always benefiting humans, either alive or dead. The most interesting thing is that the soul of the animal itself (not just the reincarnated soul of the human involved) received high merit and was very happy with the sacrifice (that is another long story). Hashem's system is rarely what it seems, but always is for the good. Death itself is the ultimate atonement for our sins (that does not include suicide or cremation which has very horrible consequences for our eternity – don't do it).

Hopefully, it will be enough to reach our rectification and avoid time in hell (yes, there is such a place as was verified in my previous discussions of near death experience and prophecy). Hell is another method of correction along with reincarnation. Hell could also be pure punishment if the soul was not correctable because of tremendous wickedness. Both methods are avoidable and should be. All we need to do is the voluntary method while on Earth which is following Hashem's instructions on how to succeed in life without requiring too much correction (more details forthcoming).

We are all, in the end of days, reincarnated individuals. Since this is the end of the line for world history as we know it, we are getting our last chance to succeed. I guess this is why I have been so adamant about taking all this seriously and wanting to reach as many people as possible. Time is just about up, but our correction is achievable without the suffering and pain that will accompany the final correction on an individual basis. I believe that once the Messiah is announced and the time of redemption is obvious to all, we will have a limited time until our actual judgment day. I, in no way, am saying that you can put off doing the right thing for now, since we will have a limited amount of time before that "too late date." I just believe that Hashem in His infinite mercy will help us greatly. The more time we spend correcting ourselves, the better our future will be.

How many times is it possible to reincarnate? Good question. The answer is: I don't know. I knew a brilliant, highly scholastic Rabbi who claims that we could only have three lives to get it straight. I have known others who say "as many times as it is needed." I personally think that this is my fourth life. I have used a method (not hypnosis, even though I believe it works) to talk to my soul and I believe I know who I was in my last incarnation. A few years ago I even had a flashback and saw very clearly, while awake, my previous life. It only lasted about two seconds, but I knew what was transpiring and where I was.

Instead, let us talk about reliable information from reliable sources. The many individuals that have used Facilitated Communications (FC), such as the autistics and severely retarded, have all known who they were in their previous incarnation. Since they are in touch with Heaven, they know why they had to come back in that condition. They also knew what they had to accomplish to complete their rectification and, in some cases (possibly all cases) they knew when this would happen, giving them the actual date of departure from Earth. Since they were in an unbearable situation, they were happy to complete their work and leave. They were totally aware of the wonderful life that follows for those who do well here. There are books on the subject. One such book is Galia. Galia was a FC miracle. The story of her messages from Heaven, her reincarnation, the correction that she needed to accomplish and her leaving this world are told by her mother on this video:

http://www.youtube.com/watch?v=PkUZcPmIxoM

The English version, 2003, book with this amazing story is called "Galia, Messages from Heaven." I highly recommend this book and "Secrets of the Soul," (2000 for the English version) the miraculous stories of many FC participants.

The essential Kabbalistic text that discusses the idea of "gilgul" is called Sha'ar Ha'Gilgulim ("The Gate of Reincarnations"), based on the work of Rabbi Isaac Luria (and compiled by his disciple, Rabbi Chaim Vital). It describes the deep, complex laws of reincarnation.

There are many famous people in history, that we know who they were before. There are books on the subject but I thought I would give you some examples:

> Moses as the *gilgul* of Abel, and Rabbi Akiva as the *gilgul* of Cain. Cain also came back as the Egyptian that Moses killed. Cain killed Abel and Abel came back to kill Cain. How's that for justice.

The Hasidic Rebbe, Moshe Teitelbaum of Ujhel (1759–1841), who was one of the founders of Hasidism in Hungary, told his followers that he had been reincarnated three times, which he recalled. His first gilgul was as a sheep in the flock of the Biblical Patriarch Jacob. He sang to his followers the song that Jacob sang in the pastures. His second gilgul was in the time of Moses, and his third gilgul, which he did not disclose out of humility, was in the time of the destruction of the First Temple in Jerusalem. His followers asked another Hasidic Rebbe, who identified the third gilgul as the Biblical Prophet

Jeremiah. In Hasidic history, his daily life especially reflected a yearning for the building of the Third Temple with the arrival of the Messiah. In his later days he wore his Shabbat clothing the entire week, anticipating the Messiah's arrival.

The contemporary scholar of Kabbalah and Hasidut, Yitzchak Ginsburgh, identifies Isaac Newton as the modern reincarnation of Noah.

This is not meant to be offensive, only to tell you the absolute truth. The Torah tells the story of Jacob and his wicked twin brother Esau. Esau hated his brother and wanted to kill him (it is mentioned many times throughout scriptures). We are told that as long a Jacob studied Torah, Esau was powerless to kill his brother. When Esau knew he would not succeed, he married the daughter of Ishmael and told Ishmael to kill Jacob. This is all prophecy since the Jews are descended from Jacob, the Romans and eventually the Christians were descended from Esau and the Muslims are descended from Ishmael. For two thousand years the Christians have tried to kill the Jews (the Inquisition, the Crusades, pogroms, the Holocaust, Jew-hatred, etc). In every country that the Jews lived they started out by staying to themselves and studying Torah. But, after a while the Jews started to assimilate into the non-Jewish society and found themselves hated and even killed. Hashem has sent a strong message to the Jews throughout history not to assimilate. The worst assimilation in history was the Jews of Europe before the Holocaust. The Jew-hatred of today is commensurate with the vast amount of assimilation. Fortunately, we also have the greatest amount of Torah study today that we have had in history.

Back to the story of the Christians. When they saw they couldn't kill the Jews, they turned the job over to the Muslims, which is what we see today (intifadas, terrorist activity, Jew-hatred). Be aware that the terrorists have been successful only with the help of all the non-Jewish nations. They buy their oil, support many of their programs and even negotiate on their behalf, always to the detriment of the Jews. There is no coincidence that the President of the United States today happens to be a Muslim pretending to be part Christian. That is the prophecy fulfilled of Esau marrying the daughter of Ishmael. Obama is absolutely the worst enemy to come along for the Jews. Obama, by the way, is the gilgul of the Pharaoh of Egypt. Also, Nimrod and Sancherev, King of Assyria. Both were very detrimental to the Jews.

There is extensive proof of how the prophecies of scriptures became the story of history. But, keeping with our topic, the Arizal said 500 years ago that Esau came back as Yeshu, the Christian deity. Rabbi Glazerson made a video showing where this is found in the Torah:

http://www.youtube.com/watch?v=vGKwTQHmv94

The last video that I invite you to watch is from a Rabbi Eliyahu Kin of Torah Ohr in California. Rabbi Kin is a fascinating speaker with many videos on a variety of Jewish subjects. This one happens to be reincarnation:

http://www.torahtube.com/video/180/Rabbi-Kin-on-Reincarnation

2.4 Leaving Egypt

The Torah uses the expression 50 times "from Egypt." What is so important about us going out of Egypt that it has to be repeated so many times? As with everything else, the Torah always is conveying a deeper message. Usually the "handbook of life" is teaching us an important concept about our lives and this is exactly what we have here.

Egypt was a place that was strictly a physical existence. As slaves, we were completely dependent on the Egyptians for our food, shelter, clothing, etc. We had virtually no spirituality until we left and traveled into the desert, received the Torah and continued to the land of Canaan. Life is the same way; we are born completely physical beings; but the Torah is telling us and guiding us on how to make the trip through life. Our lives are a trip from the physical to the spiritual – leaving Egypt and going to the Holy Land.

When we are born everything centers on meeting our physical needs. I am hungry – feed me. I am tired – let me sleep. I am wet – there needs to be some changes made around here. Clothe me, house me, entertain me, love me, etc me. Then we start to grow and learn. We get the Torah early in life, just like Mount Sinai, we start to learn about Hashem, and we spend forty years, not in the desert, per se, but progressing through life's challenges. All along the way going from a physical, trying to get closer to Hashem and becoming much more spiritual as we approach 120 years old (we expect to be as old as Moses when we change addresses).

In May of 2015, I will be celebrating (or will have celebrated, depending upon when you are reading this book) the 32nd anniversary of my 39th birthday (just past middle age according to the last paragraph). I can tell you without reservation that my physical needs have greatly diminished over the course of my life. I eat much, much less than previously; I sleep about 4 or 5 hours a night (being retired, YEAY, affords me time for naps during the day but usually not more than an hour at a time – maybe twice a day). I go to bed around 10PM and get up about 2 AM, one to see if the world is still in existence and then to study; then I go to Morning Prayer services. I recall when I was young not being satisfied unless I got about 10 hours a night sleep and I still wanted to nap during the day. My desire to study Torah has increased, since I have developed a much greater desire to come closer to Hashem. I have experienced this trip from Egypt to the Holy land, especially since I just happen to live in the Holy Land.

But what is the significance of 50 times in the Torah. 50 is a very significant number in Judaism. We count the Omer – 49 days from the second night of Pesach until Shavuot, the 50th day is the day that we received the Torah. The Israelites were at the 49th levels of Spiritual Impurity which was just above the lowest level, the 50[th.] So, even their trip had the significance of coming out of such a low spiritual level and making the trip towards the Spiritual Purity. Moses achieved the 49th level of *bina*, intellectual insights, out of a possible total of 50 such levels. The reason that Moses never reached the 50th and ultimate level of *bina* was that the achievement must parallel the effort expended on achieving the goal in question.

I forgot to mention, when I talked about reincarnation, that our present generation which is here to greet the Messiah, is the generation that was at Mount Sinai. The Jews of today (and even the lost tribes that are returning to Israel) are all reincarnated to experience the redemption. I was there, and I think I remember seeing you there, also.

Back to the subject. There are other 50's such as the Jubilee celebration that occurred every 50 years when we had the Temple. The Jubilee cycle will resume with the coming of the third Temple (soon).

One can see the tremendous significance to the number 50 in leaving Egypt and going to Israel – leaving the physical and going to the spiritual.

Does this mean that Hashem doesn't want us to be materialistic in life? What about the American Dream: cars, a mansion, maybe a yacht, vacations, drugs, alcohol, corruption, greed, higher suicide rate, splintered family relationships, looking over your shoulder often, incarceration, etc, etc, etc, etc, etc (oh, I'm sorry I think I added some extra, very realistic, commodities to the American Dream). Hashem wants us to be comfortable and have the necessities of life. But, what does a two million dollar home give me that a 500,000 dollar home doesn't? The answer is much less spirituality and more waste. There are so many people in this world that are hungry and without the necessities of life. Wouldn't the extra 1 and ½ million be better spent on helping people? If our job in life is correcting ourselves by following the will of Hashem, it seems very counter-productive to waste the opportunity to achieve a tremendous eternity in exchange for opulence during a very short time on earth. Remember the space between my fingers – that is how long life is, outside the fingers is the real life called eternity. The mansion and vacations are starting to look like a hell of an idea. They could provide you with a hot spot for travel after you leave Earth.

Go for the Jewish Dream instead, happiness, loving family, much happier children, a better education system, dear friends who help each other, great neighbors, peace of mind, good food, nice clothes including a prayer shawl (tallit) with fringe benefits, two kitchen sinks, good food (I think I said that already, but I really meant it), no boredom, great future and, the best of all, a relationship with the Owner of the universe (now you are truly a VIP). Oh, I forgot etc, etc, etc, etc, etc, etc and, one more, ETC.

Enjoy your journey through life. May you be both physically and spiritually comfortable and realize which one truly is the greater comfort.

2.5 He is Hiding Behind Nature

Why is it that we cannot experience Hashem outright? He is hiding behind this concept of nature that He created, but for what purpose?

As I have stated many times we are here on Earth to improve ourselves spiritually and to make adequate correction that will bring us to an eternity of joy with Hashem. We accomplish this task by voluntarily and willingly serving Hashem and doing all that He asks of us. If we didn't have the free will decision capability we would not accomplish our mission. Hashem did not create us as robots to just automatically do everything without a thought process. We say every day that Hashem created us in His image. This is not referring to a physical image; but, that we have personality traits that emulate Hashem and allow us to do His will. This also means that we are capable of deciding and carrying out, of our own free will, His commandments or not doing them. Without the ability to decide, the rectification to our souls would not occur. If we were aware of Hashem's presence, the system would not give us free reign to do our thing – right or wrong. So He hides and even makes everything look random just to help us.

The question is: Will Hashem continue to hide; or, when the redemption comes and the testing is over, will we experience Him as we did at Mount Sinai? It is not well known that it wasn't Moses alone that experienced Hashem, but the entire congregation of close to 3 million as well. Why am I saying "we experienced Him" instead of "we heard Him?" It is brought down that our five senses completely melded together to give us a complete experience. The fact that "We heard the light and we saw the sound" lets us know it was a miraculous experience that is indescribable. It was so scary that the Children of Israel cried out to Moses after Hashem disclosed only two commandments "we are afraid; you continue to tell us the commandments."

What will actually happen in the future when Hashem is no longer hidden? We get some insight from the Torah – the story of Joseph and his brothers. I am not going to retell all the details (if you don't know the story, you now have your first homework assignment – look it up). The important facts are that Joseph's ten brothers (Benjamin not included), out of jealousy, threw him into the pit then sold him into slavery. Joseph, who was 17 years old, was taken down to Egypt where, through a series of events, he wound up as second in command to Pharaoh (that is Yiddishe sechal – if you don't understand this statement, get back to your homework assignment). He saved Egypt and the rest of the world through his plan to horde food from a period of 7 productive years to feed everyone during the 7 years of famine that followed. His own brothers came down to Egypt to take advantage of the available food at which time Joseph put them to the test. They were not aware that this VIP of Egypt, now 39 years of age, was their brother. They hadn't seen him in 22 years, but Joseph recognized them. His biggest concern was to find out if they had repented the sins they did to him. When he realized the pain that his brothers were experiencing over their misdeeds, Joseph in a very emotional state disclosed to his brothers "I am Joseph your brother." We are told that at that point his brothers miraculously were given total insight as to what had transpired during the 22 years of separation and that Hashem was the One who had caused it (it was all part of Hashem's plan to make us a great nation and give the world His Torah to guide us). The brothers were comforted to know that it had to happen that way to accomplish the will of Hashem.

Beautiful story, but why am I bringing it up here? Let me introduce you to Rabbi Israel Meir HaCohen Kagan, who is commonly known as the "Chafetz Chaim," the name of his famous work on guarding one's tongue. He tells us that this story of Joseph is prophecy of how in the end of days Hashem will say the words again "I am Hashem, your G-d." At that time, all of history miraculously will become clear to us. We will fully understand why everything happened the way it did according to Hashem's will. I snuck in the word "again" when I said that we will hear Him. What did I mean by that? This is the second redemption with the first one being at the time we were taken out of Egypt and brought to Mount Sinai. This time will be a permanent redemption after which Hashem will no longer be allusive to us. We will be totally aware of His presence and all the pleasant changes that the end will bring. We will no longer have an evil inclination since we will no longer need free will. No more testing means no more temptation. In other words, everyone will only want to serve Hashem with joy and love. There is no decision to make when you have only one very pleasant choice. There will be no more war, hatred, sickness or death. At some future time, known only to Hashem, we will experience the resurrection of the dead; all our departed loved ones will return. There are some exceptions that will not return, but that's too detailed for our discussion here, even though you can use your imagination as to who would not be worthy of such a glorious event (it is part of the story that I am telling now entitled "How to be worthy of a tremendous future and eternity." – get it?). The overall timeline as to what is coming up and in what order is very involved, but we have been given hints in scriptures (another wait 'til you read this one, coming later).

I have given you even more reason to work on yourself before the "too late date." Take this seriously – the advantages to you and your loved ones are monumental.

There are two types of Jews in the world – observant Torah Jews and those that are not observant yet. All Jews will follow the ways of Hashem in the future but the ones who start before the choice is removed will have it the best for all eternity.

I point this out here since I believe we are closer than we think to the time of Hashem not being hidden. What is my hint? All the events that I have talked about that will happen before the redemption and introduction of Messiah, according to scriptures. It is now and so is the time of Hashem not being allusive to us coming up – be prepared. (Hopefully, by the time you read this all will have happened, B"H)

2.6 Free Will

I mentioned the importance of us having free will in accomplishing our rectification. The problem is most people really don't know what free will is or how to use it to their greatest advantage. So, what is it?

One way to gain insight of the concept of free will is to determine what it isn't. Animals, as an example, do not have free will. If an animal is hungry, he eats; if he is tired, he sleeps. If he has a choice of things to eat, he instinctively chooses the one that is more physically satisfying. He does not look at the two possibilities and reason the situation as a human might. "Well, let me see," said the animal, "I ate that just the other day; so, I think for this meal I will choose the other possibility, especially since it is more nutritious." But, is that really free will even for a human being or would we only be justifying in our mind what we instinctively really would prefer? If we wish to watch a TV show, would we reason out the situation or merely decide based on which show we favor? We have the same instinctive behavior, picking out the most satisfying or most physically comforting choice. Then if most decisions we make are for creature comfort, what is free will?

Human beings have the ability to choose something that they don't want. We possess, usually to meet obligatory requirements, the free will ability to do something not comfortable – not what we would prefer. Example, on Yom Kippur when we are required to fast for approximately 25 hours, we are capable of doing it. Our first thought is, I am hungry and I would like to eat. But, we have the ability to restrain and meet our obligation – overcome creature comfort through free will decision. Another example is on the night of Shavuot, commemorating the receiving of the Torah, we have the custom to stay up all night and study Torah. Three, four o'clock in the morning we are tired and really would like to hit the hay, so to speak. We have the tool of free will that says "I prefer to serve Hashem than to satisfy my comfort." What's really satisfying is the next day when we feel good and much more fulfilled about our accomplishments. It is said that the reward for a good deed is the deed itself (there is more to it than that). It means that we feel good about ourselves and what we have done when we know that we are satisfying Hashem's will. It's a great motivator or, at least, should be. Of course, the benefit is to our spiritual side, our soul – the real us.

The trap that we don't want to fall into is arrogance or seeking honor. We should have the proper motivation to do all deeds, especially since Hashem is watching and taking notes. An example is giving money to help the poor. When we give anonymously we are doing it for the right reason, to help people. If we like to give help directly to the person out of arrogance – "look how wonderful I am," we are doing the deed contrary to free will since it is self-satisfying and not self-sacrificing. Remember what I said about animals. Does the family pet really do anything out of love for his owner? "No, I'm in it for the treats and a good scratch on the neck." Even if a dog jumped into a body of water where someone is drowning, it is still instinctive. The dog doesn't stop to reason, as we humans do, this may be a dangerous act – but it is a very good thing and my life insurance is current and valid.

Why is all this so important? To serve Hashem and to perfect ourselves requires strong desire, motivation and action over what is comfortable. The most important thing in our lives should involve a desire to satisfy and show love for our Creator. I realize this may require a high level of spirituality, but that is exactly what our goal is and our purpose on Earth (read that again if you didn't catch on). When we exercise our free will to serve a higher level, we in essence improve and achieve that goal.

This is also why free will is not needed when the redemption comes. We have completed our task; have achieved whatever level that we were able to and no longer need the tool of free will. When we have one choice and a great desire only to do things the one way, no decision making is needed, and we are extremely happy about it.

Even though I have been speaking mostly about spiritual improvement, free will is vital for physical improvement as well. Exercise that we don't want to do because maybe it is very uncomfortable. It's more fun to be a couch potato; even though we may wind up shaped like one (was that a fat potato or an overstuffed couch to which I was referring – you decide). There are medical procedures that we might prefer to avoid but, even though very uncomfortable, are necessary for good health or even physical survival. To put this into perspective, our bodies are a gift from Hashem for the purpose of doing the commandments – our mission in this life. Therefore, the body is the tool for our rectification and requires free will decision-making to succeed – it is a win-win situation.

We should see from all this that free will is a mechanism given to us by Hashem to help us succeed in our mission of complete rectification. Use it wisely and, I shouldn't forget, – thank You, Hashem.

2.7 This Explains It All

I would like to give you some insight as to why the world is the way it is and even why history was so chaotic and full of turmoil. What I will be explaining is from Kabbalistic sources so I start off with a disclaimer: I can only give you the details as I learned them, and have no idea of the deep ramifications (it is beyond human comprehension). Am I off the hook?

Let us talk of the beginning of humankind. All my references to Adam are for all people, men and women, since Adam and Eve were created as a single being and were later separated into two distinct individuals. What is important for our purpose is that they did not start out as human beings as is familiar to us. They were at a very high spiritual level. When Adam ate from the tree of knowledge of good and evil, he did it for a very positive reason. He was very close to Hashem but wanted to be even closer. Even though he knew everything he needed to know about the world, he had a great desire to know more. Adam saw this tree as an opportunity to possibly be at the same level as Hashem. Once again, this was out of love for Hashem, since Adam was already at a very high spiritual level. What actually changed after he ate? In Hebrew there are two words that sound the same (unless you are Israeli and can hear the subtle difference) but have one letter difference giving it a different meaning. The word is "ohr." If spelled with the Hebrew letter alef, it means light. If spelled with an ayin it means skin. When Adam sinned his size was greatly reduced (he was a giant before and now was the size of a human being of today) and the covering of his body was changed from pure light to skin as we know it. In essence he went from being a spiritual being to a physical being. This is really when he became a human being to which we can relate. His knowledge was greatly changed since he was now aware of both good and evil. This is when he became aware of his lack of body covering as an example.

So far so good (I hope). Now we get into the spiritual change. The following explanation is an over simplification of a very difficult concept to understand (the part that is beyond our comprehension). Adam's soul was actually the soul of all humankind. We were all part of Adam. When he sinned, the sparks of his soul were shattered like a broken vessel and scattered throughout the world. This is the reason that the people are throughout the world since the perfection of the world requires the gathering of these sparks to bring the soul of Adam together again. Of course, most of the souls were placed in Heaven, also known as the World of Souls. That occurred with the plan that the souls would come to Earth throughout history to effect the perfection of the Earth and the perfection of each individual soul. In other words, history was a gathering of the sparks to make whole the vessel again.

A side note of interest. Where we were located as individuals within Adam's soul determined what part of the world mission for which we would be responsible. If we were the hands of Adam we would come to Earth as a skilled individual working with the hands. If we were part of his brain, we would be of high intelligence here. A soul from his heart might be a very righteous sensitive individual. I won't cover the not so favorable parts of the body – use your imagination (that may explain why we have politicians – sorry about that). The point is we as the whole of society know why the world has the tremendous variety of skills and intelligence levels. It is interesting to ponder the individual location that you may have occupied in Adam.

What purpose is served by all this? Hashem is allowing very important and wonderful accomplishments by this scenario. One is that Adam (and all of us) had to be sent down to a very low spiritual level in order to gather the sparks. By doing this we are given the opportunity upon completion to surge upward almost like a slingshot affect to a spiritual level even higher than the level with which Adam started. When the redemption comes and the perfection is put into place, eventually we will experience a level that is close to Hashem beyond our comprehension. In essence, Adam's desire to reach a much higher level will be accomplished.

There is another aspect of this plan that is not so obvious. Hashem is perfect. Within His perfection is all imperfection. Meaning, that Hashem is complete with everything. Hashem decided to demonstrate His wholeness by creating this world and us as imperfect beings. At the same time we are being brought to a level of perfection at the end, we have been the vehicle to show that all levels of imperfection exist within Hashem's perfection. We can glean from all this some of the very difficult concepts that we questioned at the beginning. Why has history been so chaotic and full of turmoil? We can now see that the gathering of the sparks had to be done at all levels including the lowest level of our existence. The levels had to include the lowest of evil to the highest of goodness. The levels had to include all the imperfection that exists within the wholeness and perfection of Hashem. Hashem is everything, there is none else. As part of Hashem, we were the vehicle to demonstrate His wholeness. The good news is all the sparks have been gathered. The history used to demonstrate His wholeness is complete. This is why I am convinced that the time of our redemption and the introducing of the Messiah are imminent. All is complete, the work is done – the future looks tremendous.

I didn't say this was going to be simple to understand; but, my purpose in trying to explain this is to encourage everyone to gain the maximum place in the sun, so to speak. We now have the opportunity to obtain the highest spiritual level that Adam craved. It is available to each and every one of us. The last minute acts of rectification will change our eternity for the absolute best. Don't waste the opportunity. Return to Hashem for everything. Know that everything that Hashem has done He has done for us and it is for the good. You and your loved ones will see a level of happiness and fulfillment that is beyond our human comprehension and that is the absolute truth. Accept it, live it and enjoy it.

2.8 Why are Jews so Intelligent?

Did you ever wonder why the Jews have such a disproportionately high number of Nobel Prize winners? Why are there so many Jewish doctors, lawyers, scientists, engineers (let's hear it for the engineers) and only one Indian chief (Mel Brooks)? There is a very legitimate reason that is not so obvious.

Jews are known as the people of the Book. For thousands of years we have studied the most complicated text ever written – scriptures.

I have a short story for you to exemplify my point. When my immediate family was becoming observant, my 18 year old son was a college student. He came to me one day to ask if he could drop out of college and go to Yeshivah. I was very proud of his feelings towards Hashem and Judaism and consented immediately – sending him to a Yeshivah in Jerusalem – an experience that completely changed his life and mine (I went to visit him and discovered that Israel was my true home). Thank you, Hashem. Happy children very much enhance the joy of life. We made this bold change even though he was lacking only four college credits to complete his degree. After a year at Yeshivah, I investigated the possibility of him getting college credit for his Yeshivah studies. There is an organization in New York that will evaluate and accredit studies. The Yeshivah was familiar with this practice and constructed a transcript of my son's efforts for the year. The Yeshivah gave him 18 credits in such subjects as general studies, philosophy, history and language. When presented to the organization for accreditation, out of the 4 credits that he needed for that college, they gave him 36 credits. They also told us how much credit would be acceptable at Harvard, Yale, University of Pennsylvania and Hebrew University. They explained to us that they are totally aware of the intensity of study that occurs at a Yeshivah. They were also aware of the devotion and willingness to learn that Yeshivah students have. There is probably no match in the world for intensive learning than that of a Yeshivah. I attended college full and part time for 16 years including graduate level studies. I have never seen the level of devotion towards studies as I have in Yeshivahs with which I have been associated. By the way, my son received his degree.

There are research studies that have been performed on the subject of Jewish intelligence that have very surprising results. They argue persuasively that "elevated Jewish intelligence is grounded in genetics" rather than being only environmental. Even though the intense Yeshivah study and even the extended study, caused by such factors as having books in the home (there is definitely much home study as well), they concluded that Jewish intelligence is 'substantially heritable." Jews, especially the Ashkenazim of central and western Europe, have been engaging for centuries in what basically amounts to selective mating and merging genes to produce children of high intelligence.

The Talmud (Pesachim 49a) says that "A man should sell all he possesses in order to marry the daughter of a scholar, as well as marry his daughter to a scholar." In the Jewish community of the Middle Ages, the smartest men often became Rabbis, and these learned men of high status were able to marry the daughters of successful merchants, thus "selecting" in favor of high intelligence. The Jewish woman who was the teacher of the house, ensuring that the children were properly and extensively educated, were themselves well learned.

At the same time, Christians were doing just the opposite: priests, monks and nuns of the dominant Roman Catholic Church, also usually among the best and brightest in their communities, were prohibited from marrying, thus "selecting out" through celibacy most of these intellectually superior men and women from the gene pool.

There is another factor that is not so obvious but is a catch 22 situation (I like catch 22's). In most countries to which Jews migrated the people were happy to have the intelligence and cleverness of the Jew, but were apprehensive about giving Jews employment for fear of them dominating and taking over businesses. The same people that held back the Jew from gaining inroads in business and even academic endeavors, helped cultivate the business savvy of the Jew. How so? Jews were "on their own" and forced, out of necessity and survival, to develop their clever ways. They became self-employed, self-educated and, in many cases, self-governing. "Necessity is the mother of invention" an expression that is the history of the Jews.

But, since I like to analyze the absolute truth, I would be remiss to not include the will of Hashem. What the Jew is and has been throughout history is, by design, fulfilling Hashem's will. The intelligence of the chosen people was totally necessary to bring the message of Hashem to the world. The correction of the world depended on its agents who were tasked to bring it to fruition. The stereotyping, Jew-hating, Jew-bashing all very much resulted from the frustration and jealousy of the non-Jewish population. It was also a message from Hashem that when Jacob is studying Torah, Esau can't touch him. A strong message to the Jews throughout history is simply: do the job you were charged with – study Torah, and don't assimilate into the gentile society. Hashem made life difficult on purpose when the Jew decided that he wanted to blend into the non-Jewish world. Jews were welcome even invited to many countries as long as they stayed separate from the local population. When the Jews said "I like the way they dress, I like their food, I like their jobs, I like their secular education" Hashem made sure the population of that country turned on them. I lived in Germany for six years, ich habe viel Deutch gelernt, I remember a speech that I heard from of all sources hitler (may his name be stricken – his name is small case intentionally since he was never a capital individual). he said "I don't want you assimilating with the German people." Who was really sending that message?

Even in Israel, the absolutely happiest communities are those that are completely observant Jews with no non-Jews or even non-Jewish behavior in their midst. When we adhere to this vital message from Hashem, no harm will come to any Jew and complete happiness is discovered. It worked for me, my family and the entire city within which we dwell. Thank you, Hashem.

2.9 What is Real?

What I am about to tell you should have one of three reactions. The intelligent person should give much thought to the subject, review the proof and realize that everything that Hashem does is for the good. The not-too-informed will think "I don't buy any of this, this guy is obviously deranged and I am finished with this book." The middle of the road person will say "I don't know what to believe – this is crazy and goes against all human logic, but I guess I need to investigate further." Do I have your attention?

Rabbi Avigdor Miller, z"tl said it best "Everything you see in front of you is only the imagination of Hashem, it is an allusion and doesn't really exist." We are not real but only the thoughts of Hashem living out the script called the Torah. He imagines everything, and miraculously His thoughts become our reality. Being an Infinite Intelligence allows Hashem to fool us into thinking that everything is real.
Since we were created in Hashem's image, we have some examples in our lives of such abilities, on an infinitely lower scale. Let me give you a scenario to think about.

Picture two couples that are leaving a house and going to a wedding celebration. They get into the car and leave.

Each one of you came up with an imaginary scenario. Since, hopefully, there are many people reading this book, there were many visualizations pictured. No two were alike. Some saw the couples living in the city, some saw a suburban scene. What type of car did they use, what color, what was the seating arrangement, what were they wearing, what did they look like, what did they say, etc? The important thing about this little exercise is we have the ability with our mind's eye to visualize situations, people and events.

What if your imagination became real? An Infinite Intelligence exists Who has that ability. Hashem decided to make a world, fill it with countless wonders and bring it to life in such a way that it became reality for the players He imagined. Why, did he do it? See above "This Explains It All," which gives some incite of what Hashem's will is for us and the world. The players, all the wonders, the entire sequence of events that is our history and even the design of everything in the universe were created with perfection to satisfy His will and to demonstrate His wholeness. It is all beyond our comprehension; but, we only need to know that Hashem designed the Earth with love and gave it to us for our benefit – to help us.

Further proof comes from the scientific discovery of a holographic universe. It was first theorized in the 1980's with much more evidence found in recent years, that the universe is not a physical place but an allusion that we experience as a holographic image. If you want the scientific explanation, the web is replete with sites, studies, experiments, etc to whet your appetite.

2.10 More science to ponder

Higgs Boson. In the 1960's a Professor Peter Higgs proposed a theory, that as we continue to study sub-atomic particles (the smallest particles of the atomic structure), we will come across a boson particle. What is the importance of this particle? It will actually be a mass of real matter that gives reality to the atom (that was an over simplification of an extremely complicated concept). Why do we need to find such a particle? Until this very day everything we see in the makeup of matter seems to be only packets of energy and wave-like behavior. We have never seen anything that can be called solid matter. A separate discipline called Quantum Physics was created just to be able to study this phenomenon. Quantum Physics provides a mathematical description of much of the dual *particle-like* and *wave-like* behavior and interactions of energy and matter. But, without the proof of solid matter, are we left with the idea that the universe is not real but strictly measurable stuff to keep the Physicist employed – of course, it is our allusion of a universe.

One comical note about the Higgs Boson. In the 1990's some clever scientist named it the "G-d particle." He wasn't aware that every particle in the universe is a G-d particle (I'm sorry, I had to get that off my chest).

Presently, the Large Hadron Collider (LHC) is the world's largest and highest-energy particle accelerator. This 17 mile long accelerator is designed to collide opposing particle beams of either protons at up to 7 teraelectronvolts (7 TeV or 1.12 microjoules) per nucleon, or lead nuclei at an energy of 574 TeV (92.0 µJ) per nucleus (2.76 TeV per nucleon-pair). That is as simple as I can make it (what did I say?). In other words, they are bringing particles up close to the speed of light, 186,000 miles per second, and smashing the particles against each other in such a way as to break down the atom into its basic components. This is all for the purpose of trying to observe real matter; but, to date they have only verified that everything must be an allusion – they still haven't found the famous Higg's boson. There are reports from LHC that they have found the boson, but in reality they have only detected energy fields that they believe contain the boson. They have never actual verified its existence, but have come up with speculation as to where it might be. I personally think it is mind over matter – if you don't mind, it doesn't matter.

Dark Matter and Dark Energy: In the 1930's there was a great change in the thinking of the concept of dark. Dark was always considered a lack of light. But, science started to view dark as having measurable energy as well as matter. This has progressed over the decades to the point where the belief that the entire universe even what was thought of as empty space is actually full of energy and matter.

What is amazing is how it totally agrees with the concept in scriptures that "the whole world is full of His glory (Isaiah 6:3, Psalms 72:19)." There is no place in the entire universe that the essence of Hashem cannot be experienced. We even say a blessing everyday "Blessed are You Hashem, our G-d, King of the universe, Former of light, Creator of darkness, Maker of peace, Creator of all things." He actually created darkness and those wonderful scientists have finally discovered it. The Torah starts out in the first paragraph talking about how

Hashem separated the light from the darkness. Hashem is everything. This is verified in Deuteronomy 4:35 Ain Ode Milvado "There is nothing but G-d!"

Another scientific concept we can peruse is "The Unification Theory," or, as I previously mentioned, "The Theory of Everything." This concept would unify all the fundamental interactions of nature: gravitation, strong interaction, weak interaction, and electromagnetism. Scientists have theorized that there is a commonality to all forces that they may actually be originating from a single source. Duh, Ain Ode Milvado says it all.

There seems to be infinite proof that everything that exists is Hashem. His infinite intelligence makes the allusion perfect and anyone who thinks that he or she can see beyond this infinite level is delusional, so to speak. This means that individual such as atheists are in total denial of the only life force that exists. To think that there is an accidental free running life producing entity in this non-existent physical world is not too intelligent. To believe that we can make up names like "mother nature or father time" to explain reality is beyond human ignorance. By the way, time is also an allusion.

The proof is overwhelming, even scientifically, that there is only a spiritual existence that provides a physical façade. The purpose is well known since the Single Spiritual Existence mercifully has given us in writing, full details of everything. The only question for each of us as individuals is "what does it mean to me and how should I be using this information to guide me through my eternity?" A loaded, but valid question. We are on our own to use the gift of this allusive world to thrive, succeed or fail. We have been given the choice of the blessing or the curse Deuteronomy 11:26, blessing if we do His commandments or the curse if not. How simple a solution to bringing happiness and everything wonderful to life.

2.11 The Scientists are Still Catching Up

You know how I laugh at modern scientific discoveries that we Jews have known about for thousands of years. Recently, I saw in the news that "The Universe may be a Computer Simulation." In other words, everything around us is only an allusion and so well organized (according to studies of radiation levels, gravitational calculations, etc), that it appears as though it was programmed by some Source – just like we might do today with a computer simulation. The randomness and chaos of the universe, including this world, is starting to look like a well-organized system that was created. What a shock!

As I stated above, we see from scriptures with scientific proof that this is not the real world but only an allusion that comes from an Infinite Source of Intelligence. The fun part is that scientists only discovered this concept in the last century when they suspected that everything around us is a holographic image. There are write-ups of this idea of "What is Real?" you can Google the subject and see how confused the scientists were, and still are.

The more comical aspect is some of their explanations for this allusion. Things like "advanced aliens came from outer space and were able to create this programming" or "in the future we might be facing extinction so, with the help of time travel, we were able to go back in time and recreate the universe as a computer simulation. I laugh at the fact that the simplest of explanations is the most rejected: There is a Deity of Infinite Intelligence and Infinite Power Who created the universe and continues to create and run everything. Why can't scientists just accept the Absolute Truth that has proof beyond any shadow of a doubt? One reason is they may be out of work if they acknowledge that all of science, with all its proofs, is in scriptures. Another reason is we live in a world of falsehood that separates "church and state," or in our case "Shul and state" even to the point of providing an education in public schools that is total nonsense. Teach lies, it is the best way to keep religion at bay and fight this concept of Hashem. Then we scratch our heads asking "why is this world so messed up?" Duh.

In all fairness, I should caveat this discussion by mentioning the Association of Orthodox Jewish Scientists. Go to their website to see how truth and science really do go together:

http://www.aojs.org/.

We should never forget that the One Who created the laws of Physics, the laws Chemistry, the laws of Biology and every other scientific discipline, was also the One Who wrote the Torah.

The Messiah is actually here already and will be introduced soon, and the world of truth will begin. Then scientists can become Rabbis (or Orthodox Jewish

Scientists) and start living reality instead of fantasy and still have a paycheck coming in.

In looking at articles in the news and on the web about this discovery of the allusion of the universe, there are some very interesting statements coming out of the scientific community. With such a proof of order, of design, not chaos, not randomness, scientists are rethinking the idea of a Designer. There is so much talk about the question "Is this proof of G-d and His creation?" that I am really having a good time – enjoying every article I read. Hashem works in mysterious ways and these messages being given to the world at this time are so encouraging. Why? I have been saying that there are many indications that we are getting close to great changes in the world. One of the most exciting changes is we are going into "The time of truth." What a delightful way for Hashem to put doubt in the minds of the people of this world than to shake up the scientific world with proof of Hashem's existence.

I would give you some classic quotes that I have seen, but they come from sources that I wish you to avoid, including news sources that are reporting such rhetoric. Also, watching certain individuals squirm about how this is messing up their minds (although a very enjoyable experience), it could border on Lashon Harah, an evil tongue, if I gave names (and we don't want that). I prefer to keep it general and not embarrass anyone. One other area of enjoyment is how atheists have gotten into the debate and how they are being made into minced meat. There are even discussions by former atheists who are seeing the light and questioning their misguided past.

The more important concept is how Hashem works and sends us profound messages. The changes to this upside-down world are becoming more obvious every day; this is just one more example.

I talked much about how everything in the universe including every one of us is encoded in the Torah. The 304,805 letters of the Torah is the genetic code for everything. Now we can modernize our terminology and add that the Torah is the computerized programming for everything. We already knew who the Geneticist is, now we know He is also a Programmer Who wrote all the computerized code for the universe and our world. I love it. Thank you Hashem.

2.12 The World is Upside-Down

There is a very interesting story in the Talmud (Pesachim 50a) which tells:

> When Rabbi Yosef miraculously recovered from a deathly coma, his father, Rabbi Yehoshua ben Levi, asked him to describe the glimpse he caught of the World of Souls where he had briefly sojourned.
>
> "I saw an upside-down world," he replied, "in which those so honored here because of their wealth were placed very low, while those so low here because of their poverty were there so highly placed."
>
> "You saw a clean world," his father assured him. "But tell me, what was the status of Torah scholars like ourselves?"
>
> "The same honor we enjoy in this world," replied the son, "is accorded to us there."

The story is basically telling us that we live in an upside-down world where what is important isn't really important and what is unimportant is really important. This is a world of fantasy and materialism and not spirituality. We are not physical beings that just happen to have a soul; but, spiritual beings wearing physical clothing which allows us to accomplish our mission in this allusion of a physical world. It is not an easy concept to convince anyone, even very observant Jews. When we get away from this gashmius world (the physical world) and start living the true ruchnius life (spiritual life), all the nonsense and craziness disappears.

So the big question is "what is your status in this crazy, fantasy world?" Take a fast test, just 20 questions – answering yes or no to each. Be honest with yourself since the only One grading you is Hashem.
Test part 1 (yes or no)

1. Did you pay attention to US Major League Baseball World Series?
2. Are you rooting for your favorite football team to go to the Super Bowl?
3. Do you know the latest pop music releases?
4. Do you have your favorite TV shows?
5. Do you know JC's mother's name?
6. If you are American, did you vote believing that you needed to help get the best leader in office (if not an American did you follow the last campaign and have a favorite candidate; someone that you think would be best to help the world situation)?

7. Did Christopher Columbus discover America?
8. Does everyone celebrate Xmas, even nonXtians, after all it is a national holiday?
9. Do you celebrate Halloween and Thanksgiving?
10. Do you know who Big Bird is?

Test part 2 (yes or no)

1. Can you name the five books of Moses in Hebrew?
2. Do you know JC's mother's name in Hebrew?
3. Do you know the names of Moses's mother, father, sister and brother?
4. Are you familiar with Shatnez?
5. Did you ever study the Mishna Berurah and Shulchan Aruch?
6. Do you know how many mitzvot are in the Torah?
7. Is your mother Jewish?
8. Do you know how many Challahs are used at the Shabbos meal?
9. Do you know the Hebrew letters?
10. Do you know what a Minhag is?

You may have psyched out my test by now and tried to answer everything in a favorable light rather than an honest answer. If you said "Yes" to all or even most of test 1 and "No" to test 2, you are most likely living the materialistic, fantasy life of this world. If you answered the opposite: "No" to test 1 and "Yes" to test 2, consider yourself a more spiritual person with a bright future. Your trip through life has been on a positive path – seeking the truth and Hashem's ways.

The problem is that the people who have not studied Torah seem to think they have all the answers. They definitely have the most distorted view of reality. Living only in this fantasy world is completely caused by a lack of scholarship of the real world, the world of truth. As long as an individual is convinced that he or she knows what reality is, that perception blocks the ability to see the truth. I thought I would go over some areas of studying scriptures and the truth of this world to hopefully help you as an individual see where you may be going astray.

Let's begin with a question: Do you understand the message of the Torah, or do you have to refer to the Talmud and 1000's of years of commentary in order to fully understand Hashem's message (and even with many years of study do you

119

still have more questions than answers)? Watch it – this is a trick question. The person who makes statements such as "I know Halachah" or "I have read the Torah (in English no less) and fully understand its message," should be avoided – that is a person with an opinion and not scholarship. The great Rabbis that I have had the privilege of knowing, and with whom I have personally studied, would never give me an answer off the top of their heads, but would always look it up before answering. I have heard many times that "the more years one studies Torah, the more one realizes how little one knows and how much more one needs to study." Torah has everything there is in life and covers everything in the universe; there is no missing subject. Do you feel that you know everything about life and every detail of the universe? I have said it before and will say it again "Torah is the most difficult subject in the world since it includes every subject in the world!!!!!"

But, human beings think they can logically figure it out, even though human logic is flawed. It says in the Bible "For My thoughts are not your thoughts" says Hashem, Isaiah 55:8. Hashem's logic is perfect, ours is greatly lacking. The final result is we get into more trouble using our own solutions than just turning to Hashem for His solution to our problems. One proof of that is personal interpretation. The Torah was given to Moshe in a string of letters (304,805 to be exact) without breaks, without sentences, without punctuation and, the best one of all, without vowels. In other words, there are so many interpretations to every word, even every letter, that to say the English translation we use gives up the deep meaning to Torah is total nonsense. We even have the problem in English that if something is written with improper punctuation or even improper emphasis, it can mean something completely different. As an example (another test question), place punctuation in the following statement:

Woman without her man is nothing

I like this example since most men punctuate it as: Woman: without her man, is nothing. (The pause being between "man" and "is")
The woman usually punctuates this as: Woman: without her, man is nothing. (The pause being between "her" and "man")
What a profound difference in meaning by just moving a comma.

What if we put emphasis on certain words in a sentence to cause change in meaning. Examples:

What do you have on your mind? Could become: What do you have on? Your mind? I added a question mark but I changed the emphasis on my pronunciation that changed the entire thought.

What is up the road ahead? Could become: What is up the road? A head?

These may be silly examples, but they make one question one's interpretation – how distant is our thinking from the truth? If we are reading Hebrew without punctuation and even without vowels, how can we be so sure that we understand the meaning – because we have an English translation? The English is always the simple surface meaning with almost no depth to its content (it is called pshat in Hebrew). We are told to rely on thousands of years of Torah scholars (the great Rabbis) who, we were told by Hashem, would give us the insight and the depth. We definitely have deeper meaning available because of Rashi or the Rambam or the Ramban or the Arizal or the Vilna Goan, etc, etc, etc. These and many other great Torah scholars throughout the years have guided us and taught us ways to see scriptures that we never could have known. Any Yeshivah student will tell you that studying the Talmud without Rashi or Tosefos, is not understanding the meaning of the text. If you are not familiar with Rashi or Tosefos, than you are exactly the individual to which I am referring.

RAV YITZCHAK HUTNER z"tl (in PACHAD YITZCHAK, Yom Kippur 5, Pesach 60 (and notes to Pesach 5:2), Shavuos 25:9) offers a penetrating insight based on the Talmud.

Rav Hutner explains that the three differences between this world and the next as described by the Talmud and by Rashi in Devarim (Deuteronomy) are inherently related to each other. In this world, we do not perceive things the way they really are; reality is blurred, and Hashem's presence is not clearly recognized by all. If we would be able to see Hashem's good and perfection clearly, His true essence as One would be obvious. In the World to Come, reality will no longer be blurred, and it will be apparent to all that everything is good. At that time, the nations of the world will proclaim Hashem's Oneness together with us.

Accordingly, all manifestations of Hashem's attribute as "One" are based on the clarity of Hashem's presence that will be evident in the World to Come.

The truth is that even in this world it is possible, to a certain degree, to disperse the clouds that blur man's perception and understanding of reality and to feel the omnipresence of the Divine will. This is because even in this world, no true "bad" or "injustice" is ever wrought. Everything that transpires is the Divine design and is intended to be for our ultimate good (see Berachos 60b). Although the ultimate purpose behind what occurs in this world is often hidden from our perception, the reality is that it is the Divine plan. When we strive to recognize the Divine plan and to accept it, we gain a "glimpse" of the Creator.

The moment at which it is most imperative that we experience the clarity of the presence of Hashem is when we declare, "Shema Yisroel Hashem Elokeinu Hashem Echad," and proclaim the Oneness of Hashem. As Rashi explains, this exclamation expresses our longing for the world in which Hashem's presence will be fully revealed and He will be recognized as One. When we recite this verse, we attempt to gain clarity of Hashem's Oneness in this world of confusion by finding the hidden, inherent good that exists in everything that happens and that exists in this world.

Several additional points that need to be made about the way we evaluate Torah in this upside-down world. Many times I have received rebuttals to subjects with the statement "this Rabbi says this or that," or "my Rabbi allows us to do this or that." Be aware that you can probably find almost any answer that you want from a Rabbi – just keep looking. Does that mean that they could be wrong? No it usually means that we are getting very superficial answers on very complicated questions – sometimes questions that have been debated for thousands of years. We very rarely get to talk to the Rabbi in depth to hear the real answer or, even more importantly, what is Hashem's opinion to that question. A Rabbi that answers off the top off his head without an in depth search into scriptures, may be giving you nothing more than his personal opinion. Sometimes the Rabbi is trying to make it easier for you to accomplish a Halachah and will give you a very lenient response that is convenient, but not the best answer. This, I know, even comes from the great Rabbis.

Rav Moshe Feinstein z"tl, one of the greatest authorities of our modern times has given lenient answers, but would not necessarily follow his own advice. An example would be about a Shabbos timer used to turn on and off various electrical appliances, lights or even heating and air conditioning systems. Rav

Moshe gave permission to use such timers saying they were halachically acceptable, but he, himself, would never use one. It comes down to a decision made by an authority of the highest level that says "I have found no violation in doing something a particular way, but to be as stringent as possible in the eyes of Hashem, I still would not do a particular act in case there is a slight doubt." We are not on the level of a Rav Moshe and in no way is he not giving us a totally correct answer, but because we do not go into the depth of life's questions as a great Rabbi, such as Rav Moshe, our complete understanding of each answer is only surface information and should be studied much deeper before we claim to have the right answer or, even worse, pass it on to others as the truth from Hashem.

I studied for years with a Talmud (a scholarly student) and former neighbor of Rav Moshe and saw the tremendous depth and scholarship with which such a brilliant Rabbi is capable. Yet, as my mentor told me, information becomes very distorted when passed down from one Jew to another or even how information can be completely misunderstood by an observant Jew. I will talk about bad habits and how people can truly believe they are doing the right thing but are, in essence, hurting themselves and others by pontificating opinions rather than scholarship.

I have been accused of not telling the Absolute Truth, but I have yet to receive any refutation of any information, with the refutation being backed by scriptural proof. This has been disturbing since I know that I have extensively researched and presented facts with complete confidence and that the individual who is making the comment is hurting him or herself with false interpretation. Saying that I am wrong on a subject without giving me a scriptural reference to counter the argument is useless to me or my readers. I am very, very open minded to the fact that I am human being and make mistakes, but I try to compensate with years of research on the one question that I always ask on any subject: "What is Hashem's opinion on that?" Giving me an answer from a Rabbi should also be supported with his deep insight from scriptures and not off the top of his head.

One more word about what Rabbis have said which is very important to this discussion is that very often Rabbis change their rulings on questions as times changes or as circumstances dictate. An example: In the 1990's there were Rabbis that cautioned about listening to the Facilitated Communications individuals as marking them as true messengers from Heaven. Why? The FC individuals were, at that time, without a track record of making statements that came true. The Rabbis were totally correct in cautioning us at that time. Here we are 18 years later and the same Rabbis have emphatically stated that these individuals have satisfied the prophecy of Bava Basra 12b, that prophecy has been given to those mentally connected to the spiritual world and the children (this is a discussion that has been discussed already) and also that they have satisfied the test of a prophet given to us in the Torah.

Another topic that I will cover is that we have the choice to be lenient or stringent on everything we do. The basic concept here is that we are watched and judged by Hashem with everything we say and everything we do. We then receive in return measure for measure what Hashem thinks we are worthy to receive. In other words, if we serve Hashem with the absolute best intentions and with complete love, He judges us favorably in the same way and life is good. If we do as little as possible, with the idea that we are just getting by doing the commandments, then we should never complain when our life is just getting by with what Hashem gives us. Pirkei Avos, the Ethics of the Fathers (Chapter 1:17), tells us that Hashem doesn't want us to study Torah; He wants us to live Torah. Of course we can't live Torah to the fullest unless we study our instructions in great depth. Bottom line, especially in the end of days is: be as stringent in doing Hashem's will as you possibly can, and do it with great joy. It may sound strange but when you are doing Hashem's will to the fullest with the best of intentions, life becomes so wonderful that you are greatly encouraged to do even more. It's habit forming.

I have received comments telling me of Rabbis who say that you don't have to be so stringent. I suspect that those Rabbis were either very misunderstood or are leading lives that are somewhat less than joyous. It is one thing to cut yourself short of a happy life, but to pass that on to others is not Hashem's way. I have had it happen to me that with the best of intentions a Rabbi gave me a watered down response to make it easier. The final result is I developed an incorrect habit that needed changing. Sometimes being more lenient is not helping anyone. I have taught people easier ways to do things, but have included the path to become more stringent. Building up to a process with baby steps is a good way to learn, but don't stay at the lower level, continue to build. As we used to say in the Army "be all that you can be." Never stop growing nor be satisfied with something less than perfection – after all, we are here on Earth to perfect ourselves, not to settle for something much less.

There is another very big misunderstanding. Issues like women hair covering, kashrus, purity and all the 613 commandments are matters of spiritual guidance. We absolutely do not know how a violation of a commandment or even performing a commandment in a lenient versus stringent way affects our soul. I received a comment from a well-intentioned woman who told me that her husband is not affected by seeing a woman's head covered in a sheitel (wig) instead of a snood or tichel. This means he knows exactly what his soul is experiencing and that is ludicrous. I know she is referring to his physical reaction but the physical reaction means nothing – it is the spiritual reaction or damage to which I am referring.

The Kirlian Camera, a device that captures the ultra-violet light in its images has been used to detect the human aura of a person. It allows us to see that what we experience spiritually and physically are two different things. As an example: a man wearing Tefillin has an aura that he didn't have before he put it on. Research on the subject has led to a consensus among researchers of the aura that Tefillin can raise a person's spiritual level, as well as protect one's body from negative external energies. The same is true for a married woman who covers her hair versus allowing the hair to be seen.

Extra note: the purpose of covering the hair is for modesty that a married woman should not attract the attention of men (attraction is reserved for one's spouse). If a wig makes the woman more attractive, since most wigs today may look better than the woman's own hair, it totally defeats the purpose. In the Eyes of Hashem that is a violation not a fulfilling of the hair-covering requirement. There are many Chabad women who believe the Rebbe told them to wear only wigs. That is a total misinterpretation of what the Rebbe said. He told women who work in an office or are in a setting where they should not look out of place (be starred at), to blend in by wearing a wig. He said the preference it definitely to cover the hair with a material garment. In other words, if you live in an area, such as the observant community within which I live, a wig is incorrect – it attract men's eyes, not the opposite.

To say we know how we feel about something is a physical reaction. To say that we know how it is affecting us spiritually is beyond human comprehension. To tell me that a Rabbi said it is all right, does not pass the common sense test of what makes it all right. I live by a very convenient motto: "when in doubt, leave it out." If there is the slightest possibility that what I am doing is not the most advantageous way according to Hashem, than I look deeper into reality and figure out the best way. It is my choice and when I don't have the slightest comprehension as to how something could be hurting me or my family spiritually, I don't question it any further, but take the safe route. This is especially true in the end of days when we need all the help we can get. Listening to very lenient advice from a anyone is shooting yourself in the foot. Even though his effort, his advice may be with the best of intentions, the result may be your getting a much lesser Olam Habah, World to Come (our eternal life).

People are weak and have very little discipline; I know, being a retired US Army Officer, about the infinite number of excuses to do things the easy way. In the military a lack of discipline can cost you your life on the battlefield. In life a lack of spiritual discipline can lessen one's level of eternity and even hurt us in this physical life. We work hard to get closer to Hashem, not to look for every shortcut to make life easier, which in turn distances us from our goal.

The spiritual level that we want and don't have is exactly what our life's work is. There is no all or nothing. Seven point three billion people on Earth are at seven point three billion different levels and each person has the obligation to him or herself, and to every family member for whom we are responsible, to work hard to raise that level. Turning to Hashem with complete trust and faith is the nicest thing one can do for oneself and family. It is not Hashem or us – we are one – on the same team with the same goal – to perfect the world. I have heard for years people tell me "I have not been too lucky in life." I have also heard and personally experienced that the more we turn to Hashem and follow His ways, the luckier we get. There is no such thing as luck; there is only experiencing everything going better and better when we work harder within the system that the Creator of this life provided. His instructions are foolproof and guaranteed to work. The problem is our misconception of His instructions. I also have heard "I follow Hashem, but I still have problems." I have evaluated many cases of people who think they are following His ways, but have made up their own set of rules. The study of Torah resulting in living the Absolute Truth is a rare commodity; but, the very undisciplined human being comes to the conclusion "what I am doing is good enough" and then follows with "but it doesn't seem to be working." Duh! Maybe you haven't reached a spiritual level that is good enough. Maybe you need to spend the rest of your days increasing that level. I am pointing out the obvious, but it doesn't make any difference since we all, yes including me, have a long way to go and are greatly clouded and deceived by this fantasy of an upside-down world. Those of us, who are cognizant of what we lack and do repentance every day to work on it, are the ones in good shape and heading in the right direction. People, who are satisfied with their level of spirituality, don't have a clue as to how much they are hurting themselves in this life and all eternity. Get with the program and experience true happiness. Hashem guarantees it. Try to see this world right-side-up as described in the Torah and see what a difference your life will be.

Remember my finger display:

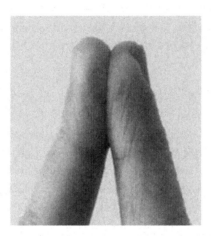

It lets you know that the space between my fingers is how long life is on earth. The space outside of my fingers is eternity and the length of our eternal life.

We work so hard to make life on Earth as pleasurable and successful as can be, and we ignore the real life which goes on after we change addresses. We do live forever but the time in this upside-down world is very limited and is the only opportunity to get it right for all eternity. Be as skeptical as you want about the truth; but, be aware that a day is coming soon that you will know without a doubt what the truth is and you will have to live with whatever you provided for yourself.

2.13 Measure for Measure or How to Change the Weather in the US

I have mentioned the idea that Hashem's system in this world is measure for measure. Whatever we do will result in what will happen to us. Action –

reaction. When we follow Hashem's ways we are blessed, when we think we know better and follow our own flawed human instincts, contrary to Hashem's instructions, we face life's challenges and troubles – life just doesn't go so smoothly.

The same is true for the nations of the world. As it says in the Torah, and expounded upon many times in Jewish scriptures, "those who bless you will be blessed and those who curse you will be cursed." What is my proof? If we review events that happen around the world, we will see a definite pattern of measure for measure, especially in the way countries treat Israel. More specifically is the way the US of A's has tried to help Israel with the most destructive policies possible. This is just a very partial list to shed some light on the reality of this world:

These storms were NOT a coincidence, and got many hecklers mocking that possibility, to say the least. Here are examples of instances where disasters or storms, or sometimes considered just plain political nuisances, afflicted the United States JUST when it attempted to divide the Land of Israel. One might call these coincidences (which there is no such thing considering that Hashem reacts measure for measure), but the number of incidences takes the chance out of the equation.

1991, 30 October - The Oslo Accord

President George H. W. Bush, Sr. promoted and proudly signed the infamous Oslo Accord at the Madrid Peace Conference on October 30, 1991. The Oslo Accord was labeled a "Land for Peace" accord that demanded Israel award their land to the Palestinian murderers and terrorists in exchange for peace. The perverse Oslo proposition was simple: give us your land and we'll stop killing you.

1991, 31 October - The Next Day – The Perfect Storm hits:

A very rare huge storm starting in the north Atlantic, moving east to west (wrong direction for storms to move – although in the Bible, the Holy Spirit and history move east to west). This storm was so unusual and contrary to typical weather patterns it was immortalized by the book The Perfect Storm by Sebastian Junger and later a popular movie. Amazon says of the book The Perfect Storm, "Meteorologists called the storm that hit North America's eastern seaboard in October 1991 a 'perfect storm' because of the rare combination of factors that created it. For everyone else, it was perfect hell. In The Perfect Storm, author Sebastian Junger conjures for the reader the meteorological conditions that created the 'storm of the century' and the impact the storm had on many of the people caught in it."

Interesting, one of the first places The Perfect Storm hit was Kennebunkport, Maine. Waves over 30 foot demolished the home of guess who – President George H. W. Bush, the instigator of the Oslo Accord.

1992, 23 August

A year later, President Bush literally picked up the pieces from Oslo attempting to rob Israel again. Meeting in Washington DC, Bush and crew again attempted to "sell" the fictitious Madrid "Land for Peace" agreement.

1992, 23 August – Same Day - Hurricane Andrew visits Florida

Hurricane Andrew smashes and crashes into Florida. Andrew causes over $30 billion in damage while destroying over 180,000 homes. At that time, Andrew was the worst natural disaster ever to hit America.

1994, 16 January

President Bill Clinton meets with terrorist and Israel hater Syria's President Hafez el-Assad in Geneva. They talk about a peace agreement with Israel that includes Israel giving up the Golan Heights.

1994, 17 January – less than 24 hours - 6.9 Earthquake rocks California

In less than 24 hours, a powerful 6.9 earthquake rocks Southern California. This mysterious quake, centered in Northridge, is the second most destructive natural disaster to hit the United States, behind Hurricane Andrew.

A disaster of another kind, but destructive just the same.... Impeachment.

1998, 21 January

Israeli Prime Minister Benjamin Netanyahu meets with President Clinton at the White House and is coldly received. Clinton and Secretary of State Madeleine Albright refuse to have lunch with him.

1998, 21 January – the same day – the Monica Lewinsky scandal erupts

After Clinton's rejection of Israeli Prime Minister Benjamin Netanyahu, later the very same day, the Monica Lewinsky scandal breaks out, destroying the Clinton presidency and resulting in his impeachment.

1998, 28 September

Secretary of State Madeleine Albright finishes the final details of an agreement which requires Israel to surrender 13 percent of Yesha (Judah and Samaria). President Bill Clinton meets with Yasser Arafat and Netanyahu at the White House to finalize another Israel "land for peace" hoodwink. Later, Arafat addresses the United Nations and declares an independent Palestinian state by May 1999.

1998, 28 September – Same Day - Hurricane George hits Gulf Coast

Hurricane George blasts the Gulf Coast with 110 mph winds and gusts up to 175 mph. The hurricane hit the coast and stalled until the agreement was finalized and Arafat addressed the UN. Then it hit and caused $1 billion in damage. At the exact time that Arafat departs the U.S., the storm begins to dissipate.

1998, 15 October

Arafat and Netanyahu meet at the Wye River Plantation in Maryland. The talks are scheduled to last five days with the focus on Israel giving up 13 percent of Yesha. The talks are extended and conclude on October 23.

1998, 17 October – Two days later - Tornadoes hit Texas.

On October 17, heavy storms and tornadoes hit southern Texas. The San Antonio area is deluged with rain. The rain and flooding in Texas continued until October 22 and then subside. The floods ravaged 25 percent of Texas and left over one billion dollars in damage. On October 21, Clinton declares this section of Texas a major disaster area.

A Financial Disaster... (3rd worst day in financial history)

1998, 30 November

Arafat arrives in Washington again to meet with President Clinton to raise money for a Palestinian state with Jerusalem as the capital. A total of 42 other nations were represented in Washington. All the nations agreed to give Arafat $3 billion in aid. Clinton promised $400 million and the European nations $1.7 billion.

1998, 30 November – Same Day - Financial Disaster

The Dow Jones average drops 216 points, and on December 1, the European Market had its third worst day in history. Hundreds of billions of market capitalization were wiped out in the U.S. and Europe.

1998, 12 December

President Clinton arrives in the Arab-controlled section of Israel to discuss another "land for peace" fiasco.

1998, 12 December – Same Day - Clinton impeached

The U.S. House of Representatives vote four articles of impeachment against President Clinton (even though it did not include removal from office, it was a very big embarrassment for Slick Willy).

1999, 3 May

Yasser Arafat schedules a press conference to announce a Palestinian state with Jerusalem as the capital.

1999, 3 May - Same Day - Powerful Storms in Oklahoma and Kansas

The most powerful tornado storm system ever to hit the United States whips through Oklahoma and Kansas. The winds are clocked at 316 mph, the fastest wind speed ever recorded. Arafat postpones his announcement to December 1999 at the request of buddy President Clinton. In his letter to Arafat, Clinton praises and encourages Arafat for his "aspirations for his own land."

2001, 8 June

President George W. Bush sends Secretary Tenet to Jerusalem to promote his "Roadmap to Peace," the continuation of the failed Oslo Accord.

2001, 8 June – Same Day - Tropical Storm Allison hits Texas

Tropical storm Allison hits Texas the home state of President George W. Bush. Allison causes over $7 billion in damage and closes George Bush Airport for two days. Allison continues for five long days. When Tenet leaves Jerusalem, Allison settles down.

2005, 23 August ...

This was one of the saddest days as I watched and listened to Jews being evicted from their homes in the most beautiful of places.... Gush Katif was paradise. And it was destroyed by those who took it over.

Israel completed the evacuation of the Gaza Strip and gave it to the Arab terrorists. The Gaza Strip evacuation came directly from President Bush's "Roadmap to Peace."

2005, 23 August – the Same Day - Tropical Storm Katrina appears

August 23, a small insignificant tropical storm slowly appeared in the Atlantic below the Bahamas named Katrina. From her beginning meteorologists stated the U.S. had nothing to fear. Katrina packed little punch, plus the computer forecasts kept Katrina calmly corralled in the Atlantic. Defying the computer models, Katrina turned south-east, scraped the south tip of Florida and then with the vengeance of a runaway freight train Katrina took an unexpected turn into the warm Gulf Coast. Meteorologists tracking Katrina's unusual path labeled Katrina one of history's most bizarre hurricanes.

2005, 29 August - Hurricane Katrina hits New Orleans

Katrina raced directly toward New Orleans, harnessing deadly strength every moment. Literally recording wind strength "off the scale" On Monday, August 29, the nation watched in horror as deadly Katrina slammed and slaughtered the fragile Gulf Coast. Destructive Katrina left beautiful homes as piles of worthless rubbish. Deadly Katrina tossed bodies like litter along the highway. When Katrina ended her deadly mission, America suffered the worst disaster in her storied history. As I saw the thousands of homes destroyed, my mind kept going back to those U.S. ordered bulldozers destroying the Jewish homes in the Gaza Strip. As I saw the thousands and thousands of United States citizens being evacuated from their land, my mind could not keep from remembering the Jewish people crying and literally begging to stay in their land. America found no mercy for the Jewish people.

With no mercy, Katrina completely "bulldozed" tens of thousands of homes. Katrina completely "evacuated" the celebrated city of New Orleans. Hundreds of thousands are homeless, helpless and hopeless. The greatest displacement of U.S. citizens in history occurred. Over 10,000 people are estimated dead (Note: there were 10,000 Jews evacuated from Gaza and Samaria). Over 400,000 jobs were wiped out. President Bush has requested $50 billion from Congress for the first round of Katrina's expensive bill. Estimates put Katrina's final bill – over $150 billion.

Most reporters described the aftermath of New Orleans worse than anything they've ever seen.

Could it possibly be true what is written? That the Almighty is watching over HIS own little land.

Measure for measure....

> "They have said, Come, and let us cut them off from being a nation; that the name of Israel may be no more in remembrance. So persecute them with thy tempest, and make them afraid with thy storm." Psalms 83:4, 15

These events are the tip of the iceberg considering that everything that happens in this world is the result of "measure for measure."

How about outside of the US of A. If I got into the rest of the world I would be writing a book. One of the most dramatic examples of this is that in 2011 Japan had two newsworthy events. One was the idiotic treatment of three Yeshivah boys who unknowingly were arrested for drug possession. The details are too extensive for discussion here; but, it was a blatant disregard for Jews. The second incident that occurred at that time was Japan officially coming out in support of the Arabs in Israel, the so-called Palestinians, and saying that they support Palestine (wherever that is). What followed these events was the worst earthquake, 9.0 on the Richter scale and a tsunami that caused loss of life and great damage. The worst part of the damage is still occurring since the tsunami caused extensive damage to the Fukushima Nuclear Facility north of Tokyo. That plant to this day has been spewing out radioactive waste to the extent that the Pacific Ocean is losing all its life. Even worse, is that the radiation has travelled and already has reached the west coast of America and Canada. Fukushima is so unstable that the future devastation could affect the entire world. The details here also are too much to cover, but suffice it to say that this all came about immediately after the unfair treatment of the Jews and Israel.

I reiterate: all nations, all organizations, all governments and every individual on this earth is under Hashem's system of "**Middah K'neged Middah**," measure for measure. Take seriously what it says in Genesis 12:3:

> "I will bless those that bless you, and him who curses you I will curse; and all the families of the earth shall bless themselves by you."

And what is the secret to receiving Hashem's blessing? Do His will; live by the "handbook of life," the Torah – that is the true key to happiness and success.
All that said, how am I suggesting you can change the weather in the US of A? Take away Secretary Kerry's frequent flyer membership. If you can complain to the government and prevent Kerry from visiting Israel in his attempt to destroy our homeland, the sun will shine more in the US. Of course, then there are the rest of the government shenanigans – the White House, the Pentagon, the Congress, the Senate, etc, etc, etc.

Alright, I guess the only way for a Jew to survive the mayhem of the US and every other country in the world is to come to your real home, Eretz Yisroel. If you stop believing the propaganda of the terrorist organizations, such as the news media, then you will realize that Israel is the only safe place for a Jew in the world.

One disclaimer: Israel and all the people living here are under Hashem's system of measure for measure. If one comes here and desecrates the Torah, as many secular Jews and non-Jews have done, chas v'shalom, then that individual is subject to whatever fate he or she has caused. The unusual snowstorms in Israel were a very good message from Hashem. The areas where observant Jews live saw the storm as a beautiful blessing. The areas that saw many problems were the non-observant or even non-Jewish areas. Gaza, as an example, had horrible flooding. I wonder why? You may think that it was because there are more secular people in the lowlands and the observant happen to be in towns that are higher elevation. You are right, but ask the question: Who put them there?

One cannot hide from Hashem's system by living in Israel, but one surely can enjoy His abundance here more than any other place. Guaranteed in writing!

2.14 Kabbalah

The Talmud speaks of a Rebi Chanina ben Dosa, a miracle worker from the time of the Second Jewish Temple. Story after story is told of the miracles he performed or of miracles that were performed for him. Reflecting on these stories one can't help but ask oneself; wouldn't it be nice to be able to perform miracles at will as well?

The truth is he was not the only one from his time period who could. According to tradition, the greatest Rabbis of that generation could perform miracles at will. It was the time of the great Rebi Akiva and Rebi Meir Bo'ol HoNeis - Master of Miracles - to name two. They were a perfect example of the famous principle, "A righteous person wills and Hashem fulfills." The Talmud even speaks of times when someone who died was revived soon after, as if in the normal course of events.

However, after learning some Kabbalah, which reveals the spiritual infrastructure and material of reality, the question is no longer, how did they perform miracles; but, why can't we perform them as well? (Caveat: we are talking about performing, not experiencing miracles which we all have stories to tell – to be discussed later).

The most obvious answer is: Because they were far more righteous and on a much higher spiritual level than we are. We do not merit the kind of Heavenly help they enjoyed to perform their supernatural feats.

Without a doubt, that is true. But it is also over-simplistic, because it makes a faulty assumption: the physical world is a fixed reality that can only be changed through physical means, or miraculously; that Hashem does this for us by "breaking" the rules inherent in Creation. Apparently, that is one of the privileges of being Hashem: the physical world melts before His will.

However, as science is beginning to discover, the physical world is not so static. At the basis of everything in physical existence is energy which in itself is not physical, but spiritual. Scientists don't even understand what energy is, though they use the term freely as if referring to something as basic and discernable as air.

What is just beginning to dawn on the world of science has been accepted fact in the realm of Kabbalah as long as we have known it, for at least 3,327 years. For, a central tenet of Kabbalah is that the basis of all of physical Creation is a completely spiritual light called Ohr Ain Sof – the Never Ending Light.

Rabbi Yitzchak Luria, more commonly known as the Arizal, explains that prior to any hint of Creation, even the completely spiritual aspects, there was only Ohr Ain Sof (It represented the will of Hashem to reveal Himself to created beings). Though that would be only at the end of a long and complex period of Divine creating, man would be the crowning touch on the Creation-process on Day Six. But, it was with him in mind that Hashem created everything else - physically and spiritually - during the previous five days.

Thus, as physical as all of Creation appears to be, and as spiritually void as it seems to be able to become, the truth is, the Ohr Ain Sof permeates everything at all times. Absolutely nothing can exist, even evil, if the Ohr Ain Sof is not at its core. If the Ohr Ain Sof were to be removed from something in Creation, it would immediately and completely disappear.

Thus, even the term, Yaish M'ayin - something from nothing - which is used to describe the leap from a completely spiritual level of existence to the physical one, is not an entirely accurate one. It implies that at some point the light went from being totally spiritual to something physical. In truth, the core light – the Ohr Ain Sof, the source of ALL energy in existence – remains completely spiritual, like a soul within a body.

What happened instead is that, as the Ohr Ain Sof moved further away from its Source, it became layered with other less spiritual levels of light, like clothing worn by a person. The more layers added, the more physical the outward manifestation of the light became, and in this sense, the Creation Story is an account of the adding of layers of light to make Creation increasingly more physical. The story seems to flow horizontally along a timeline when in fact it is about light descending vertically.

Thus, everything in existence is a function of spiritual light, including people, something that was perfectly apparent in the Garden of Eden prior to the sin. For, prior to the eating from the Tree of Knowledge of Good and Evil, the skin of man was Ketonet Ohr - Clothing of Light (ALEF-Vov-Raish). As a result

136

of the sin additional layers of less spiritual light were added to man - Ketonet Ohr - Clothing of Skin (pronounced the same way but spelled differently: AYIN-Vov-Raish) , causing his "physicalization."

The advantage is this: unlike a concrete, physicality, one made of spiritual light can be manipulated at will, which is what the Rabbis of the Second Temple era were able to do. Being experts in Kabbalah it was clear to them that Nature is more allusion than fact; they were not fooled by what their eyes perceived: an incredible sense of solidity and permanence projected by the physical world. The question for them was not, "why can we walk through walls?" but rather, "why can't others as well?"

The answer to this question is an issue of free will, as it says, "The secrets of Hashem to those who fear Him" (Psalms 25:14): one must earn the right to know Torah on its deepest levels. And there can be no greater secret than the nature of the physical world and how to spiritually manipulate it.

It also says, "All is in the hands of Heaven except for the fear of Heaven" (Brochot 33b), implying that it was for this that man was created, and that the only area in life that our free-will impacts is in the building up of fear of Hashem, the key to the secrets of Hashem. Thus, regarding this the Talmud states that someone who knows much Torah but lacks fear of Hashem is like one who has the key to the outer chamber - Torah in general - but lacks the key to the inner one - the secrets of Creation to which the verse refers, and to which Torah is meant to lead a person (Shabbat 30b).

However, there is also a tradition that, at the End-of-Days, it will be a special time, and that some of the rules that may have applied to previous generations will be waived in the final one. Time may simply run out, and as the Talmud explains redemption may no longer be a function of merit, but of need and at which time Heaven will "subsidize" what is lacking to bring it about (Sanhedrin 97b).

As physics begins to reveal what Kabbalah has always known, that time may be now.

3.15 Conclusion

We do have the ability to cause things to happen that may seem beyond our physical world. In the next section I will talk about how prayer causes energies to flow and hence we can cause things to happen. Healing the sick, causing positive events to occur are within our capability, but require much effort and proper attitude to succeed. Unfortunately, improper language and negativity cause thing to go wrong in our lives and the world; that ability, we seem to be much more proficient at accomplishing. Our personal growth in our Judaism and living our daily lives according to the Torah and the Will of Hashem produces great and very positive results. It doesn't take long to see these results and to learn what happiness in this world can be. We will get into specifics to accomplish the positive.

Part 3 - What Does This Mean To Us?

3.1 The Key to Happiness

What is the purpose of this world and our lives within it? How is that for a loaded question? The world is imperfect and human beings are imperfect. We are here to perfect ourselves and the world. The way to perfect ourselves is by serving our Creator, by doing His will. Simply, observe the commandments of the Torah, 613 for Jews, 7 for non-Jews. A very important aspect of Hashem's system in this world is testing. We are constantly tempted, coerced, bribed and many other concepts that are for the purpose of testing. If we react to any test in accordance with Hashem's will, we pass; if not, read below. The commandments are the tools, the instructions provided to accomplish our individual missions on Earth. This leads to a very interesting aspect of living on this planet and how we can go about perfecting ourselves for all eternity.

According to Rabbi Avigdor Miller, Z"tl, we have two choices as to how to accomplish our mission – voluntarily or involuntarily. By voluntarily doing the commandments, studying scriptures, proper praying, giving charity, helping others and repenting all our mistakes (which includes working hard to correct them), we receive the correction that we need and will thrive in this life and all eternity. If we ignore all of Hashem's instruction and do our own thing, we will still receive the correction that we need (this does not apply to pure evil), but it will be through involuntary occurrences. Sickness, accidents, misfortunes, financial difficulties are examples of ways that Hashem helps us.

A very misunderstood concept about this world, that only those who diligently study Torah comprehend, is that there is no such thing as luck, coincidence, chance or by accident. We bring these concepts on ourselves and our families. I know that you know much better, and that you might believe what I am saying sounds like nonsense, but if you want to gamble that this is not Hashem's system, then you will pay the price.

There are a couple of concepts to remember about this world that will serve your best interests. One thing is nothing is random. The infinite intelligence level of Hashem makes everything in this world seem random, but it isn't – it is exact, measure for measure. To allow us to experience free will, we have to see everything as random. Hashem wants our love and service by our choice. If the system were that every time we do the right thing, we immediately get rewarded and every time we make a mistake (or sin on purpose), we immediately get correction (or downright punishment), we would be as robots and not able to live life with free will. We do, measure for measure, get reward and correction but in a very random appearing manner; it cannot be so obvious. Another very important fact to remember is **if you don't believe it, the truth doesn't go away.** I have known many people who will tell me "I don't believe a word you are saying." But, they never investigate what the truth really is. When things go wrong, however, they are the quick to ask Hashem "why are you doing this to me?"

Am I saying that if I do everything that Hashem asks of me in this life, that life will be much easier, more enjoyable, successful and rewarding? No, Hashem is saying it. It is the basis of our Torah instruction. It works for me and many, many others that I have observed for decades. I have paid so much attention to what I am telling you that there is no doubt in my mind that this is the key to happiness for me and my family. Mind you, I am human and I do make mistakes (everyday). Hashem is totally merciful and is more interested in our intensions to serve Him and our love for Him than our final performance, even though performance is of the utmost importance. **Hashem doesn't judge us by what we know, but how we grow.** The newly observant individual is given more leeway and allowed to make more mistakes than us more experienced people. The more important thought is that as we learn and put more meaning to what Hashem wants from us, all becomes much easier. We are creatures of habit, why not have good ones. Not understanding why we do something does make it more difficult to accomplish. An example would be keeping Kosher. We keep Kosher because Hashem told us to. The deepest reasons are spiritual and beyond our comprehension. Non-kosher food is to the soul as poison is to the body. We need not question the idea; we only need to be reassured that Hashem knows exactly what we need. To fully understand every aspect of this concept would require years of study.

We do see problems happen to good people. Abraham, Isaac and Jacob had many hurdles to overcome but one must know that everything is for the good and gives us in this short life exactly what we need for a perfect eternity. Books have been written about this subject and, obviously, I cannot cover all aspects in a single volume. An interesting aspect of the testing we get in life is the more righteous a person is, the more difficult the tests may be. Why? Hashem in His mercy gives

140

the righteous person much greater opportunities to excel and thrive. The eternal quality of life is what is at stake. Why not shoot for a better, much higher quality of eternity. Abraham was so high in spiritual level that Hashem gave him tests that would project him to even higher levels that most of us couldn't even comprehend.

I am only covering the ground rules not all the details. Just know that we have much more control over everything that happens in our lives than we think; and, by following the handbook of instructions, the Torah, we can perfect ourselves, our families (we are the ones who guide our offspring) and the world.

To help understand this a little deeper, let me talk about prayer. Prayer absolutely works (some of the deep dark secrets that allow for success are coming up); and, if done the proper way, we can have everything we need and even everything we want in life. I personally believe I have more than I deserve (bli ayin harah – such a statement should be said "without the evil eye" affecting me). I do not have any complaints with my personal situation in life, but I feel the pain of others who have all the opportunities that I have and are too stubborn to take advantage of it. This is, perhaps, one of the biggest reasons that I wrote this book. The other big reason is Hashem commands me to help other people less fortunate than myself. Even though I will give more detail on many of the subjects on which we all need to work, I submit this insight as to how prayer works. It puts prayer and life into perspective:

I asked for strength and HASHEM gave me difficulties to make me strong

I asked for wisdom and HASHEM gave me problems to solve

I asked for prosperity and HASHEM gave me brawn and brain to work

I asked for courage and HASHEM gave me dangers to overcome

I asked for love and HASHEM gave me troubled people to help

I asked for favors and HASHEM gave me opportunities

I received nothing I wanted; I received everything I needed

My prayers were answered.

I've heard people question: isn't it enough that I am a good person, do I have to do all of Hashem's commandments too? Let me give you an analogy to try to put everything into perspective. Let us consider that this world is a giant corporation and Hashem is the CEO, the Big Boss, Numero Uno. Would we ever say to our boss at work "isn't enough that I am a good person, everyone around here likes me, I help increase morale; do I also have to do all the work that you want me to do? That is also a system of reward and punishment. Do a good job and get raises, promotions, who knows what. Ask the boss that question and the only raise you get is the raise off the premises. The entire system of measure for measure is "do what the Boss asks of you, and the reward is beyond belief." One last note on the subject, we do not perform Hashem's will for reward, but strictly out of love for Him. That is the way to better results.

A very important idea about all this that requires mentioning: Hashem doesn't need our praise; He doesn't need our prayers; Hashem needs nothing from us; He is an Infinite Intelligence, with Infinite Power. Everything that He wants us to do is for our benefit. We praise Him to gain complete faith and thrust that He does everything for us and for our good. We pray to Him for our benefit since He gave us a system that gives us everything we want. Prayer also lets us evaluate what we truly need – humans have much clutter and confusion in their lives and need to sort it out.

All is done to be in awe of Him and results in fulfilling His will of total goodness in the world – for us. We are part of Him and therefore partners in creation. When you catch on to His system and His purpose, you achieve total happiness, satisfaction, peace of mind and success.

We can have it all, for us and our loved ones as soon as we get over the stigma that we know what we're doing and especially if we think we know better. If we rely on our human frailties and believe that we do not need Hashem, we have thrown it all away and will bring devastation to ourselves and our loved ones.

He loves us trillions of times more than we could ever love Him. By just following His will, using the tools that He gave us, you will experience the most positive results and discover what true happiness can be in this life and forever. None of this is conjecture, but proven over thousands of years of total success. All I ask is be open-minded and not to argue with success. We are talking about the happiness of you and your loved ones. Please, don't take it lightly. Learn about it and give it a try, you won't be disappointed. Live life voluntarily, not involuntarily.

3.2 Prayer Works

Are you ready for one of the best kept secrets of the world (this is secret, so make sure you tell everyone)? **Prayer works.** Not just sometimes; but, when done correctly, every time.

How do I know? Hashem told us. In the Talmud there are many stories of miracles from Rav Hanina ben Dosa. Whatever he prayed for, including impossible nature controlling events, it happened – his prayers were successful. The message that Hashem is giving us through Rav ben Dosa is: **If you pray correctly, it works!**

Another proof, that I personally have, is many years of success with my prayers, and observation of tens of thousands of people over decades. I have observed that when individuals pray according to Hashem's instructions, they are successful and when they don't, use your imagination.

Two things one needs to know about successful praying is (1) why it works and (2) how does one pray properly. The why is easy to explain. I mentioned that we are partners in creation with Hashem. He created the universe, according to scriptures, by looking into his Torah, His blueprint of the universe; and, by simply uttering the words of Torah, the universe came into being. But, as we say every day in prayer, **Hear O Israel: Hashem is our G-d, Hashem is One.** This is a very profound statement that declares that everything in the universe is one within Hashem. That has a much deeper meaning, but what is important to us is that when we speak, Hashem gave us the ability to cause things to happen. Our prayers are not ascended to Hashem for the purpose of Him making a decision, whether He should say yes or no. Our words actually cause energies to flow and bring about positive or negative results. Hashem already knows well in advance what we will think, say and do. Prayer is for us to actually verbalize our thoughts and cause the results. It is a gift from Hashem that is so under used, but even worse, abused. For, even when we are not in prayer, every word we say causes energies to flow and things to happen. Improper language is not just a means of expression, but cause for very negative occurrences. Words of love and hate translate into positive and negative reactions. Earthquakes, tsunamis, hurricanes, etc (what we like to call acts of Hashem) are acts of Hashem's system caused by us. It is the reason that the world is in such dire straits at this juncture in history.

I am sure that I have many skeptics on this subject, but let me touch upon some very obvious proof. There was a very impressive discovery made a few years ago in Russia. Simple words and thoughts can have an effect on changing the DNA of a person. It was in the news with the headlines "Faith Healing Explained." There are several write-ups on the web if you want to check it out.

It is well known that when people get together to pray for the speedy recovery of a sick person, there is improvement. Medical science has discovered that humor, as an example, can spark the immune system. When we laugh, we can become healthier.

Even more outlandish is how plants can grow better and healthier when one talks nicely to them or even sings to them. What has been demonstrated in a lab environment is that positive statements, such as compliments, words of praise or of affection, cause the formation of crystals such as these:

An ice crystal formed from water exposed to the words "Thank you very much."

An ice crystal formed from water exposed to the words "Love and appreciation."

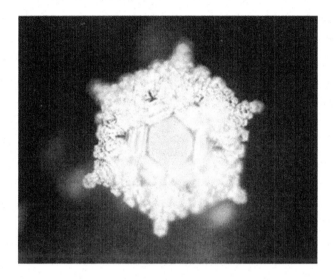

An ice crystal formed from water exposed to the word "Idiot."

An ice crystal formed from water exposed to the sentence "You disgust me; I'm going to kill you."

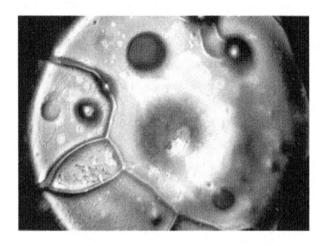

I think that last sentence would affect anyone. It says in the Torah "Those who bless you will be blessed; and, those who curse you will be cursed."

I already have talked about the idea that every natural disaster that has occurred in the world has immediately followed a negative occurrence in Israel or even negative words said about Israel or the Jews. Now you know how that happens within Hashem's system for this world.

We also have many statements and miracles from Rabbi's and other holy people who will testify with many examples as to the effectiveness of proper praying. It wouldn't mean much to anyone, but I personally have experienced miraculous results including immediate results in time of need. My stories are extensive but only your own experiences would solidify the validity of prayer. I used to teach a class on prayer when I lived in the states. Many times Hashem had setup my students by performing miracles for them after praying. It made my job easy, convincing people that prayer works. Hashem is always there to help.

Let me tell you about three tools that I personally have used for health problems. One is called a Pizmon which is nothing more than a statement that I say repeatedly that convinces my soul not to give me pain (I will discuss this later). Pain is in the mind and the mind is in the spiritual realm. By simply convincing the soul that the pain is unjustified, it goes away. I have witnessed this on a man who had a slipped disc, a woman with migraine headaches as well as using it on me. In all cases the medical problem wasn't totally solved, but the pain was eliminated. I have a friend that we got together every day to study, but he could not sit still for long because of a knee pain. After I taught him the Pizmon, pain disappeared and studying was no longer interrupted.

Two other techniques that I have used are NAET and EFT (Google to get more information including what the acronyms stand for). These techniques are involved, but have been totally effective in solving just about any medical problem one might have, without drugs. Through a practitioner, NAET is described as an alternative treatment for the permanent elimination of food and environmental allergies. I, however, have used it for many other purposes. It diagnoses the problem and then cures it. EFT is a form of acupuncture without the needles. It is used for almost any medical ailment and, the best part of all, one can perform the procedure by him or herself without a practitioner. Both techniques include words being said and souls being talked to – very spiritual, very mystical, but very effective. They are a form of prayer or meditation and they work. These tools as well as everyday prayer have served me and my family well. Even though I never needed it for these purposes, all three techniques have proven effective in weight loss and/or smoking cessation.

A fascinating story with which I was involved that demonstrates the power of prayer. I received a call, years ago, from a friend in the states who was totally distraught that his wife had developed mental problems. My wife and I knew this woman and believed her to be a very lovely, calm and pleasant person. The husband was telling us that a psychiatrist determined her to be crazy and even non-functional. They were ready to take her away from her family and institutionalize her. A Rabbi in the town that we lived suggested that she should make a trip to Israel and see a particular very mystical Rabbi who had the ability to cure with words. The husband arranged the trip and I arranged the meeting of the woman and the Rabbi. After two days of prayer and chanting of certain verses from scriptures (in which the Rabbi was totally trained), the woman was completely cured and back to her pleasant self again. The explanation was that we do have good and evil forces that can enter our spiritual makeup, and that prayer can enhance or eliminate as needed. This woman actually had demonic forces invade her and the Rabbi knew the remedy. You may think this is all hocus pocus fantasy (I used to), but after I experienced this situation first hand, I became totally convinced of its validity.

The next question is: what are some of the tools and techniques that make prayer work? Your prayers won't be perfect; but, I have seen tremendous results right away in others and, of course, my own personal experiences. Once I learned some of the secrets, vast changes came into my life and the lives of my loved ones. One caveat: my prayer is not perfect and still improving after 68 years (I started to learn about prayer when I was three years old). Hashem in His mercy makes it easy for you to succeed if you have the proper attitude, even if you need much improvement – you will see positive results rapidly. Here again the subject is so extensive that books have been written. I can only give you a cursory look at the subject.

The most important concept in proper prayer is: "knowing before Whom we are standing and taking it very seriously." If we were standing in front of an important king of flesh and blood, we would be scared to death. We would never turn around and talk to a friend, start reading something that does not pertain to our meeting with the king, dress improperly, act silly, drink something, talk on the cell phone (that is a biggie), etc. We would believe that if we acted improperly at such a moment, the king might give the ever so familiar "Off with his head!!! (G-d forbid)" command and that could ruin your whole day. Even if we were put in front of the owner of a large corporation, the CEO that just happens to be our employer, the big boss, we would also be in fear of our livelihood, if we messed up. But yet we stand in front of the King of Kings, the Owner of the universe, the Big Big Boss, three times a day (not to mention being observed by Him 24/7) with the consequences of damaging our eternal life forever and ever, and we do not act accordingly. How many people do you know that pray realistically in fear and love with a sense of urgency and trepidation knowing that the outcome of this event will determine their entire future?

Let me turn this completely around and give a very different approach to the situation. We have been given the gift, the privilege of a private audience with Hashem three times a day, morning, afternoon and evening (of course, He is available 24/7 to help those who simply turn to Him). This golden opportunity, if done correctly, will make our lives much more pleasant, productive, successful and enjoyable forever and ever. Wow, what a gift. But the way we treat this is similar to someone giving us a million dollars that we put in a safe that we don't have the combination. Yes, we own the money, but never can use it since we made the mistake of putting somewhere out of reach.

I know that praying three times a day for us creatures of habit becomes a very routine act and very often results in lip service. We pray very quickly with the attitude of "let us get this done and get out of here, we have more important things to do," or do we? What is even worse is that our minds drift and at the most important time of praying, the silent devotion when we get to request all our personal needs and wants. We think to ourselves "I have to pick up some bread on the way home or I am going to fix that broken appliance today." We end this particular important part of prayer with the statement "Let the words of my mouth and the meditations of my heart be acceptable to You." But there is nothing in the prayer that says "please ignore the part about picking up the bread or fixing the appliance." If our prayers are not focused properly, we are wasting the most important opportunity of the day.

A hint to avoiding the mind drifting is to prepare in advance. We have prayers for everything – for people that we know who are sick, for those who are financially in trouble, for those who are in trouble with the law, etc, etc, etc. If we prepare in advance with a plan to think about each individual that we want to help as we come to the prayer that pertains to that individual (it is very important to picture the person in your mind as you pray), it works. We channel our minds away from the trivia and accomplish our intended request.

Of course, don't forget the prayers that simply say thank you to Hashem or praising Him. They should be prepared in advance as well. To thank Hashem for everything is OK but to thank Him for something specific that recently happened is much more meaningful. That shows the idea of extra thought and inspiration going into your prayers. Making our prayers work for us and totally successful is much more gratifying than lip service. All distractions must be eliminated. It is one of the biggest reasons that men and women should not pray together. Show me a man that says he is not distracted and completely can concentrate on prayer with a woman in front of him, and I will show you a liar (or a homosexual). The other problem is when men and women are together it is usually in more of a social gathering where there is more trivia talking than praying. Complete concentration makes prayer effective. Distractions take away the gift of communing with Hashem.

Our prayer service is designed with perfection and covers all our needs. It has been handed down for thousands of years as a proven way to achieve everything we need and want. Although there are books written about the ways to maximize your effectiveness during prayer, there are certain suggestions that I have that will help greatly. The topics that I would like to mention are areas that are very misunderstood and even perpetuated as bad habits that many observant Jews do unknowingly. Changing a bad habit is extremely difficult, especially if one is not even aware of how detrimental that behavior is. But for the newly observant Jew who is just getting started, developing good habits from the beginning is extremely important and will serve one well.

To begin: prayer should be in the proper order from beginning to end without skipping. People who come late and/or leave early lose a lot of potential in their prayers. Why?

The Midrash Tanchuma says that there were four steps to Yaakov's ladder (I know there were many more, but we only are talking the first four rungs here), and the Zohar teaches that these four rungs parallel the four main stages of Morning Prayer. This begins with the earthly reality and slowly moves upward and inward to a higher, deeper level of connection and unity with Hashem. At the outset of prayer, we begin by standing on the first rung, and through the course of the prayer service, we climb the ladder toward spiritual perfection and elevation.

The four stages of Morning Prayer are as follows:

1) Morning Blessings (Birchas Hashchar) which reflect our dawn of our awareness.
2) Verses of Praise (Pesukei DeZimrah) which cut away any negativity and awaken our emotions.
3) Reading of the Shema (Kerias Shema) which internalizes our emotions.
4) The Silent Standing Prayer (Amidah also known as the Shemoneh Esrei) which is a deep encounter with the Divine in a quiet space of union, ultimately reaching a place of oneness.

The stages of prayer parallel the worlds of creation as well as the levels of our soul:

1) The world of action (Asiyah) and the soul level of physical/functional consciousness (Nefesh).

2) The world of formation (Yetzirah) and the soul level of emotional consciousness (Ruach).

3) The world of creation/context (Beriah) and the soul level of intellectual/cognitive ability (Neshamah).

4) The world of unity (Atzilus) and the soul level of transcendental consciousness (Chayah) which is reflected as our inner most deepest will and desire.

Yes, this is deep and very mystical, but simply put: doing prayer in order and completely is the design that Hashem gave us to maximize our efforts. Coming late and skipping may be nice, but far from the best way to connect to a much higher level of spirituality – losing out on the effectiveness of prayer. The worse problem about this bad habit is the individuals who do it daily, not just occasionally being late, but every day.

The next bit of advice is: remain in one place and do not walking around (within 4 cubits, about 2 meters or 7 feet). Many of us are familiar with the concept of "Makom Kavua," a permanent place. Typically, we trivialize and neglect its significance, mainly thinking it to be important because of convenience. However, there's a lot more thought involved. Below is just a small collection of Halacha and thoughts relevant to the concept of "Makom Kavua":

1. The first makom set aside for prayer we know about was Avraham's. The verse in Genesis 19:27 says Avraham would wake early in the morning "to the place where he had stood before Hashem." The verse indicates Avraham had a designated spot where he would go to speak with Hashem.

2. Since prayer is when we converse with Hashem and establish a connection with Him, setting aside a space for prayer demonstrates while everything else may change, our connection to Hashem is constant and absolute.

3. The Talmud (Berachos 6b) teaches Hashem takes care of someone who sets aside a place for prayer -- Hashem destroys his enemies. There is much more discussion in the Talmud (Berachos 6 to 8) about the importance of a fixed place for prayer.

4. The Shulchan Aruch (90:19) and the Mishnah Berurah on 90:19 (59,60) mention the fix place of Avraham as the reason we must have a fixed 4

cubits. Even if one prays at home, there should still be a permanent fixed place for prayer.

5. The Zohar tells us that we are like the Alter in the Temple that our prayers rise like the smoke and the fire comes down like Hashem's abundance, the fulfillment of our prayers. This also alludes to the fact that the Alter was in a fixed position and, when in use, never moved. We too must be fixed and not walk around.

6. There are other places that you will find references to praying within 4 cubits, but one that says it all is Tanya. The *Tanya* is an early work of Hasidic philosophy, by Rabbi Shneur Zalman of Liadi, the founder of Chabad Hasidism, first published in 1797. It states very definitely that if you go outside of your 4 cubits, the Shechinah, "The Divine Presence," is lifted from you. When we have a quorum, or minion, of ten men, the Shechinah comes down and is in our presence. If we walk around, it is almost like we are not part of the quorum – the Shechinah has left us. That is quite serious since we want to have every advantage in getting our prayers fulfilled.

Another negative habit worth mentioning is talking or studying or any other activity that has nothing to do with prayer. A good common sense test is, as mentioned above, pretend that you are having a private session with a King, a Prime Minister, a President or any very important dignitary, would you say to that person: Occupy yourself for a little while, I want to talk to my friend or I want to go read something. Sounds silly; yet, we are in a private session with the King of Kings, the only Infinite Source of Power in existence, and we take dangerous liberties that are very contrary to our mission of praying. Then we wonder why ours prayers were ineffective.

These items of misconduct are covered in the Shulchan Aruch and Mishnah Berurah with a very common theme, that of disturbing others around you. It is one thing to degrade your own prayer; it is not nice to mess up someone else's prayer just because you want to talk or even study Torah (Shulchan Aruch 90:18), which is a distraction. The wording for not talking is interesting in the Shulchan Aruch (101:6) because it even covers the idea of praying too loud. Your voice should not be heard for several reasons, one is that Hashem is not hard of hearing (I was told that decades ago), and two, it is difficult to concentrate on one's prayers when the person next to you is louder (of course that also includes nonsensical talking). Hearing another voice is compared to hearing a false prophet, for it was their custom to shout loudly to their idols. There is more detail, but you get the idea.

It is brought down in many places, unless you follow all of Hashem's instructions on how to pray correctly, your prayer will not work. That means correcting all the bad habits that people take so lightly. They show absolutely no fear of Heaven when they say "there is no problem with the way I pray." Instead, one should be in great fear of doing it incorrectly. Talking, walking around, studying, doing anything that is not prayer, not standing or sitting at the proper times, not observing the 4 cubits (daled amos) of those around us, not wearing the Tallit or Tefillin properly, etc, etc, etc are all violated by most who pray. One should check out all the possible mistakes that one makes; it makes a very big difference between having successful prayers or just wasting one's time. If you can say "everything that I do during prayer is OK," you are probably one of the violators. Study the Mishnah Berurah, the Shulchan Aruch and many other guides to serving Hashem properly, which teaches us how to pray correctly; you may be very surprised at how many mistakes you are making.

Using a proper prayer book is also important. Scriptures tell us that you can pray in any language, but you must understand the language you are using. Only Hebrew, which is the best for prayer, can be used without knowing what it means word-for-word (learning what it means is definitely beneficial). After all, as previously mentioned, the words are what cause the energies to flow and bring success. Hebrew is the best formula for that success. Hashem's system of prayer is perfect and anything we do that detracts from that system makes our efforts less than perfect.

I have heard all my life "I talk to Hashem every day, but in my own words from the heart." That is all well and good and should definitely be continued, Hashem wants to hear from us always. But, such praying or meditation should be supplemental to the real thing and not a substitute. Only praying with a proper quorum of at least ten men in a proper synagogue brings you to the perfect praying and the best results. (I know the Torah is sexist but let me break the myth by letting you know that it is completely in favor of women, not men – to be discussed).

Another secret that perhaps is the most important aspect of successful prayer is how we say the many names of Hashem. Throughout prayer there are many places that a name of Hashem is used, each one has a different meaning and is pertinent to the particular prayer being said. Two important actions must occur. One is to say each name clearly; and two is to think about what that particular name means (examples are one of Hashem's name is a name of mercy, another is of judgment). Since words and sounds are the key to positive energy flow, this becomes the most important part of prayer, speaking His names. This is more difficult than it sounds, but should be given great effort. Our drifting minds and our natural speed inhibit our effectiveness in praying. Believe it or not, books have been written on the deep meanings of Hashem's names, so anything that I explain here is just a cursory look at what needs to be reviewed more deeply. The good news is, when you start to improve these two actions (proper pronunciation and meaning of names), results happen quickly. I admit, perfection is difficult, but working on it will result in visible improvement. I myself have much room for improvement, but my attitude towards loving Hashem and serving Him by wanting to improve, gives me the edge. Reminder: It's not what we know, it's how we grow.

We have all heard the expression "watch what you ask for, you may get it." I only bring this up since asking for the wrong things can also work, but result in problems. Everyone is convinced that if they were very wealthy, they could handle it. I believe the opposite to be true. Money is evil. Many people who find themselves instantly rich tend to develop bad habits: drug habits, drinking habits, family problems; even the suicide rate is higher amongst the wealthy. Hashem gave us a system to satisfy our needs and our wants. We are obligated to use it for the right purpose. Since the system on Earth is measure for measure, we should only pray for things that will be according to Hashem's will; otherwise, He will make sure we get correction for all our improper deeds. The secret here is to always want to help others. If wealth comes upon us, congratulations, but only if we have a great desire to help the poor, sick, elderly, hungry, orphan, widow, etc, etc, etc. I only use money as an example (probably the best example), but everything we do and acquire in life should be used for everyone's benefit and to serve Hashem. That is what Hashem wants and that is why He gave us prayer. True success is when we demonstrate that we are unselfish. Take notice that most of our prayers are in the plural, saying "we" instead of "I." And, be aware, Hashem is listening to every word we say and watching every move we make. The good news is when we pray for others, and really have the proper attitude toward others, Hashem makes sure to take care of us.

One additional note. I stated that prayer is an exact science. One might ask: then how can prayer be different for different groups of Jews? The prayer book of a Sephardi Jew is not the same as an Ashkenazi Jew. The answer actually demonstrates how scientific and how specific the requirements are for prayer and everything else.

Rabbi Moshe David Valle (1697-1777) was a Kabbalist who wrote many books. One of the subjects, for which he is known, is stating the differences required by different Jews. Jews are very much influenced by their environmental conditions with which they grew up. A Jew in Northern Africa obviously has a very different situation from a Jew in Europe. Differences such food, water, air, climate, customs, etc actually cause differences to be needed by the soul in every activity in life. Prayer is very much included in the dichotomy, and therefore even requires different words and customs. You can't get more exacting and scientifically accurate than that.

3.3 Being Positive

Positive attitudes generate positive occurrences with positive results and I'm positive about that. Of course, negative attitudes generate negative occurrences with you know the rest. We talked about the tremendous benefit of proper prayer, but we must also concern ourselves with every moment that we are awake. If we have positive thoughts, words and actions, all will result in a very happy and enjoyable experience in this life.

In 2006 there was a film called **The Secret.** It consisted of a series of interviews related to the idea of thinking. It states that everything one wants or needs may be accomplished by believing that one will receive that outcome, by repeatedly thinking about it, and maintaining positive emotional states to "attract" it. Although this was a secular movie, it very much touched upon the spiritual realm. In other words, everything they professed can be found in scriptures and leads one to a very positive attitude that Hashem exists and that His system does work very positively in our favor. When you apply the information in the movie by using prayer and meditation to cause the energies to flow (as I mentioned in previously), the outcome is even more successful.

Positive attitude is really a display of faith and trust in Hashem. I know that He wants the best for me and my family and always will be there to help. When my thoughts, words and actions are all according to Hashem's will, the tools He gave me to cause positive results bring those positive results. As an example, I retired ahead of my years because I had such a positive attitude that Hashem will help me in whatever I needed to accomplish. I discovered how important it is to help people and bring them to the ways of Hashem (for years I was invited to give lectures and I invited many people to my home – especially for the Shabbos). This definitely was more important and rewarding than doing Research and Development on electronic equipment (the plight of an Engineer). Being ahead of retirement age, meant that I still had about 6 years to wait for my full retirement pay. But, I just happened to have some stock that I purchased eight years earlier that was going nowhere. After praying and asking for Hashem's assistance, both stocks went up to a point where I was able to sell and put a down payment on a house (and all the expenses needed to move). The house more than doubled in price allowing us to sell, move to Israel and live on the profit until retirement time. The true miracle was that these stocks were owned by many of my fellow employees before I retired; but, I was the only one of the group that made money on those stocks. After I sold them, both companies went bust – no it wasn't because of me, or was it? Everyone lost their money except for the individual that turned to Hashem for help – me. This has happened several times in my investment career letting me know, once again, there is no such thing as luck or coincidence.

When people make negative statements, they very much set the pace for what will happen. We have all said "I hope this happens, but I really don't think it will," or as I have heard with my suggestion about prayer, "I'll give it a try, but I am not expecting too much." And then when it doesn't happen as desired we feel justified in our prediction. Positive attitude is saying and knowing beyond a shadow of a doubt that it will happen the way we want. Why? Because I prayed that it will and my very positive prayer caused it to occur.

Prayer is just one tool. Other very positive actions that Hashem gave us to do is study Torah, give charity, do repentance, help others and do the commandments. These are all positive actions that give positive results in more ways than one can imagine. Praying for someone's speedy recovery is greatly enhanced by studying Torah in that person's name.

I am about to tell you a fact that you may or may not believe, but it is absolutely true. Since the words of Torah are the genetic code for the universe, if at any time there isn't someone in the world studying Torah, the universe would collapse and cease to exist. It is so well known by the Torah observant Jews that the continued existence of the universe is dependent on the words of Torah being said continuously (difficult concept to grasp, but absolutely true). There are many places (such as the city where I live) where study groups cover all 24 hours a day with Torah activity. Fortunately, Hashem provided a globe to live on with 24 time zones and Jews all over the world to accomplish 24/7 Torah study. When that study is channeled to a particular need, such as helping sick people, it works. One additional hint to helping the sick and many other situations, is reciting Psalms. Which Psalms to say: stay tuned for the answer.

Giving charity is an interesting event; for the Torah tells us, when we give to help others, we get a return that is 10 times the value. I don't believe that one; because, I have always experienced at least a 100 fold return (even thousands of times the return). Lucky me? No this happens to everyone with a positive attitude working within Hashem's system. They say "you can't take it with you." I don't believe that either. The best investment in this world you can take with you is the money or possessions that you use to help others. This investment has the best return with the highest yield dividends possible. The best part is the payoff is forever and ever.

Both repenting ones mistakes, correcting them with words and actions, and living the commandments, are so positive a way to live that the reward is beyond comprehension. The reason is: it will be rewarded on Earth, but it will continue for all eternity.

Everything I am mentioning here has to be done with a very positive attitude in order to be effective. If one studies Torah with complete joy, gives charity willingly, with a very positive attitude towards helping people, and performs the commandments with complete love and devotion to Hashem, life will be totally successful in every way.

A very important personality trait that helps greatly is humility. One should not think that positive attitude means being arrogant. If one is boastful about his or her accomplishments and not open minded to learn new things, Hashem does not look at that person favorably. Having a positive attitude does not mean "look at how great I am." Judaism is always concerned about embarrassing others. It is not always easy, but one should consider everyone's feelings and treat every person with respect, not disdain. If someone is impossible to get along with, just avoid the person, if possible. Revenge or even making fun of someone should be considered a very negative act and doesn't get you points in Hashem ledger (He keeps track of everything for everyone).

I personally experienced Hashem's reaction recently. I was very pleased at the fact that my blog, that I mentioned, seams very successful. My count of new countries and visitors has exceeded my expectations. I bragged about this to my wife and others and Hashem sent me a message soon thereafter and wiped out my counter. I had to reinstate the count by reapplying for a new counter account. At first I was greatly disappointed, but knowing that everything happens for a reason and for the good, I thanked Hashem for the message and did repentance for my boastful mistake. I have mentioned that there is no such thing as coincidence as proven by the fact that this should happen exactly at the time that I wanted to talk about arrogance.

One of the most important messages from the Torah is not to speak Lashon Harah, literally "the evil tongue." It pertains to talking about someone, or gossip. Talking about people, even if it is something good, is dangerous and not a positive act. Words are a powerful weapon and when used to hurt others, one loses favor with Hashem. When we say something about another person it is often believed. If it is a negative statement, whether true or not, that person's reputation can be harmed. Even if it is a positive statement, it could harm a person since the individual may not live up to the statement that was made or may even fail miserably – disappointing everyone who heard the gossip. There are so many ramifications about gossip that once again many books have been written. The subject is a very important to Hashem, since He wants us to be nice to each other. Rule of thumb, just don't talk about someone unless it will greatly help the person you are telling, and is not gossip. Example would be to warn someone that so-and-so is planning to kill him. That's not gossip.

Let me tell you a secret about Lashon Harah. When we leave this Earth on our judgment day, we do appear in the heavenly court to plead our case (not a myth). The accusing attorney presents all the evidence against you of what wasn't done correctly on Earth. What he will be saying is Lashon Harah unless it is against an individual who never spoke Lashon Harah. He cannot testify against such a person. That person gets to speak directly to Hashem and obviously is destined for a wonderful eternity. Don't take this lightly, it's your eternity.

One last word is that Hashem not only pays close attention to every small detail in our lives, but He sends us messages to help us. Learning to recognize messages from Hashem and reacting to them is a very positive habit to have. It does help us greatly through life.

3.4 Psalms

What is a good way to help sick people and, for that matter, solve many other difficulties in life? I'm glad you asked. Actually, I have been asked this question many times over decades.

We talked about prayer and how effective it can be. To be more specific about how to help those in need, Hashem gave us an additional tool that works, Psalms. Not replacing, but supplementing prayer, the 150 psalms also are the powerful words that I have mentioned that cause energies to flow and problems to be resolved. This chart tells you the best Psalms to say for the purpose you wish to help.

FOLLOWING IS A LIST OF PSALMS
WHICH ARE RECITED ON SPECIAL OCCASIONS:

	CHAPTER
To find a mate (shiduch)	32, 38, 70, 71, 72, 82, 121, 124
On the day of a wedding	19
For healthy childbirth	4, 5, 8, 20, 35, 57, 93, 108, 142
Upon the birth of a child	20,139
On the day of a circumcision	12
For recovery from illness	6, 13, 20, 22, 23, 30, 32, 38, 41, 51, 86, 88, 91, 102, 103, 121, 130, 142, 143
For livelihood	23, 34, 36, 62, 65, 67, 85, 104, 121, 136, 144, 145
For peace	46
For success	112
For the Jewish People	43, 79, 80, 83
For thanksgiving	9, 21, 57, 95, 100, 116, 138
For Divine guidance	139
For repentance	51,90
For help in troublesome times	20,38,85,86,102,130,142
Prayer recited when traveling	91
Psalm of thanksgiving for a miracle	18
Psalm of thanksgiving upon being rescued	124
In a house of mourning	49
At a gravesite or on a Yahrzeit	33, 16, 17, 72, 91, 104, 130
At the dedication of a monument	1

159

Although, as in the daily prayer, it is best to say these in Hebrew, any language that you understand fully can be used. All languages originate from Hashem and work. Saying these Psalms in a group in unison enhances the cause. One reason is, like prayer, some people are weak and others are strong in both pronunciation and determination (please, don't think that individual effort isn't effective – it is). All prayers are heard, but the strong help the weak and make the group reading more effective. Like prayer these words should come from the heart with a very positive attitude that the words will help. Also like prayer, lip service is far less powerful in helping others. With confidence and maybe even with tears in your eyes say the Psalms and think about the person or people who need help. This will help you pour it out with greater feeling. You will succeed if you feel the pain or even the joy of the people for whom you are reciting Psalms. It works.

3.5 Why Keep Kosher?

To give you the bottom line right at the top: "Jews must keep Kosher because Hashem commanded us to keep Kosher." The word Kosher actually means "proper or fit." In other words, anything that is done correctly according to Jewish law makes it Kosher. That means not just food, but it pertains to a Torah, the prayer shawl, other things to we do and wear, etc.

A wonderful source of information about Judaism is from Aish Hatorah, a yeshiva in Jerusalem with offices and programs worldwide. Here is a very good write-up giving us concise reasons for keeping Kosher (this only is covering the dietary law concept of Kosher).

1) Hygienic: There are many laws that promote health. Judaism forbids eating animals that died without proper slaughter and the draining of the blood (which is a medium for the growth of bacteria). Judaism also forbids eating animals that have abscesses in their lungs or other health problems.

Shellfish, mollusks, lobsters (and yes, stone crabs) which have spread typhoid and are a source for urticaria (hives) are not on the diet. Milk and meat digest at an unequal rate and are difficult for the body; they are forbidden to be eaten together.

Birds of prey are not kosher – tension and hormones produced might make the meat unhealthy.

2) Moral Lessons: We are taught to be sensitive to others' feelings – even to the feelings of animals. A mother and her young are forbidden to be slaughtered on the same day, and of course "don't boil a kid (goat) in its mother's milk."

The Torah prohibits cruelty to animals. We must not remove the limb of an animal while it is still alive (a common practice, prior to refrigeration). When we slaughter an animal, it must be done with the least possible pain; there is a special knife that is so sharp that even the slightest nick in the blade renders it impermissible. This prevents pain to the animal. (I will cover this subject separately, with the proof that ritual slaughter is totally painless and even of great benefit to the animal. You don't believe it? Stay tuned).

And we are reminded not to be vicious, by the prohibition to eat vicious birds of prey.

3) National Reasons – the Jewish people have a mission of Tikun Olam, repairing the world (or "healing the world"). A special diet reminds us of our mission and keeps us together as a people to fulfill it. (Intermarriage is kind of hard when you have to take your non-Jewish date to a kosher restaurant, or if you go to a prospective mother-in-law's home and you won't eat her food...)

Keeping kosher is also a reminder of gratitude to the Almighty for taking the Jewish people out of Egypt, and a symbol of the holy covenant. (see Leviticus 11:45-47)

4) Mystical -- The Torah calls the Jews a "holy people" and prescribes a holy diet (see Deut. 14:2-4). You are what you eat. Kosher is God's diet for spirituality. Jewish mysticism teaches that non-kosher food blocks the spiritual potential of the soul.

Kosher animals properly slaughtered and prepared have more "sparks of holiness" (according to the Kabbalah) which are incorporated in our being.

161

5) Discipline -- If a person can be disciplined in what and when he eats, it follows that he can be disciplined in other areas of life as well. Kashrut requires that one must wait after eating meat before eating milk products and we may not eat certain animals or combinations of foods. (Even when you're hungry!) All of this instills self-discipline.

To expound on number 4, Mystical, the deepest reasons for keeping Kosher are beyond human comprehension; but, I guarantee that Hashem knows exactly what is best for us (He gave us the guarantee in writing – iron clad). Non-Kosher food to the soul of a Jew is like poison to the body. As we would never consider eating arsenic laced food or serving it to our family or friends (it definitely has negative effects on the physical well-being of the human being), why would we serve poisonous food to our soul? Physical death can ruin your whole day. Spiritual death lasts forever and ever. If you think this is an exaggeration, I highly suggest you don't test it. You will not know the truth until a time that is called "too late."

When it says you are what you eat, we actually pick up the personality characteristics of the food we eat. It is totally a spiritual concept that from the soul of the food we are eating, our soul is affected. As an example, a cow is a very docile animal (I have never seen an attack cow being used to guard anything). A pig is a slob and even a very deceptive animal. He has one of the two physical characteristics of a kosher animal (split hooves) but hides the fact that he is not Kosher (he doesn't chew his cud). This trait of being deceptive, by displaying his paws and pretending that he is a kosher animal, is transferred to the eater (not a favorable personality trait). We don't eat birds of prey because we should not be people of prey (only pray).

What confidence do I have in this information? Total, since it comes from Hashem. But, let me give you a more miraculous confidence measure (in case you require more help in believing). It says in the Torah that we can eat from any animal that has two physical traits. The animal must have split hooves and chew its cud. If you don't know what that means, Google it. That is really all the information that is needed, but yet the Torah continues to tell us a warning. It says "beware there are four animals that have one sign but not the other."

- The camel, for being a ruminant (ruminants are mammals that are able to acquire nutrients from plant-based food by fermenting it in a specialized stomach prior to digestion, principally through bacterial actions.) without their hooves being divided.

- The hyrax, for being a ruminant without cloven hooves. The Hebrew term for this animal - שפן *shaphan* - has been translated by older English versions of the bible as *coney*; the existence of the hyrax wasn't known to early English translators. The *coney* was an exclusively European animal, not present in Canaan, while the *shaphan* was described by the Book of Proverbs as living on rocks (like the hyrax, but unlike the *coney*).
- The hare, for being a ruminant without cloven hooves.
- The pig, for having cloven hooves without being a ruminant.

This sounds like very good information to help us identify kosher versus non-kosher animals. But, wait a second. Is this implying that whoever wrote the Torah knew every animal that ever was, is and will be? Is the writer of the Torah willing to lose total credibility if there are other animals not mentioned here that can be found with only one sign? You bet!!!!! The miraculous answer is there has never been another animal found in the 3327 years since Hashem gave Moses the Torah on Mount Sinai (there are variations of the above animals but they are still in the same family). I guess the credibility goes completely to the One who happens to know every animal throughout history (since He created all of them).

Let's go one step further. It says in the Torah that the requirements for a fish to be Kosher is that it must have scales and fins. Once again, that is enough information to recognize a kosher fish. But in the Oral Torah (the Talmud) it warns us that there are fishes that have fins, but not scales and they are not kosher. It goes on to let us know "but don't worry there are no fish that have scales but no fins." Wait another second. Is this implying that whoever wrote the Oral Torah knew every fish in every sea, lake and river that ever was, is and will be? Is the writer of the Oral Torah willing to lose total credibility if there are fish that can be found that have scales but no fins? You bet, again!!!!!

Simple conclusion is that we know beyond a shadow of a doubt Who dictated the Torah, letter by letter, to Moses. If the miraculous information here testifies to the total credibility of the writing of the Torah, the information that is in the Torah is also totally credible. There are, by the way, an infinite number of miraculous bits of information in all of Jewish scriptures – this was only one example.

Don't mess with the commandments especially since they are for our own good. They are the tools to succeed in this world and for eternity. You owe it to yourself and your loved ones. Just be aware that for a Jew to observe the dietary laws is not just a cute tradition handed down for thousands of years, they are vital instructions for survival. There are dire consequences for not doing what Hashem asks of us and they last for all eternity. Once again, we should never argue with success. When you treat this information as a gift from Heaven to help us be happy, we should say "thank you" rather than ask "do we have to?"

3.6 Jewish Ritual Slaughter

Now, hopefully I convinced you that keeping Kosher is not just an old Jewish tradition that you can take it or leave it, but a commandment that is a matter of survival. One might bring up a very controversial subject that we find in the news these days: Jewish ritual slaughter. After all, the Torah is supposed to be very humane in the way all of Hashem's creations are treated; how come there is so much debate worldwide about this method of slaughter?

A quick description. Jewish ritual slaughter, called Shechita, involves using a very sharp knife to cut the carotid artery at the neck of the animal. It is interesting that this method is totally painless for the animal. How so? The blood flowing in the carotid artery is directly connected to the blood flowing in the vertebral artery at the back of the neck to the brain. This causes immediate cessation of blood to the brain and instantly renders the animal unconscious. There is absolutely no pain felt by the animal because the unconsciousness occurs immediately (actually within a second or two, but definitely before the brain gets a signal of pain).

What is fascinating is that this connection of the carotid artery directly to the brain only exists in all animals with cloven hooves that chew their cud, meaning those that are kosher animals. Hashem designed kosher animals to allow a totally painless slaughter. A non-kosher animal's carotid artery is not connected directly to the brain meaning it would not fall unconscious and would experience great pain. This method was commanded by Hashem and given to the Jewish people 3327 years ago at Mount Sinai. It is the only humane method of animal slaughter in the world. It is only out of complete ignorance and the growing Jew-hatred in the world that it has become a topic of debate in recent years.

A definite requirement in the process is that the knife, by Jewish law, must be an extremely sharp, smooth blade with no nicks. This along with the very quick forward and reverse motion ensures the animal's total lack of pain. There have been testimonials from surgeons that perform emergency medical treatment, that a quick, sharp cut using a sharp knife is essentially painless. You may have noticed that when you cut yourself, it is generally when the blood starts to flow that the pain is felt, usually a couple of seconds after. The most reassuring proof is that the animal does not complain as with other methods of slaughter which result in obvious outburst of animal crying. If the procedure is done improperly causing pain, the animal is declared not kosher.

Non-kosher methods of slaughter on the other hand undoubtedly cause pain to animals. Very often they use numbing techniques such as an electric shock, which supposedly prevents any feelings of pain. It actually fries the animal's brain, and definitely causes unnecessary suffering. Another method is a bolt to the head which surely causes suffering. This can be even worse when delivered inaccurately, whether due to poor aim or an unexpected movement of the animal's head. Clubbing animals is also a very inhumane and extremely painful slaughter. There is no doubt that the only method used in the world today that provides sensitivity and compassion to the animal is the Jewish ritual slaughter.

There is yet another very interesting difference between kosher and non-kosher animals. A study conducted years ago demonstrated that horses, dogs, and other animals resist being brought into slaughterhouses because they sense their approaching death. They become agitated, and may even kick and fight until they are killed. In kosher slaughterhouses, this phenomenon is almost non-existent. For example, lambs present at the slaughter of other lambs do not show signs of fear. A calf allowed to roam freely during a period of Shechita did not attempt to run away, even though the door of the slaughterhouse remained wide open. In addition, cud-chewing animals will cease to ruminate when they are under stress. However, cows in a Jewish slaughterhouse may even sit and ruminate while members of their own species are being slaughtered around them. All this indicates that not only do kosher animals not suffer during ritual slaughter; they do not even experience emotional discomfort before the act, and have absolutely no sense of their impending deaths.

Still, since there is always the possibility that one of such animals will be more sensitive than the others, Jewish law forbids killing an animal in the presence of another, in order to prevent even the slightest chance of suffering to the one remaining alive.

There is still more.

Meat slaughtered for consumption must be kept hygienic and safe throughout the duration of its storage, both for health reason – to avoid food poisoning – and economic ones – so as not to needlessly waste food. In general, the higher the quality of the meat and the fresher that it can be kept, the less the need for discarding of the meat, ensuring that fewer animals need to be slaughtered. According to some researchers, Shechita ensures higher quality meat than other forms of slaughter. Shooting, for example, leaves an excess of blood in the carcass, due to the time lag between death and the bleeding of the carcass. This causes the meat to spoil faster. In other non-halachic methods of slaughter, the situation is even worse. (With regard to this topic, we should note the halachic requirement to salt meat after slaughter in order to extract the remaining blood. This act is derived from the prohibition against consuming blood – primarily a spiritual commandment, which has obvious health benefits as well.)

There are other very big advantages to the animal being killed according to Jewish law that are obscure and would not even be considered. I will discuss this later when we talk about the ritual slaughter that was done in the Temple (3.24.1). Animal sacrifice has some additional characteristics that are virtually unknown but very beneficial to the animal.

I have one more question that needs attention. Why, if Shechita is painless and the most humane to kosher animals, is the world so blind that it wants it stopped? Simple answer, Hashem is sending a message to the Jews "It is time to come home." If, eventually, the only place in the world that a Jew can be a Jew; serve Hashem and observe all of the Torah is ISRAEL, (you finish this sentence). Thank you Hashem – Your message is clear.

3.7 Shabbos

Of all the topics that I could talk about, Shabbos, or the Sabbath as you English speakers say, is definitely the most misunderstood concept. In fact most people reading this have no idea what Shabbos is. You may ask: Isn't Shabbos the day of rest, a day that we can't do any work, a day that we are totally restricted from everything? If you ask that question, then you are exactly the individual who needs to be educated about Shabbos.

First of all you should know that Shabbos it the greatest gift from Hashem to the Jewish people. Even though we are commanded to remember and observe the Shabbos, there is nothing more enjoyable than Shabbos if you do it correctly. We see that the seven Noachide laws given to the non-Jews do not include Shabbos. The fact that the Muslims celebrate their Sabbath on Friday and the Christians on Sunday is no accident – it is from Hashem. Saturday the day that Hashem finished the creation of everything and rested was designated as a gift for the Jews of the world to join Hashem.

The word used in the Torah to tell us it is not a day of work is מְלָאכָה which translates to craftsmanship or created effort. When the Israelites were building the portable Tabernacle in the desert, they performed 39 different skillful activities in making the Tabernacle. When Hashem told us to rest on the Shabbos, He referred to those 39 activities.

That is why turning on a light switch is forbidden, but moving furniture around to accommodate guests is permitted. Moving furniture is not a creative activity of the 39, but building or destroying is. Modern interpretation shows that completing an electrical circuit is a building activity and should be avoided (there are other authorities that equate closing an electric circuit with starting a fire, or at least the idea of a transfer of energy which is one of the 39 activities to avoid). If you don't see switching on the light as a building process, then you have proven that you have not studied the interpretation of the great Rabbis who are giving you the word of Hashem. Even if something is a precautionary effort just to make sure, you are showing Hashem your willingness to adhere to His will, and you will come out in His favor. Never forget that this is the world of testing and Hashem notes everything you do to serve Him or not. Anyone who doesn't agree with the great Rabbis, over centuries, is not serving Hashem, since we know that Hashem is the One Who put the guidance into the minds of the Rabbis and made them the authorities to help us.

Let us talk about the more spiritual purpose of Shabbos. We are actually given an extra soul on Shabbos to bring us to a much higher spiritual level. Until you experience this higher level of spirituality, my words mean nothing. It's like trying to describe a new taste that you have not experienced. The only way for you to appreciate that taste is to put the food in your mouth and enjoy. The extra soul has a very hidden advantage. We are told that with this extra soul you can get a taste of paradise right here on Earth. Once again, that is meaningless unless you try it.

Shabbos has another great advantage that is also very hidden. We start on Sunday to prepare for Shabbos. The entire week is buying the food, preparing the food, getting clean clothes ready, setting up timers, setting heating and air conditioning controls, inviting guests (or accepting invitations), cleaning the house, preparing words of Torah to be talked about at the Shabbos table, etc, etc, etc. This is the greatest lesson in preparing us for the real world – the World to Come. I have mentioned that this world is only a place of testing and perfecting ourselves. When we prepare for Shabbos we must not overlook one thing. Why? Because whatever you did to set up for Shabbos is what you have available when it starts. We cannot fix things that we forgot to do in preparing for Shabbos. You have to live with your effort you completed Sunday through Friday. You cannot fix something in this world, in this life after you leave it. What you did in this world is what you are blessed with or stuck with forever and ever. What a valuable lesson for setting up your eternity is practicing with Shabbos.

Another example that might be more familiar. After months of counting the days, vacation time is here. You are planning a trip about which you are very excited. The preparation was nerve-racking, but it is all done and you and the family are ready to go, go, go. You have your plane tickets, you packed everything (hopefully), you made hotel reservations, ground transportation arrangements, someone to take in the mail, feed the dog, make the house look lived in (to trick the burglars), travelers checks, travelers insurance, etc, etc, etc. Whatever you did is what you will live with. If you forgot to make a reservation and the hotel is full; if you forgot to take the money that was sitting on the dining room table and the bank account is drained, if you forgot to... You got the idea. A successful, enjoyable vacation (or holiday if that's what you call it) is all based on the preparation before the event. Just like Shabbos, just like life – now and forever, you must prepare and make sure everything, and I do mean everything, is done properly. Fortunately, Hashem gave us a roadmap to get us totally prepared. It is up to us NOW to use it.

What about the restrictions of Shabbos? The fact is, it is just the opposite. During the week we are slaves to this materialistic world. Whatever we need we have to do something to accomplish it. On Shabbos, everything is done. The food is cooked the house is ready even the lights and heating system is set and doesn't even need our effort. Best of all, the world goes away. There is nothing more emotionally upsetting than looking at the news and seeing all the chaos and turmoil happening in the world. In the 1960's (I know, I am showing my age), there was a Broadway show and also a movie entitled "Stop the World, I Want to Get Off." The world sometimes becomes so tense that we think the same. On Shabbos the world goes away. My bills go away, my work problems go away. I love it. I am not restricted; I am free from the craziness of this world and the harsh requirements to live on it. I know Shabbos ends and the world comes back. That is when I start my countdown to the next Shabbos.

I should mention that Shabbos is the best day of the week to study. The phone doesn't ring, no traffic outside (cars and buses are not allowed to operate in my hometown on Shabbos). There are many study groups and lectures available. Many friends are available with which to study, who are not always available during the week. No school, so the children and grandchildren get extra attention and study – they love it also. Of course dad and grandpa (me) also get extra attention.

A little caveat: There is one vehicle that travels through the streets in our city – he is the Shabbos goy. A non-Jewish fellow who will fix, adjust, change, turn on, turn off, you name it. He knows the Halachah as well as, if not better than, most of my neighbors, and therefore will get the job done without any worry of a Shabbos violation.

What is one of the most special days of the secular year in America? Thanksgiving. Why? It is a beautiful day of being with your loved ones, eating scrumptious food, relaxing and above all the world seems to go away. Jews have 52 Thanksgiving celebrations a year (more if you include holidays, WOW). A big difference is that the family is truly together – in the same room, not in different worlds, watching football. We are forced to pay attention to each other on Shabbos. My wife and children didn't know each other until we got into the Shabbos phenomenon. We also could be four individuals together in separate worlds. But on Shabbos, we sing, we talk Torah, we laugh, we smile, we have a very, very good time. The best part is we have become so close a family that when the grandchildren came into our lives, the Shabbos was the ticket to love and happiness with the new generation. A very hidden pleasure in the Jewish community is a much lesser generation gap.

If anyone tells you they don't enjoy Shabbos, they are doing it wrong. There is nothing like it in the secular world. I thank Hashem so much for this gift, a gift that is so great, you have to experience it to understand what I am saying. My words mean nothing, your experiencing Shabbos means everything and you get good marks on your final report card from Hashem, the Gift Giver.

3.8 What did Becoming an Observant Jew Really Mean to Me?

Obviously, my spiritual level has changed and I am much more aware of Hashem and His goodness. Many times I have received His help in rough situations. It would take me hours to tell you all the miraculous occurrences that I have experienced; but, I would prefer to concentrate on some specific areas of my life.

The greatest and most enjoyable improvement was in our family life. Before we became observant, my wife, two children and I would sit and watch television together but never realized that we were four people in different worlds and miles apart. We didn't talk to each other or share life together. We only went through motions and pretended to know one another. Suddenly, when we began observing the Shabbos, there was no television and fewer distractions. We sat around the dinner table and actually started to talk to each other. We shared Torah issues that we had learned and found ourselves teaching each other. We sang, we laughed and, best of all, we discovered how much we love each other. To this day my wife and I couldn't be closer with our children, but to really talk about pure happiness is grandchildren. Even though we only had two children, we now have 17 grandchildren. The best part is that our children and grandchildren are very good people. They are beautiful, intelligent (bi-lingual), totally respectful and very pleasant to be with (this is an unbiased opinion). They don't fight, they don't argue and they always help each other. This type of behavior isn't limited to my family. Children that I have met in many observant Jewish communities are the absolute best in the world. The expressions: "kids will be kids" and "teenagers will be teenagers" are meaningless to me since they are usually excuses for misbehaving.

My wife and I grew up in secular communities. We attended regular public schools. I went through a military career, living in 5 states and two countries.

170

We have been observant for about 23 years which means we have extensive experience with both worlds – secular and observant. So, why would so many of the problems that we experienced in secular communities not be prevalent in an observant community? The city we live in, of about 50,000 people, is 100% observant. The Mayor is a Rabbi. His staff consists completely of Rabbis and observant women. The major industry is studying Torah. There are about 150 places to pray and study Torah. I personally live about a four minute walk to 12 places of worship. It goes past 20 if my walk is increased to 10 minutes.

Television is not allowed and children are not to have computers. There are many computers in this city, but they are used mostly for business and by retired people like me who keep up with the world using the web (and write blogs and books). My son who uses the computer for business uses a kosher web service. All filth is blocked by the service; meaning, that if his children see the screen, it will not have improper content. The children are excited about learning and they actually use books. Most of all, they are happy children.

You may think that this seems archaic; but, let us look at the results of such a pristine society. We have no police force in this city. Stores often leave merchandise outside over night or receive deliveries overnight to be taken in at opening time. There is no theft. There are times that people need items that are left outside the store; they are permitted to take what they want since the owner knows that they will return to pay for it when the store opens. All grocery stores and supermarkets only carry kosher products – that makes shopping much easier. The bus service within the city and those buses that travel to other cities have separate seating. Women sit in the back because they do not want to be looked at by men. Am I saying that even observant men can't control their emotions? It so happens we are also human; and, we appreciate not being able to look at women on the bus, or during prayer. This leads to an interesting situation since women enter the bus by the center door; they scan their own card to pay for the ride. There is a separate machine at the center door and it is completely on the honor system even for children who use that door. I remember a situation recently where my son took a taxi home and realized he didn't have money on him. The cab driver said "no problem, I will stop by tomorrow and you can pay me."

This city has no drug problems, no teen pregnancy (dating starts when we are ready to get married), a very low divorce rate; gossip isn't allowed or any other prohibition in the Torah. Even music is completely in praise of Hashem and is

171

very popular. Lots of music can be heard and on special occasions I've seen dancing in the streets (the men of course since men shouldn't watch women dancing). 24/7 is serving Hashem.

These are the happiest people on Earth. Very honest, very generous, people always trying to help others, very good parents to their children and, of course, very good grandparents to their grandchildren, is the norm in my neighborhood. All the negative stereotypes that we have heard about Jewish people are non-existent. Jew hatred doesn't exist. Even when secular Jews or non-Jews visit, I have noticed such an atmosphere of respect and even emulation since the people are so friendly and lovable. The only disagreement I have had with neighbors is when they try to pay me for thing and I don't want the money. The reverse has happened many times that someone does something for me or my family or gives us something, even at great expense, and they won't take any money in payment. Niceness between people should be my worst problem in life.

When we lived in the states, we also lived in a city that was about 60,000 people with about 40,000 being observant. Any crime that occurred came from outside the community and it was obvious. I used to invite guests to my house, especially on Shabbos, to share the observant experience. Very often it was a secular Jew or secular Jewish family that we wanted to teach about Hashem and His ways – let them experience the true joy of Shabbos. I constantly got comments such as: "Your neighbors are such nice people," or "Jews aren't this way where I live." Any time I had a guest, there would always be a neighbor trying to steal my guest or guests for a meal. I always got comments such as "I can't believe that total strangers want to feed me and my family and treat us like we are their family." It actually is enjoyable since I, myself have stolen guests (that's a secret, so make sure you tell everyone).

The most telling comment was when we went for prayer service on a Saturday morning. There were always young children there who were praying. The service would last about 2 ½ hours. My guest would notice how intense these children would be praying to Hashem. They would comment: "Adults could put on an act, but the children don't lie – these are well adjusted children that really want to serve Hashem." When it came to doing outreach work and helping people, my neighbors and especially the children (especially my children) were the best assets I had.

One incident that I want to relate involves a situation where two families were living in one house. It was very crowded and did not afford the individual families privacy. The observant Jewish community wanted to help, so they made a city wide collection. They raised enough money to buy a separate home for one of the families. There is no better way of serving Hashem than helping others, and that was one of the most inspiring acts I have ever witnessed.

When someone tells me about an observant individual who was a crook, I explain that the individual they are talking about had a "secular moment." Observant crook is an oxymoron; you can't do the commandments and violate them in the same breath. I can't put on a stethoscope and walk into a hospital and call myself a doctor. Likewise, I can't call myself an observant Torah Jew, and not follow the commandments of the Torah.

We are products of our environment. If we grow up surrounded by goodness and happiness, than that is what we become. If we are surrounded by evil; well, you get the point. Jewish stereotypes usually come from people who really have never met an observant Jew. A non-observant Jew can have the same bad habits as a non-observant gentile, but if the one seeing the individual with bad habits knows that he or she is Jewish, it becomes an "all Jews are that way" scenario.

Someday, I hope to invite each and every one of you to my home (don't tell my wife I said that). Seeing is believing (unless it is something reported in the news). This will sound strange; but, I don't want you to believe a word that I am saying. If you ever get the chance to go to an observant Jewish community and meet the people, I can give you an "I told you so." That experience will be worth a thousand of my words.

3.9 Orchard

The Torah was given to Moses on Mount Sinai 3327 years ago in a fiery display. The 304,805 letters were in a single string and Moses put the spaces between the words. How do I know? It says so in the Torah. How do I know it's true? Since I have shown unshakable proof that the Torah is Hashem's creation by verifying that the number of bits of information in the Torah that no human (or alien) could have known is infinite, I would say we have pretty good odds that it came from Hashem. The most miraculous thing about the Torah is that it can be studied at different levels. At the same time that we can read the simple meaning, the Torah can be studied at levels so deep it goes beyond human comprehension. That, in itself, hints to the fact that it could not have been a product of human hands.

There are basically four different levels that the Torah can be studied and are called by the name:

Pardes (Jewish exegesis)
Pardes refers to (types of) approaches to biblical exegesis in rabbinic Judaism (or - simpler - interpretation of text in Torah study). The term, sometimes also spelled PaRDeS, is an acronym formed from the name initials of the following four approaches:

> Peshat (פְּשַׁט) — "plain" ("simple") or the direct meaning.
>
> Remez (רֶמֶז) — "hints" or the deep (allegoric: hidden or symbolic) meaning beyond just the literal sense.
>
> Derash (דְּרַשׁ) — from Hebrew darash: "inquire" ("seek") — the comparative (midrashic) meaning, as given through similar occurrences.
>
> Sod (סוֹד) (pronounced with a long O as in 'bone') — "secret" ("mystery") or the mystical meaning, as given through inspiration or revelation.

Each type of Pardes interpretation examines the extended meaning of a text. As a general rule, the extended meaning never contradicts the base meaning. The Peshat means the plain or contextual meaning of the text. Remez is the allegorical meaning. Derash includes the metaphorical meaning, and Sod represents the hidden meaning. There is often considerable overlap, for example when legal understandings of a verse are influenced by mystical interpretations or when a "hint" is determined by comparing a word with other instances of the same word. Some thinkers, such as the Tolaat Yaakov, divide Pardes into Peshat, Remez, Din (law), and Sod. According to this understanding, Derash is divided into the homiletics, which are classified under Remez, and legal interpretations, which are classified under Din.

Examples:

Pshat
{Gen. 1:2) And the earth was empty (tohu) and formless (vohu).

Rashi - The Hebrew word 'tohu' means astonishment in English and the word 'bohu' means emptiness and next to emptiness. Thus the phrase is 'amazement and desolation'. This means that a person would be amazed and astonished at anything that was there.

Remez

(Gemara Makkos 2b) Q. A hint that the law of conspiring witnesses is in the Torah, where is it?

A. There is no such hint, because it is stated explicitly (Deut 19:19) You do to them what they conspired to do to the accused.

Q. But a hint that conspiring witnesses receive a whipping [if they cannot be punished by doing to them as they conspired] according to the Torah, where is it?

A. As it says (Deut 25:1-2) They caused the righteous to be righteous and the evil to be evil. And therefore the evil get whipped.

Q. Because they caused the righteous to be righteous and the evil to be evil. And therefore the evil get whipped?

A. But there must have been witnesses who testified that the righteous were evil. And other witnesses came and caused the righteous to be known as righteous as they were before, and caused the previous witnesses to be known as evil. And therefore the evil get whipped.

Derash (Midrash)

(Gemara Makkos 23b) Rabbi Simlai deduced that there were 613 mitzvot (commandments) taught to Moses at Mount Sinai. The verse says that (Deut 33:4) Torah was given to us through Moses at Sinai. The gematria of Torah is 611. And one should add to them the first two of the Ten Commandments that were given directly by G-d to the Jews [this is known because they are written in the first person singular], making the total 613.

Sod

(Guide for the Perplexed, book 2 section 30) "Adam and Eve were at first created as one being, having their backs united: they were then separated, and one half was removed and brought before Adam as Eve." Note how clearly it has been stated that Adam and Eve were two in some respects, and yet they remained one, according to the words, "Bone of my bones, and flesh of my flesh" (Gen. 2:23). The unity of the two is proved by the fact that both have the same name, for she is called ishah (woman), because she was taken out of ish (man), also by the words, "And shall cleave unto his wife, and they shall be one flesh" (2:24). How

175

great is the ignorance of those who do not see that all this necessarily includes some [other] idea [besides the literal meaning of the words].

Association with paradise

The Pardes system is often regarded as mystically linked to the word Pardes (Hebrew פַּרְדֵּס), meaning orchard. "Pardes" is etymologically related to the English word "paradise." It occurs only three times in the Bible, namely, in Song of Songs 4:13, Ecclesiastes 2:5, and Nehemiah 2:8. In the first of these passages it means "garden"; in the second and third, "park." In the Talmud the word is used of the Garden of Eden and its heavenly prototype.

I never said that the study of Torah was easy. If you were wondering why I called this section Orchard, sorry to make you wait so long to find out; but, now you know.

A very important concept to learn from all this is that the Torah is the most complicated text in existence. Many of us went to a Sunday school, as an example, and at the age of 5 we heard for the first time the Bible stories – Adam and Eve in the garden, Noah and the ark, Abraham, Isaac and Jacob's escapades and, of course the story of the Exodus (which we know well from the movie version – extremely inaccurate). We grow up and by the time we are 20 or 30 years old we are still stuck with the stories we learned at age 5. Most people see the Torah at the Peshat level and go no further. If I asked someone to tell me about Quantum Physics or corporate law or differential equations or brain surgery (that's enough – we get the point), most would answer "Oh, I've never studied those subjects." But, if I ask them questions about the Torah or the Bible, everyone would have an opinion. Even worse they would tell me "I'm skeptical as to whether that really happened." To know that the Torah and even all of Jewish scriptures are so deep and even beyond comprehension, it doesn't compute – after all "I read it once and know all the 5 year level Bible stories."

I know that ten lifetimes of Torah study would only scratch the surface of what the deeper meanings are. What is even worse is we study in English, which is Peshat personified. The true, deeper meaning can only come from the mystical and miraculous letters of Hebrew.

There are no wasted words or even wasted letters in the Torah. The 22 Hebrew letters of the alphabet are basically consonants. (The first two letters are Alef,

176

Bet hence the origin of the word alphabet – not the Greek alpha beta since Greek also came from Hebrew). Vowel sounds are added by symbols beneath the letter which means that every word has several meanings by just changing the symbols. The Torah has no symbols beneath the letters so a variety of translations are possible. Sometimes the hidden message of a word would come from pronouncing the word differently. Examples of this could fill volumes but here's a good one:

The story of Abraham taking his son Isaac to the alter, as Hashem commanded, includes a very interesting statement that Abraham tells his servant Eliezer and Ishmael who accompanied them to the foot of the mountain where the alter was. He told them "You stay here with the donkey and I and the boy will go to that place." With the donkey? No wasted words in the Torah? The words in Hebrew for "with the donkey" are "eim hachamor" (ch is the guttural sound not available in English). If I changed the vowel sounds under those words, not the spelling, (remember there are no symbols for vowels in the Torah) and pronounce it "am hachomaer" the translation changes to "a people of materialism." Abraham is saying a very profound statement that you are physical, materialistic beings of this world while he and his son are spiritual beings. To complete the thought, Abraham says "I and the boy will go to that place." The Hebrew word in the verse being translated as "place" is actually one of Hashem's names which solidifies the idea of Abraham and Isaac approaching the spiritual.

Another type of coded message (going down a letter in the alphabet) can be exemplified using the very famous verse of "An eye for an eye." Is it really telling us that by law, which the Torah accurately guides us, that if someone were to take out my eye (may Hashem protect me from such horror), that I can just reciprocate likewise (de-eye him)? The actual translation is more accurately "an eye below, or substituted, by an eye." The message is: the three Hebrew letters for the word eye are in the alphabet below three Hebrew letters that spell the Hebrew word for money. In other words it is hinted (Remez) in the translation to substitute the letters according to the alphabet and you will see what the law is. Physical damage is subject to monetary compensation (as thoroughly discussed in the Talmud).

One more example, that shows how, by putting the words together and making new spaces, one can gain insight into the meaning or even see prophecy. In the book of Numbers, Moses is told by Hashem that "you are not getting this land because of your righteousness, but because of their wickedness." The paragraph ends off with the famous statement "you are a stiff-necked people." If you look at the Hebrew of that expression, remove the spaces and put in new spaces, you see the name "Arafat." Wickedness personified and a very prophetic message for our time.

OK, one more really cool example. This is not even in the Torah but is in the commentary of Onkelus. Onkelus, who lived about two thousand years ago, was a Babylonian who translated the Torah into Aramaic. Aramaic was the language of Babylon and also, the language that is used throughout the Babylonian Talmud to this very day. His translation is so important that most copies of The Five Books of Moses include the Onkelus translation. Aramaic uses Hebrew letters so Hashem even provided messages in Onkelus's commentary. My favorite example appears in the book of Numbers (the portion of Shoftim) also where Onkelus is talking about judges but if you take on particular sentence and push the letters together and make new separations, you will read this sentence that alludes the idea of "today being Diana's funeral." Every Shabbos throughout the year we read a portion of the Torah divided as such that over a year's time we read the whole Torah. The portion that we read on the day that Princess Diana was put to rest contained that sentence found in Onkelus.

There are no coincidences. Hashem's messages are very spooky sometimes.

We live in a time that we should look for deeper meaning. We read the entire Torah every year but need to delve into its meaning in a more profound way. It is our handbook of life and truly is our guide to total success and happiness. We say during praying "It is a tree of life for those who grasp it, and all who support it are fortunate. Its ways are ways of pleasantness and all its paths are peace. Cause us to return to You, Hashem, and we shall return; renew our days as of old." Such good advice – thank You, Hashem.

3.10 Sexism in Scriptures and in Life

One subject that I have found to be a big myth is the stigma of women in the observant community. The secular world is convinced that women are treated as subservient citizens and it is all because the Bible treats them as such. I had the exact same belief before I became observant, since I had only lived in secular communities (about 48 years' worth) which perpetuated that stereotype. I didn't know any observant Jews and could only believe what I had heard about them. Then two things happened in my life. One was a deeper analysis of what scriptures really says, and the other was moving into an observant Torah community, meeting these wonderful people and experiencing the exact opposite of what I was led to believe.

First of all, let us review what it says in scriptures. The most amazing thing that I discovered was it is very one sided, but against men, not women. "Women are at a higher spiritual level than men could ever be." What is the basis for that statement? Because women can experience life in them and men can't. It is the primary reason that women are not obligated to fulfill many of the commandments. Women are above the need for many commandments.

We see throughout scriptures that the women are more righteous than the men. The original sin was mostly due to Adam not repenting his mistake. We have additional insight into how a wife should assist her husband. Hashem separated Adam and Eve and said that she should be "ezer kenegdo," a helper parallel to him (Genesis 2:18). This has an interesting connotation that in English we stress the first word a "helper" almost making her sound like a servant to him. More accurately, the second word "parallel" or, I have even seen it translated as "against" him. This makes her totally equal a partner who should even keep him straight when he makes mistakes. She is there not to serve him but to work together on an equal basis and maybe even keep him out of trouble. The concept of keep him out of trouble is perpetuated throughout the Bible, actually alluding to the fact that women make better decisions than men – they should, they are at a higher spiritual level. Maybe it isn't so equal after all, which is why we call our wives "our better half."

Examples: We are told that Sarah was more of a prophetess than Abraham being a prophet (Rashi states that). Isaac was not aware of the deception of his son Esau but Rebecca was able to help Jacob achieve the birthright and perpetuate the will of Hashem. Both Rachel and Leah were very wise and of great help to Jacob. When the father of Moses, Amram, a leader in the community, decided to prevent further killings of the Jewish male babies, he required the men to divorce their wives. It was the wisdom and foresight of his daughter Miriam that changed his mind. As a result of the prophecy that she experienced, her brother, Moses was born -- the deliverer of the Jew people. Shifra and Puah (who were actually Yocheved and Miriam) acted as midwives and saved many Jewish babies. The greatness of Queen Esther in her role that saved the Jews in Persia (the celebration of Purim) or Yehudit the one whose bravery helped save the Jews (the celebration of Chanukah) or the greatness of Chanah, Chulda, Michal, etc. The fact that the women were not in favor of building the Golden Calf or that they did not believe the negative reports of the spies are very indicative of the much higher spiritual level that women have throughout history. Many are not aware that because ten of the spies did come back with a negative report and the fact that the men didn't have the high level of faith and trust in Hashem as the women did, there were two punishments that resulted. One is that the Israelites would have to remain in the desert for 40 years, one year for each day that the spies were away. The other is that, from that time on, when men pray they will require a quorum of ten men in order to bring down the Shechinah, the Divine Presence of Hashem, one man for each negative spy. Never think that women cannot be counted as part of a minion is a sexist of prejudicial act. It is that women are at the higher level and don't require this punishment of ten in order to pray to Hashem. Women should never lower themselves to the level of men by wanting to be included in the minion. (It's interesting that this spirit of Hashem is a feminine word, which negates the poor English translation of Hashem as He. Hashem is neither a He nor She. But, the different qualities of His essence are considered masculine or feminine and the words demonstrate those qualities that men and women are individually blessed with from Hashem). You get the idea.

The roles that women played and their tremendous sacrifice that we see throughout scriptures is very much in favor of the Jewish woman and not men. One incident in Torah that shows the weakness of men is when the righteous Joseph was confronted by the wife of Potifar. Joseph was said to be a very handsome man that the women swooned over. When he was made a servant in the house of Potifar, the captain of the palace guards, Potifar's wife made a play for the handsome Joseph. Joseph knew that men, including him, were not strong and could give into temptation, ran from the house. Sometimes one passes a test by running from the situation.

One of the most important roles of the married Jewish couple is to "be fruitful and multiply." Bringing new Jewish souls into the world is a very prominent factor in the process of perfecting the world. The world will not be perfected until all the Jewish souls in Heaven have come to Earth and have been rectified individually (this is much more involved than what I am saying here). The woman takes on the very important role of teacher of life within a household. Her nurturing of the children is the greatest element for the success of the family

180

and in turn the entire Jewish community. The training of Jewish children to become righteous adults can be attributed to the high level of righteousness of the Jewish woman. What I have experienced is that Jewish men hold their wives in high regard since most households are very successful in bringing fruition to the will of Hashem.

There is another great misunderstanding in the customs of the observant community – the separation of men and women in prayer service. As demonstrated in the story of Joseph, men are weak. When you have a situation such a prayer that requires complete concentration and not lip service to perform it properly, no man could ever convince me that he can handle the great spiritual involvement with a woman in his site. I've said it before, any man that tells me he can handle it is either a liar or a homosexual. There are other hidden factors in the separation of men and women. One is Hashem wishes no individual to be embarrassed. When men and women sit together it becomes obvious if you see a single man or a single women sitting alone – people gossip. They look at the individual, especially if the person is older and wonder why that person doesn't have a spouse. We eliminate any possibility of embarrassment by having men sit with men and women sitting with women. Another embarrassment is that no individual should touch a Torah if he or she is ritually impure (this would require much explanation as to what impurity means. But, whatever you think it is you are probably incorrect, since it is a spiritual matter not physical). The time of the monthly cycle renders a woman impure. If a woman was in seat in the synagogue that she could reach the Torah or could be asked, as the men are, to take the Torah out of the Ark, it would be an embarrassment if the woman declined or shied away from the Torah and everyone suspected the reason. Extra note: if men are impure because of a seminal emission or other reasons, he also must go to the ritual bath for purification before touching a Torah (but it would not be suspected for embarrassment purposes if he avoided touching the Torah).

It is fascinating to know that for thousands of years men and women were always separated in prayer service, even in the church. When the enlightenment came in the mid-1800s, the church modernized, so-to-speak, and combined the sexes. The Jewish Reform movement, which mimicked the church in most of its customs, followed suite. This is the only reason the so-called modern Jewish movements have combined seating. It is definitely against the will of Hashem. It is sinful to pray to Hashem while one is violating His will.

Tefillin are a most wonderful way to bind oneself to Hashem. But, it is only for men. Where do women come in? On a most simple level, the reason for the commandments is to establish a link with Hashem. The most profound way to do this is to resemble Him. There is one unique way that women resemble Hashem in a way that no man could ever hope to. Only a woman can create within her body. Only a woman can bear a child. In this sense, a woman partakes of Hashem's attributes more intimately than any man. The Kabbalists teach us that the hand Tefillin represent the feminine element. The single hollow can be said to represent the womb, and the coils, the umbilical cord. What man partakes of with an object, woman partakes of with her very body. The box of Tefillin is called a Bayis – literally a house. The woman also has her Bayis, the home in which she raises a family. One could say that a woman's home is her Tefillin.

There are two basic elements in Judaism, the home and the synagogue. Judaism treats the home and synagogue as being co-equal. Some of our most important rituals belong exclusively to the home, such as the Seder, the Succah, the Sabbath table, the Sabbath candles, the Chanukah lamp, etc. The continuity of Judaism rests on the home more than anything else. This Bayis, the home, is a woman's Tefillin. It is her contribution to the overall picture of Hashem's purpose. It is interesting to note that Hashem told all, from Moses to Jacob, and teach the sons of Israel: "If the Torah does not enter the Jewish home first, there can be no continuity of Judaism. This spirit of Torah in the Jewish home (Bayis) is the same as the parchments of Torah in the Tefillin box (Bayis). But this is the domain of the woman.

Additionally, the Tallit or prayer shawl is a reminder to men to perform the 613 commandments. Women do not need this reminder and are therefore not obligated to wear a Tallit. Woman who would like to wear either a Tallit or Tefillin are lowering themselves to the level and weaknesses of a man. Let us do things the way Hashem commanded and not attribute any custom to the arrogance of men or the misconception of prejudice to women.

I probably could never fully articulate the true aspects of the high attributes of Jewish women – after all, I'm a man; what do I know? But having had a very extensive comparison of the way women are treated in the secular world to the pedestal treatment they receive in the Jewish observant world, I can say without reservation that they are not even close. I have observed such prejudicial treatment of women in secular life, at school, in the military and at the work place. This behavior would be considered appalling to the observant Jewish community.

When people believe that it is the flawed rules and customs made up by men that we follow instead of the perfect guidance of Hashem, they are greatly deceived (and uneducated). When they realize that Hashem's system is perfect, only then can they also enjoy the happiness that the system of this world has to offer. The observant Jewish community has the happiest people in the world with the best behaved children (most of whom actually have two parents, a mother and a father – what a novelty in today's society), the lowest divorce rate, the most successful marriages and by far the greatest peace of mind. When you follow and trust Hashem, it is easy. Are we perfect in following Hashem's system? Definitely not but that is what life is all about – perfecting ourselves so that our eternal life can be the best. Yes, we make mistakes; yes, observant Jews sometime have "secular moments." "Be all that you can be" is not just for the US Army.

Why are we so adamant about studying Torah, studying Hashem's guidance for this life in this world, it is not to have a lot of information in our heads, it is to know how to live Torah and be totally successful in this life and forever. I know, I repeat myself; I know, I repeat myself, but if you are not catching on to the absolute truth of everything, you haven't caught on to the purpose of this book. The truest accomplishment of that motto of being all that you can be in this world is with the observant Jewish community. Don't argue with success.

3.11 Reward and Punishment

I have mentioned that we are under a system of reward and punishment (to save typing hereafter will be referred to r and p), measure for measure (hereafter m for m) for what we do. But, as with everything in this life, there are many more details to be discussed. The basis for the system is: if you follow the commandments (hereafter I will start calling a commandment "mitzvah," plural "mitzvot." It's time to start introducing some Hebrew into the picture), you will be rewarded; and, if you violate the mitzvot, there will be retribution. When the Torah talks of m for m it is referring to everything. Every word, every act, no matter how small, is recorded and will result in r and p. The system, however, is strictly help from Hashem in our mission to correct ourselves and the world. Human beings require discipline to behave properly, so Hashem provides us with a totally workable system to succeed. Hashem wants us to have an eternity of goodness and joy, but created us in His image meaning we have the capability to do the right thing or not based on our own free will. This entire world was created for us; so, we have the opportunity to make it right or not, hence, the system or r and p.

There are three aspects that need to be clarified. What will happen to us as r and p? When will we receive r and p? Where will the r and p occur? To preserve our free will, nothing can be obvious. Example from the Torah is the telling of Miriam receiving retribution for saying something against her brother Moses. I'm not going to get into the details except to say that she was put outside the camp for seven days and afflicted with tzaraat (described as a condition of disfiguration in chapters 13-14 of Leviticus – unknown to us today – many times incorrectly translated as leprosy – it wasn't). The entire assembly of Israelites were about to make their next move, but were delayed one week to wait for Miriam. Why? Miriam was 87 years old and highly loved and respected, but when she was 6 years old, 81 years earlier, she did the mitzvah of waiting in the Nile River to see that her baby brother Moses, who was in the basket, would be retrieved and taken care of by Pharaoh's daughter. Her reward, so to speak, was an m for m act of the people waiting for Miriam because she waited for her brother 81 years earlier. Not so obvious, but the important point is every positive act will be rewarded positively.

I think you get the idea that if r and p happened exactly at the time of the mitzvah being done or violated, we would not have free will. If we actually saw reward immediately we wouldn't have a choice but would, like robots, be programmed to react only one way. What is wrong with that? Hashem wants us to correct our errors in order to perfect ourselves – that requires self-determination through free will.

Can positive results happen immediately? Absolutely, when it is imperative and it happens as a result of turning to Hashem. I had a friend who was driving in Israel and he mistakenly drove into Ramallah, home of the PLO and probably as dangerous for a Jew as driving into Gaza. He was captured, brought to a spot where a crowd gathered and threatened. A gun was put to his head. My friend, who is a devout Jew, immediately started saying Psalms, in other words, his immediate and only reaction was to turn to Hashem. At that exact moment, an Arab soldier ran into the area and said "forget about him, we have a problem and I need help." They abandoned my friend who immediately ran to his car and escaped. It was so obvious to my friend what had happened – Hashem is always there to help. My friend followed up the incident with a big thank you to Hashem by giving charity. When you experience something like that, your faith and trust in Hashem is greatly enhanced.

An important word about punishment is that Hashem is merciful. We are not referring to someone making a mistake. If mistakes are made, Hashem helps us with correction, but does not punish us. Punishment comes from deliberate and willful violation of the mitzvot. If someone knows, as an example, that he should observe the Shabbos, but inadvertently didn't realize today is the Shabbos and started to perform many acts of violation, that is forgivable. If the individual knows it is the Shabbos or knows that he or she is eating non-kosher food and performs violations maliciously (or even out of ignorance), in other words, in defiance of Hashem's mitzvot, that will bring punishment. Important to note that one's personal violation of a mitzvah is carried on to one's children, who rely on the parent for proper guidance in life. If the child continues the Torah violation into the next generation, retribution continues, but the original parent receives even more retribution for passing the violation along – Hashem sees the entire future and what future generations will do as a result of our rearing.

An additional word about timing. When Hashem knows that our free will is only directed at doing His will, the r and p does become more obvious. If we are in a dire situation, as my friend was, and pray to Hashem for help, the very act of always turning to Hashem for help is important, but it must be done with the proper conviction to get immediate results. I say with proper conviction and even proper intention since the person who thinks "I am going to fool Hashem to get my way, that person is a fool." Tricking or bribing Hashem is counterproductive and never works. The person who thinks praying is: "do this for me Hashem, and I will go to synagogue every Shabbos from now on" is probably a Hell of an individual. Hashem is infinitely smarter and cleverer than all of us combined.

I have personally experienced immediate results on a fairly regular basis. I find I don't have to wait 81 years to have my prayers answered, if I need something on the spot. If you remember when I talked about prayer, Hashem gave us a system that our very words can cause energies to flow and results to occur. The important thing is knowing exactly where the source of energy originates – there is only Hashem.

Let me give you some examples I've experienced. I have 100's, if not 1000's, of stories that I could share (or bore you with), but will offer on two stories just to get my point across. I was once at a meeting at work on a Friday afternoon. I was getting a little panicky since I had to leave (Shabbos was coming). The boss was standing at the exit door. How could I, without making a scene, leave? We were on a conference call with other individuals using the phone. I turned my attention to Hashem and thought "if we could lose the phone connection." With split second timing, as I thought the word "connection," the phone went dead. The boss asked "what happened?" I proudly said "I think we lost the phone connection." The boss said "let's take a ten minute break to reconnect and we'll continue." I went back to my office, got a friend to replace me at the meeting and off to Shabbos. Thank you, Hashem.

There was another incident where my car broke down about 13 miles from home on a highway. You guessed it. It was Friday afternoon and I had to get home for Shabbos. Fortunately, I don't care for, nor did I have, a cell phone. Why? If I did and called a towing service I would have been late. I took my attaché case out of the car (yes, I used to carry an attaché), locked the car and with a big smile on my face said "I wonder how Hashem is going to help me with this one?" I put out my thumb and within 10 seconds a big truck stopped. This was a surprise since big trucks don't usually stop for a guy in a black suit, black hat and beard. I figured "Hashem works in mysterious ways" so I climbed up into the truck to see that the truck driver was wearing a Yarmulke. He just happened to be going to the town where I live and proceeded to take me right to my front door. Thank you, Hashem. I have even more miraculous stories, including things that happened that violated the laws of Physics, but they are much longer and give me the chills when I think about them. When we meet some day, I will bore you for hours.

We are told, as an example, that if an individual is destined to go to Hell, it does not have to be for punishment, but could be strictly for correction before they enter Heaven. To make it even easier, we are told that when we recite the prayer, Shema Yisroel, twice a day, if we do not slur our words together but meticulously separate words as told to us in the Talmud (the places of separation are defined in our prayer books), Hell will be cooled for us. This place that we have a picture of being very hot and torturous doesn't have to be, if one is sent there for correction and not retribution.

Let me talk more about the when and the where. Even though the system is for both here on Earth and for all eternity, most of r and p occurs after we leave this Earth. This is also a merciful thing because r and p are far more intense in the afterlife. On Earth we always have the possibility of further correction through our efforts. When we leave this life, our need for further correction or, may Hashem forbid, retribution is well defined. The possibilities are we go to a Heavenly existence; we receive correction as needed, hopefully, in as pleasant place; we return to Earth for another life; or, we go to a very harsh place for pure punishment. Each of those choices has many levels involved. The important idea for our discussion is that this is usually when most of the r and p is dulled out. The good news is correction is usually swift and not difficult (depending, of course on how much needed). Punishment is also anywhere from short to extensive (use your imagination on that one). Reward, however, is forever. For our good deeds, our fulfilling Hashem's mitzvot while on Earth, we are rewarded forever and ever and at a level that is beyond our comprehension. Doing Hashem's will on Earth has such a tremendous payback, that we truly would lose our free will if we could experience one second of our eternity. That is all it would take to make us the most observant individuals possible. More so, is the giving such a wonderful gift to a spouse and, of course, children and grandchildren.

We very often think about what it would be like to win the lottery on Earth and have everything we ever wanted (financially). I like Steve Wright's line about that: "If I had everything, where would I put it?" Yet, we have a guaranteed lottery winning ticket available; all we need to do is purchase it. It is waiting for each of us and the payoff is eternal. Wow, eternal Powerball. Thank you, Hashem.

What is the reward or punishment that usually happens? Similar to Miriam, it is usually something related to the act we performed. She waited for her brother to be taken car off, everyone waited for her affliction to be removed – they wouldn't leave without her. As an example, if we give charity, we will receive financial help when we need it. In Egypt, the Egyptians were punished or not punished in the plagues, m for m for what they did to the Israelites. When it says those who bless us will be blessed, and those who curse us will be cursed, it is m for m according to what they do (or we do). Once again, intension is primary. If you give charity because you really want to help people, Hashem really wants to help you. If you give charity because you think you discovered a trick to get great reward, the trick will be on you. Hashem knows exactly why we do each mitzvah (He even knows better than us).

One last concept to know about doing mitzvot. "A mitzvah is its own reward." On Earth the feeling of doing Hashem's will or helping another human being is extremely rewarding in itself. This leads us to the most important concept of all "we do not do mitzvot for reward; we do them because we love Hashem and want to do His will." If Hashem knows that we are doing His will for personal gain, it diminishes the purpose of why we serve Him. But, if we do it for its own sake out of love for Hashem, we get it all and that includes the wonderful feeling of just serving Hashem with joy. That is true happiness and there is no greater reward for us and our loved ones.

3.12 Habits

There are basically two types of Jews in the world – those that are observant and those that are not observant, yet. All Jews are destined to serve Hashem since it says in the Torah that we are a "Nation of Priests" (Exodus 19:6). With some it is at birth while others it happens later in life. Since we are also creatures of habit, I thought I would address what that means to the two types of Jews.

Two new words to learn – machmir (stringent) and meikil (lenient). Everything we do to serve Hashem should be as machmir as possible. Why? As with anything in life, we manage to do just enough to get by; or, we can be with an attitude that we want our efforts to be the very best, to excel. Since we are on a system of measure for measure, we will be treated in return by Hashem as machmir or meikil as well. When we pray, do repentance, give charity, study Torah, observe the mitzvot, keep the laws of kashrus and of purity, observe the Shabbos and holidays, our success is completely dependent on our effort put forth. As an example, when we go to prayer service, do we get there on time, early or late? Do we pray with kevana (another new word meaning passion, intensity and feeling) or is it lip service – just saying the words quickly to get out of there as fast as possible? Do we feel the trepidation of standing in front of Hashem or is our mind on the groceries that we remembered to pick up on the way home?

What do I mean by having the right kevana in giving charity? When someone comes to the door to collect do we run to the door with enthusiasm about helping others or is it with disdain? Having the opportunity to help others and the convenience of it coming directly to our front door should be considered a pleasant opportunity, not a burden. Whatever our attitude, Hashem is noting measure for measure. I've always lived by the adage "let gratitude be you attitude." I don't know if I made that up or not (I have said for many years), but I like it and it serves me well.

There is a story about a shtetl (Yiddish for a little town) that only had 10 Jewish men living in it. There was a small shul (Yiddish for school but used to mean the synagogue) that always had a minion, all ten men showed up every day for prayer. Then an 11th Jewish man moved into the shtetl. From that day on they had trouble getting a minion. There were always two or three men who thought "I am not needed now that we have another to help with the minion." Unfortunately, many are in the habit of thinking it will get done without me. One should always consider in every situation that his or her help is needed. With a minion, with giving charity, with helping the shul or the Jewish community with an abundance of tasks – they just don't happen by themselves.

Let's talk about the two types of Jews. It is of extreme importance when one is becoming observant to learn correctly and get into the right habits immediately. Having a very inspirational teacher who leads you in the right direction from the very beginning can make or break your experience. This should be someone who knows what to teach you, when to teach you and to control the speed at which things happen. If a person becomes observant at a very slow and comfortable pace, he or she will not really notice big changes in life and will experience great success. This can be best done with an educated guide to take you every step of the way. If the teacher shows you all kinds of shortcuts and tells you don't have to worry about ever doing this or that, the student will be handed bad habits immediately and not too rewarding an experience. It is good to learn how to learn. In other words, to know what are the best books to read and best references to use when a question arises and your teacher is not available.

The other group is the already observant individual who has either a machmir or a meikil approach to everything. What I have observed over many years is that the machmir Jew is the machmir teacher. Fortunately or unfortunately, it is very often the children who benefit or suffer. Individuals who are always late to prayer service or habitual talkers during prayer service usually have children who follow in their footsteps. The biggest problem is that bad habits are generally not even recognized as bad habits, but are engrained in one's daily routine. How many times I have heard "my father did it that way" as if that gives us permission to act improperly. So, not only do we have bad habits, we justify in our own minds why it is OK.

My biggest suggestion for both the observant and the newly observant is to know the proper sources for answers, if a Rabbi or teacher is not available, and to use them frequently. There are two main sources, the Shulchan Aruch and Mishnah Berurah, which are used extensively for answers. The Mishnah Berurah, written by Rabbi Yisrael Meir Kagan (1838 – 1933), who was known popularly as The Chofetz Chaim, is perhaps the best and most complete compendium of laws and explanations on just about every subject a Jew needs. Although there are many Rabbis over the millennia that we study their commentary, there are certain Rabbis that are considered to be the best authorities on Jewish law, halachah. A Posek (plural – Poskim) is the term in Jewish law for "decider" – a legal scholar who decides the halachah to be followed in cases of law that previous authorities are inconclusive or in those situations where no halachic precedent exists. In the observant or Haredi world, each community will regard one of its *poskim* as its Posek HaDor ("Authority of the present Generation"). For the Lithuanian-style Haredi world it is probably Rav Yosef Shalom Eliashiv, z"tl. For the Sephardi Jews it is probably Rav Ovadia Yosef, z"tl. The Chofetz Chaim, the Chazon Ish and Moshe Feinstein are three that have been published extensively and can be relied on for halachic guidance. The names that I am using have all been within the past century, giving a more modern interpretation. After all there are many questions that come up regarding more modern apparatus, such as electricity, electrical appliances, elevators, time clocks, lighting, water urns, heating and air conditioning, etc, etc, etc on Shabbos.

When I was living in the US, my Rav was Simcha Bunim Cohen, Shlita. This Rabbi, who was a student of Rabbi Moshe Feinstein, zt"l, and is the grandson of Rav Avigdor Miller, zt"l, is a Posek of our generation. He has written or has been involved in the authoring of many books (I highly recommend all of his books). Since most of his books are on Shabbos alone, Rav Cohen is considered one of the world's experts on the halachot, laws, of Shabbos. About 18 years ago, I had a Shabbos question for the Rav. I posed it to him and he answered "Let me look it up and I'll get back to you." What, the world expert has to look it up? I learned that day the difference between opinion and scholarship. Rav Cohen would never give me an incorrect answer. Unless he was absolutely positive, without any question, he would look it up and get back to me. When I got the answer I was confident in its total accuracy. Sometimes he would look it up in one of his own books, but he never relied on his memory when it came to the importance of giving guidance to a fellow Jew. That is what I mean by machmir, since I myself try to do the same thing. I try to look things up even if I am sure of the answer. I consider my present Rav in Israel a genius. His memory of halachic answers is very impressive. Yet, when I ask him a question he goes directly to the source, not to tell me the answer, but to show me where it is and how it is worded. Talk about confidence in getting answers.

I tell you all this to impress upon you the importance of good habits. If you are starting out, get into the proper way of doing things. It is just as easy to do everything correctly as doing things incorrectly. If you have been observant all your life, review on a regular basis your halachic accuracy – you may find much improvement can be done and at no extra cost. You owe it to yourself and your family. The Jew who serves Hashem in a meikil way may not even know that he is losing out on his efforts or that he is giving bad advice to others. As mentioned many times we are here to perfect ourselves and to setup as wonderful an eternity for us and our loved ones as possible. When Hashem assigns us to our place in the World to Come that we will live forever and ever, we should all strive to be in the machmir section and not the meikil section. The assignments are handed out measure for measure according to our efforts and habits we display in this world. Make the best of it – we only get one shot.

Something that I have paid attention to for many years is the specific design of my life. How everything that happened to me in life was meant to happen. The places that I found myself – I needed to be there. The people that I've met and when I met them, was all destined. The many years that I spent as an engineer organizing and perfecting, was a great learning experience and was time well spent. My career as a military officer served one very important purpose for my life; it taught me discipline. A strong lesson that one learns in the military is that one's very survival is dependent upon his or her ability to follow all the rules and regulations. Peace time consists completely of training the soldier's ability to carry out a mission with complete discipline. If one deviates from mission requirements, one could be putting himself and his fellow soldiers in jeopardy when on the battlefield. Discipline in the military means life or death on the battlefield – success or failure in winning the war.

Habits that I talked about are no different from disciplining oneself in a military mission. The big difference is that doing the mitzvot correctly will result in life being successful, both our life on Earth as well as for all eternity. Getting into bad habits or even being lenient with the learning of others can be more detrimental than the discipline required for success on the battlefield.

I have heard about Rabbis who allow this or that leniency. If a Rabbi is trying to make it easier to serve Hashem by releasing an individual from stringent obligations, he is not doing that individual any favor. His intentions may be admirable; but, if it results in bad habits for life, he has caused the individual harm.

According to Pirkei Avos (Ethics of the Fathers) I am old enough to give mussar (new word meaning: teaching moral conduct, instruction or discipline). For years I have been very unsuccessful in doing so. We are in a time, as it says in the Talmud, that "the old will get up for the young." There are individuals that I have tried to help by giving them mussar. The effort resulted in these individuals not talking to me anymore. I experienced the same thing when I lived in the states. There were very prominent Rabbis who gave mussar and were rejected. It is interesting to me that you can give individuals very good advice in an effort to help them greatly in life – resulting in such a statement as "who are you to tell me what to do?"

I am a people watcher. Also, I have studied psychology and sociology for many years (close to a college degree that I will never get). My observations have shown that the individual who has many problems in life is also the same type of individual not disciplined properly in serving Hashem. As an example, I have a neighbor who has been married multiple times, has had several business failures and has been plagued with sickness. He is a very good person, but is not too well disciplined in his obligations as a Jew. When I confronted him with improvements that would create tremendous improvement in his life, he wouldn't hear of it. I have seen it numerous times just how obvious the lenient observer of Judaism is plagued measure for measure with problems in life. It is frustrating to me when something is so obvious and I can't help the situation. The greatest frustration is that I am talking about very nice people who could have a much better situation in life if they were more stringent about their observation of Judaism.

Am I saying that I am perfect and do not make mistakes? No, I am actually human and make many mistakes. The difference is I am aware of my mistakes and my human frailties and work hard on a daily basis to correct them. My study of Torah very much has been directed at practical efforts for self-improvement. I have mentioned that Hashem does not judge us by what we know, but how we grow. The secret to complete success and happiness is knowing what you are lacking and working to correct it. A stubborn attitude of "what I do is good enough" is very counterproductive. A desire to perfect one's habits to serve Hashem better is truly the way to success. The most important aspect of all is that Hashem will greatly help the individual who has the correct attitude towards improvement.

Rabbi Avigdor Miller, zt"l, told us that it is possible to have a type of hell in heaven. He said that we could achieve heaven, but be aware that we could have had a much higher level of heaven. We would suffer with the anguish of knowing that if only I had done more on Earth, I would have brought myself closer to Hashem. This holds true for our eternal level of The World to Come (forever and ever).

My great concern for every human being on this earth is with love and a desire to help each individual achieve his or her perfection and a very happy and joyous eternity. Good habits are just as easy to achieve as bad habits. With the proper effort and discipline we can have it all. Why settle for less?

3.13 What should I study?

I have mentioned numerous times how important it is to study Scriptures. I have been asked the question "what should I study?" What's interesting about the question is that I asked the exact same thing years ago. When I first arrived in Israel I met a very prominent Rabbi and asked for his help in setting up a study program.

The question of what I should study resulted in two basic answers. One was to learn the details of my daily activities; in other words, studying everything that I do in a day to make sure that I develop good habits in serving Hashem. Improving everything I do to serve Hashem is so important, since it allows me to meet my goals in life and my eternity, and makes my goals more achievable and joyful. This advice holds true even for someone who is observant from birth. We tend to think that what we do every day is good enough, and will get us the best possible Olam Habah (the World to Come). But, never being satisfied with our observance and wanting to improve every day has a great impact on the outcome, and brings an even greater sense of accomplishment. I always found a deficiency in Yeshivahs, which study very important subjects that need studying, but ignore the basics. Most observant Jews believe they are doing things correctly, out of habit, and that it is good enough. Am I going to tell someone who has been praying every day for the last 30, 40, 50 years that he needs to improve his praying ability? The question that I like to ask is "are all your prayers fulfilled – do you get positive results with every prayer request? If the answer is: well, not everything, then I will be glad to tell that person (in a very nice way, of course), your performance is lacking and you have room for improvement. This is just one example but it holds true for everything we do in a day. Are the results exactly what we wanted? If not, how many of us ask the question: "what should I do to improve – what should I study that can help achieve better results? Most people believe "I thought I knew it all but, obviously, I am lacking something." When we can be that honest with ourselves, we are on our way to maximizing this experience called "Life." This goes hand in hand with my previous discussions on positive attitude and good habits. They should be a high priority area of study and improvement, daily.

The other subject area of study that the Rabbi suggested was: what I enjoy the most. Study of the Scriptures must be done with complete joy. If I spend my time being fascinated by what I learn, my time is pleasant and productive.

A very big consideration was my age. I knew that I would not have the time to do everything. When I was in the states I was involved with a study group that we covered two chapters of the Talmud in about 2 1/2 years. We were not learning the Talmud; we were learning how to learn Talmud. The time was well spent and was very enjoyable. When we had a Siyum (which means "completion" which includes a celebratory get-together) at the conclusion of the two paragraphs, I gave a speech and stated that at this rate we should cover all of Talmud in about 375 years.

When I arrived in Israel I decided to join a group that studies Daf Hayomi. Daf Hayomi is a program that was started in the 1920s where the study group covers one page (daf) of Talmud a day (yom). In a 7 1/2 years cycle, the 2711 pages (5422 sides) of the Talmud are covered (This is not the entire Talmud since there are other Mishnahs that are not included). This is not really learning the Talmud but gives a great overview of its contents. After my first 7 1/2 year cycle, I had a very general overview of all of the Talmud and a great feeling of satisfaction that I have reviewed the Oral Torah. Continuing with another 7 1/2 years cycle has allowed me to get even deeper into the material. At my age this is a perfect way to get an overview of the oral Torah and feel a sense of accomplishment. There are presently 100's of thousands of men worldwide doing this program. Imagine that someone in South Africa and someone in the United States are working on the same exact page of Talmud every day. When the 7 1/2 year cycle is completed, there is a worldwide Siyum celebration in stadiums and theaters around the world to commemorate the occasion. It is exiting and it gives Hashem lots of nachas (Yiddish for a high level of joy or blessings, pride especially from One's children – and we are Hashem's children).

The Daf Hayomi generally only takes about an hour a day. The rest of my study includes the self-improvement mentioned above and the fun portion of my learning – the subjects that I enjoy the most. As you can see my background pointed towards interest in such subjects as Torah codes, numerology, the Holy Tongue and, of course my favorite, science versus scriptures. My personal library contains many books dealing with these subjects. It has been, and continues to be, a fascinating area of discovery for me. Since it includes so many areas of discovery, I think I will need the 375 years that I mentioned above to exhaust the topics (I know that a thousand years wouldn't be enough). The most important accomplishment is bringing myself closer to Hashem everyday while doing something that I love.

Some additional notes on my daily self-improvement routine. It is not just studying the proper way to pray (which has been extremely successful in giving me a wonderful life); but, also improving my performance of the mitzvot, better and more effective repentance and any other subject that I need to improve my life in the service of Hashem. I devote much time to learning the best ways to help my fellow Jews, which includes passing on this information to them as well. Teaching is a very rewarding endeavor and is what Hashem wants from us. I have always known that when one person teaches, two people learn. This is why the popular method in Yeshivahs and study groups is for two to work together in learning. Teachers learn from their students – this book and my blog have been just that for me. I have said it before and I will say it again, I have been very impressed with the level of intelligence of my blog readers and, B"H, have learned from those readers (B"H, baruch Hashem, means "Blessed be G-d," or more accurately that G-d is the source of all blessings). The research that I have put into this book and the answering of questions that I have received on my blog (over 6,000 comments and Emails), have been a very important and enjoyable part of my daily learning experience. Thank you.

Some references that I suggest for learning. I have mentioned the Mishnah Berurah which is probably the best compendium in the world for the laws, observances and customs of Judaism. There are thousands of reference books available, but they are not on the same level. The great Rabbis of today should always be the source of what is best for learning. The true test of reference material is to know that the author is giving a compilation of Torah and scriptural sources and not personal opinion.

Another suggestion, that I have used, is the Guidelines series from Rabbi Elozor Barclay and Rabbi Yitzchok Jaeger. They wrote books in a question and answer format that is easy reading, clear presentation and totally accurate (mostly from Mishnah Berurah and the Shulchan Aruch). They cover a variety of subjects and are very usable for the newly observant as well as the seasoned observant Jew. My list of references is extensive but, here again, it depends on the level of observance that you personally possess.

One additional suggestion is for women. My wife had for years a study group in our dining room with about 15 women, who were taught by a very learned woman. There are several excellent classes given weekly, but the best learning that my wife has enjoyed has been with a study partner. Whatever the method (including reading on one's own), women should not miss the learning opportunity. The mitzvot that pertain to women are so important to the family and the Jewish community, that Jewish women should realize that their learning is vital and has been for the survival of the Jewish people.

The greatest part of my study program has been enhanced by the realization that I have a lot more to learn. I look forward every day to my learning and treat it as an opportunity to improve. I will never want to have the feeling that I have achieved my goal. There is always more to learn and more to improve and that keeps my level of excitement about learning very high. I have always been able to jump out of bed in the morning, no straggling, no attitude of "do I have to get up?" Why? I know that every day I am going to discover something fascinating about life and it makes my day very exciting. I also know that the right attitude towards serving Hashem invites His help with everything that I do. That is evident to me every day and keeps a smile on my face. I joke with my fellow Jew when they point out to me how happy an individual I am. I tell them that "if I didn't know any better, I would think this is Olam Habah." Imagine how great it will be when I get to the real place (I can't imagine).

3.14 Tests: Why Hashem Gives Them

All that befalls us in this world, the good as well as the bad, are tests...
Rabbi Moshe Chaim Luzzatto (The Path of the Just).

Everything that happens in this world has a purpose and a deeper message, because everything is from Hashem and everything is a test. This holds true for every individual, group, country and all the people on Earth collectively. We can even learn much about what we need to do as individuals just by paying attention to all that befalls us, good or not-so-good and doing repentance; Hashem is telling us what our weaknesses and our strengths are. Testing is given to us with great mercy and serves to help us.

Our testing in the end of days is extensive. Why? This is the time for finals and the "too late date" coming up will be the report of the test results (our report card). We will find out measure for measure how we did, and what our future is. It's not too late to cram – after all we do want the best test results, it's our future.

3.14.1 Testing Tips

Here is some additional insight as to why we are tested, and how one can pass life's tests.

We have talked fairly extensively about how life's learning experience is one of our main missions in our effort to perfect ourselves. Everything we do in life and everything that happens to us in this world is putting into practice the knowledge that we have achieved, which allows us to demonstrate how well we are applying what we've learned. I've said many times that Hashem does not judge us by what we know, but how we grow.

It says in Pirkei Avos (Ethics of the Fathers, Chapter 1:17), Hashem doesn't want us to just learn Torah; he wants us to live Torah. In order to gauge how well we have translated our learning into life, we are tested. I have mentioned, I cannot put on stethoscope, walk into a hospital and say that I am a doctor. It takes many years of medical school, internship and practice to hone one's skills properly. When you consider that every patient a doctor sees is a test to see how well the doctor is growing in his or her skills, we see the necessity for testing. Nobody would like to go to a doctor who was fresh out of school with about a 70% average and no experience. What confidence could you have in such a doctor?

In life, to say that we are good people doing the right thing can only happen when our growth is perfected through testing. When life's experiences are performed because we've learned our lessons well from Hashem's book of instructions, only then could we say that we have become a better person. We have studied Hashem's instructions, we have gauged our proficiency in life by what happens to us every second and we have used the test results to improve.

So what little tricks do we need to know to help us pass life's tests? First of all, we need to be aware that Hashem only gives us tests that we can pass. We are not at the level of *Avraham Avinu*, our forefather Abraham, who was tested with ten trials and withstood them all. He demonstrated a high degree of love for Hashem with tests that are beyond the capabilities of most human beings. Why should such a tzadik need to go through such testing? Hashem provided Avraham with the growth that he would need to introduce Hashem to the world. Avraham was chosen to carry out one of the toughest missions ever given to a human being. But, Hashem knew in advance that he would be able to handle the task. Similarly, we see the testing that was necessary for Isaac, Jacob, Joseph, Moses and everyone else throughout history that would continue to bring the will of Hashem to fruition. Every test is by design – for us and for everyone who has ever lived on this earth. Hashem makes this world look random, by chance, by coincidental, by accident and even events that appear to be by luck; but it is all an allusion, since everything is 100% by design.

With that said what are examples of testing and how do we pass.

I once worked for a Colonel in a government office. My fellow workers always acknowledged that he liked me and my work. One day he gave me a hard time and started to chastise me for the most minor nothing (I don't even remember what it was). This animosity continued for a few days to the point where everyone around me asked "what happened to your good working relationship with the Colonel?" I started to get very frustrated and finally said I don't need this aggravation – I can get a good job elsewhere. Then I thought, wait a minute, Hashem is testing me – that is what is going on. Immediately, this Colonel was back to his old loving self even to the point where my fellow workers said "it looks like your back in the Colonel's good graces." It was such an immediate change that I knew without a doubt what had transpired.

People you deal with are only agents of Hashem to carry out tests and help you reach Tikun. When you acknowledge the fact that you are being tested and thank Hashem for the help, you may find a difficult person that you are dealing with becomes more docile. Try it and realize that everything is from Hashem even your interaction with other people. Please, don't do this with a negative attitude such as "I'll try it, but I don't think it is going to work" (you just made sure it will fail). The most important part of passing this type of test is turning completely to Hashem for help with complete confidence, and fully understanding why something is happening.

An important Torah lesson is that everything is from Hashem and he is the only one that can help us out of any difficult situation. So, important tip: recognize that you are being tested; you will more clearly understand why you are going through a difficulty.

Every tzadik is faced with the most difficult tests. Our great sages say that the higher one's level, the more challenging the testing could be, since Hashem will give this person the opportunity to climb to an even higher spiritual level (that is what happened to Avraham). There is no tzadik that exists that wasn't tempted, and didn't face sin head to head. We think that because they are righteous they were never normal human beings, just like us, facing the simple temptations that we do. Yosef Hatzadik covered his face and ran away from Potifar's wife. Here is an example of passing the test by running away from it. The person, who says "I can control my desires completely and I can handle the temptation," will fail the test. It is not within the human psyche to stand up to temptation and succeed, especially because it is the soul being affected, not just the physical person. Important point: no matter how much we think we can handle a situation, we have no idea how it will affect our soul – our spiritual side. The best way to handle temptation is to avoid it and run from it. That is how Yosef pass the test and that is how we must also react. This sometimes applies to the example I gave above. Dealing with a very difficult person is sometimes solved by going away from that person. Obviously, a casual acquaintance is much easier to avoid than a difficult boss, but that is where we must figure out exactly what the test is that Hashem is giving us, and work accordingly. So, tip: if you can, run from the test to pass it. Admit that you will not be able to handle the test, and that you can avoid it.

An important aspect of our lives with which we need work is our personality traits. The perfecting of the soul is a nebulous concept that we may not have a grasp of its meaning. The perfecting of the way we consciously do everything in life is what we need to perfect and that will result in spiritual perfection. As an example, are we kind, caring, considerate individuals who are truly concerned about the welfare of others? Or do we have a selfish, greedy, me, me, me attitude?

Unfortunately, we are the worse judges of ourselves. We may believe that we are doing everything in the best interest of others, but are in fact only looking out for ourselves. So how do we learn more about ourselves and what to do about it? Hashem tells us very definitely by how we are tested constantly throughout the day.

If you want to know what Hashem thinks your weak spots are, and what needs work, pay close attention to how you are being tested. Most of us who do repentance every day are not always sure of our weak areas. What needs the most repentance, meaning what needs the most correction, is sometimes very allusive to us, especially if we think that we are good to go on a subject but really need improvement. As an example, if you notice that your prayers are not being answered in a positive way, you may find Hashem is telling you that great improvement in praying may be needed. I use this example because it is probably the area of service to Hashem that most of us believe we are doing everything correctly and need no improvement. I am here to tell you that I rarely find anyone praying correctly. It is one of the least studied subjects that needs the most correction and is, perhaps one of the most beneficial gifts from Hashem. We are stubborn and always think this doesn't pertain to me, it is for the other guy.

Another example: one of the worst testing mechanisms that we have in life is money. It is the most difficult commodity to deal with, but it tells us much about ourselves. If you find that you are greatly lacking the funds you need in life, check to see if your personality is the cause of your shortcomings.

Giving charity is a test. If you give with a complete desire to help, even giving anonymously, you should find that you are well compensated in return and that you should not have a financial deficiency. If you say "I give charity all the time, but I still have many bills that I personally can't pay," it is time to check your true attitude towards giving and wanting to help. I think you are probably seeing where this is going. The test will always give you the results that are commensurate with the attitude with which you handled the test.

Also, be aware that there are many levels of giving to be judged. Did you ever give someone a loan, and when you went to collect you found the person was still in such dire straits, that you told the person to forget about paying you back? That may sound like a very high level of kindness and consideration, but if done with the proper attitude, it is a test passing that will have very positive results.

If your act of kindness is not resulting in your feeling good about the way you handled the situation, the test is a very strong message that needs evaluation. Do you really have enough, but are a greedy individual who wants more, more, more? Pirkei Avos answers the question: "Who is rich? With: The one who is satisfied with his lot." In other words the poor person who is happy with what he or she has is much richer and happier than the rich person who has enough, but wants more. Testing results give you the answer and a hint as to what needs further effort, if the answer is not satisfactory.

That was an example that can be applied to everything we do in life. Not just money, but having the time to work with someone, teach someone, help someone with whatever is needed (for good purposes, of course). When someone desperately needs our help and we answer with "I don't have the time," are we really saying I don't want to? That is especially true if we have the time and lied to the person – that is not a way of passing Hashem's tests.

Another very important point to be made is "Don't ask to be tested." King David asked Hashem to test him. Hashem answered him that he would not be able to withstand the test. Later he was given the test of Bat Sheva, which apparently he failed. In truth, he could have withstood it, but Hashem had already informed him that he would not pass the test. Hashem deliberately caused failure in order to prove that one should not ask to be tested. Hashem sees us asking for tests as a display of arrogance. He will make sure that we do not pass that test. We even say in prayer every morning "Do not cause us to be tested or brought to disgrace." So, tip: don't ask to be tested. Be humble with Hashem and people.

To summarize, we can see that testing, like mitzvot, are tools for our growth to help us reach perfection. If our study of Torah is performed properly, life's activities will be done more correctly and require less testing. We may receive testing to bring us to an even higher spiritual level (as mentioned above with tzadikim), but with more Torah we are aware of reality and aware that the testing is for our good and for our growth. I said many times the "too late date" is coming up on us rapidly; after that, the testing will end. We don't want testing; but, when it happens, which is every day, we want to pass the test and we want to learn what the deeper meaning is for each test. This will come with the study of Torah in the same way that a doctor can be more professional by learning from each patient and performing by capitalizing from his or her experiences.

This didn't cover every type of test or even talk about the yetzer harah (the evil inclination) within each one of us (which is actually an agent of Hashem to provide temptation and testing). The important thing to know is that if you approach every test knowing from Whom it came, and what the purpose is, the Torah answer will always be the right answer. It's our lives; it's our eternal future – let's make the best of it.

I recommend your read "Life is a Test," by Rebbetzin Esther Jungreis. It truly helps you understand how to meet life's challenges successfully.

3.15 The Law (halachah)

Halachah is so involved and so complicated to figure out, there is no way that we can ascertain final Halachic ruling by studying the Talmud. The Talmud argues every aspect of the law to show how Hashem wanted the Torah to be interpreted. It is very rare that you see the word opinion in the Talmud; but, instead, the arguments are almost always what information was handed down over the years by the Rabbis. Most statements are said as "Rabbi So-and-so said in the name of Rabbi So-and-so." In other words, the Rabbi heard the ruling from his Rabbi, who heard it from his Rabbi, etc. That is telling us that the information traces back to when we were in Bamidbar (the desert) for forty years where the Jews first learned it from Moses, who learned it from his Teacher, Hashem. Most of the information was not just remembered, for they were living the details every day. When you live the Torah on a daily basis the information is very fresh in your mind and is easily transmitted to the next generation. That is what has happen for the past 3327 years since we learned the halachah from Hashem through Moses.

I have said that figuring out the fine details from the Torah is the most difficult subject in the world, making subjects like Nuclear Physics, Brain Surgery, Business Law, etc child's play. No one in the world can derive final Halachic ruling from the Talmud which is why Hashem gave us codification (the final answer) over the millennia in the Shulchan Aruch, Mishnah Berurah, Rambam commentary, Arizal commentary, etc. The Talmud serves to teach us how we derived much of the final ruling; but, it is far beyond our human capability to draw the proper conclusions.

Studying Talmud serves other very important purposes that I have already talked about such as helping to keep the universe running (we are partners in the creation). Learning is also a very important part of our development and reaching Tikun. The benefit that our soul derives from learning Hashem's ways is invaluable and perhaps the greatest gift mankind (and womankind) has ever received.

The Talmud is not just deciphering the law, but is a discussion of every aspect of life. There is nothing missing about life on Earth. If it is missing from the Talmud, it doesn't exist. I am not talking just outright information since I have already talked about the Pardes (the four levels) that one could study. Just be aware that since the Talmud includes everything (including all of science and mathematics as I mentioned), it is the most difficult text in the world and the most challenging (I am talking both the written and oral Torah and even the rest of Jewish scriptures).

I told the story about my son wanting to drop out of college to go to Yeshivah. The important message was how valuable and accepted the level of learning is considered by places like Harvard, Yale, University of Pennsylvania and Hebrew University. The intensity and depth of study that occurs at Yeshivahs is unmatched in the world. Also, the devotion and willingness to learn that

Yeshivah students demonstrate is unparalleled in the world. I personally can attest to the level of devotion and intensity of study since I attended college full and part time for 16 years including graduate level studies, and have witnessed the comparison.

Today, however, most people are computer non-thinkers and are always looking for the easy answers. The problem is (and I have seen it on my blog and every other blog) what the people who have an opinion of what they think Judaism is and what they think the Torah says about this or that.

An analogy that comes to mind is the difference between a cook and a chef. Someone who prepares a meal by just following a simple recipe is obviously not of the stature of a great chef who studied the culinary arts for years. The tremendous attention to detail that is needed in preparing a sumptuous meal such as picking the proper, fresh ingredients, combining those ingredients in the proper sequence and proportions, proper seasoning, proper moisture level, knowing your cooking or baking equipment and exactly how to use them (timing, temperature, etc), knowing portion control for the size group that you may be serving, keeping things at the proper serving temperature, an appetizing appearance being presented to your guests or customers, etc, etc, etc.

It sounds complicated and it is, in fact it is an art; but, it is a far cry from just following a simple recipe. Or, as I do, which is to take the wonderful leftovers that my wife prepared last night, microwave it, serve it and then tell everyone that I prepared dinner. No I am not a chef, I am not even a cook but I do operate a mean microwave.

My whole point is the detail at which I learn Hashem's word can result in a sumptuous meal fit for a king or a fast food serving fit for no one. What is the best recipe for life, success and happiness is not cookie-cutter learning but years and years of deep and dedicated hard work. I've said it before, what we achieve in this life is measure for measure what we put into it. We have the greatest opportunity to excel for all eternity. Why not take it? One last note: Hashem is not interested in what we learn, but how we live our lives – in other words, how we apply what we learn. A brilliant Torah scholar does not make a tzadik; but, a tzadik makes a brilliant Torah scholar, since he is obviously putting his learning into the most beneficial action.

Summary: The law is fixed. It is exactly as it was given at Mount Sinai. It was interpreted by our great sages throughout history with complete guidance from the Law-Giver. Even guidance into the 21st century is still from Hashem. No modernization has been needed by those who do not know the law or its purpose. Living the law as Hashem intended is the key to success, since it guides us completely through life – the best life possible.

3.16 More Simple Truths

I have mentioned the need for people to be helping people. It is more important now than ever. The world is in trouble and Hashem is watching us and testing us to see how we react. Reaching out to the needs of others is a vital test to pass – so simple a lesson, yet so important to all.

In Parshat Re'eh we find a very pertinent message from Hashem (Deuteronomy 15:7-11):

> 7 If there shall be a destitute person among you, any of your brethren in any of your cities, in your Land that HASHEM, your G-d, gives you, you shall not harden your heart or close your hand against your destitute brother.
> 8 Rather, you shall open your hand to him; you shall lend him his requirement, whatever is lacking to him.
> 9 Beware lest there be a lawless thought in your heart, saying, 'The seventh year approaches, the remission year," and you will look malevolently upon your destitute brother and refuse to give him - then he may appeal against you to HASHEM, and it will be a sin upon you.
> 10 You shall surely give him, and let your heart not feel bad when you give him, for in return for this matter, HASHEM, your G-d, will bless you in all your deeds and in your every undertaking.
> 11 For destitute people will not cease to exist within the Land; therefore I command you, saying, "You shall surely open your hand to your brother, to your poor, and to your destitute in your Land."

Simply put, Hashem is not just giving us people to help in order to test us, but He is giving us an opportunity to help ourselves. An open hand and an open heart lead to great reward for the giver. We do not do Hashem's mitzvot for reward, but when we do His ways, the payoff is great. I have been saying again and again that the only way to true happiness in this world and for all eternity, for us and

205

our loved ones, is by following Hashem's instructions and living His Torah. This is one big example and it works beyond your wildest imagination.

3.17 Here's to Your Good Health

How about solving medical problems, both physical and mental. Since I have written about the subject, and even successfully assisted some of my readers on an individual basis, I thought I would share some of my secrets with you. Wait a minute. You might ask: what does an Electronics Engineer know about solving medical problems? All medical solutions are in scriptures.

Let's begin by describing how most of the body works, and what is often the cause of medical ailments. The body works by electro-chemical reactions that cause signals to flow throughout. In other words, it is one big electrical circuit. But, like a battery that creates the electricity through chemical reactions and then allows the flow of electricity by providing a completed circuit path, the body reacts in a similar way to allow for proper functioning. When the electricity doesn't flow properly (signals getting from brain to the organs and limbs, as an example), medical problems arise. There are two ways to treat such problems: one is to cause proper chemical reactions to affect circuit completion and signal distribution; or, to perform some other procedure to complete the electrical flow.

Most of the world uses the chemical method better known as medicine or drugs. Why? Because, there is good money in it. The pharmaceutical industry is one of the most lucrative industries in the world. A big reason that the US and many other nations became such a haven for drugs is that we are indoctrinated from birth with the idea that to solve a medical problem all you need is a pill. The fact is Hashem created the human body with everything it needs to heal itself. The problem is that medical science has turned the healing process into a multi-billion dollar industry. They don't want you to perform self-healing – there is no money in it for their stockholders.

I have a lifelong friend who became a detail man for one of the world's largest pharmaceutical companies. His job was to visit doctors, hospitals and pharmacies to introduce his customers to the new products that his company developed. This friend told me much about the medical system in the US. The item that many of his customers were interested in was the placebo. Why? Doctors, as an example, knew that the body could cure itself as long as the mind believed there was a cure being administered. But the sad part was that the doctor was not interested in curing the patient, but just making the person feel comfortable which promotes future business. The doctor makes much more money by having his patients return than curing them. Unfortunately, the medical profession is a very lucrative industry that has made many people very wealthy.

We lived in Europe for six years and Israel for 12 years. We have experienced leaving a doctor's office without a prescription. In the US most people would say: "that doctor wasn't any good, he didn't prescribe anything." To have a doctor tell you "eat a particular diet, get some rest or do this exercise and the ailment will take care of itself," is unheard of in the US and, after all, return business is the key to success in the medical field. (The best thing about the medical services in Israel is that we have no trouble finding a good Jewish doctor). I thought I would throw in a joke here to demonstrate the system in the US: Obamacare (end of joke).

So what am I recommending as a way of curing your ills that is totally effective and in most cases free of charge. I got your interest?

Let us break it down into different categories of medical help that is needed and simple techniques that truly work. The basic cause of medical problems is emotional instability. When people are stressed out, worried, out of control, the body reacts with physical problems. Why? I'll tell you later. Suffice it to say that most medical problems are solved when we become very emotionally stable and happy. This emotional stability enhances the completion of the electrical circuits mentioned above and solves many of the physical ailments that we experience. The more technical term that describes this is meridian zones of energy. Acupuncture, as an example, has been used for thousands of years to realign these meridian lines of energy causing a flow which results in solving medical problems. What if we had a technique to do acupuncture without the needles and even without a person to administer the treatment, in other words, a self-administered procedure?

Let me introduce you to The **Emotional Freedom Technique® or EFT** which is an approach to healing that has gained attention from medical professionals and laypersons all over the world and often gets results when nothing else has worked. There are many excellent websites that tell you all about this technique and the easy procedure to be done to affect healing. I need not say any more but invite you to look at some of the sites available.

The many available sites can introduce you to the concept, and help you get started. The testimonials that exist of all the medical problems that have been solved using EFT are overwhelming. Stay with it with complete confidence – it works. It does take persistence and may require several tapping sessions before it works, but it works. Whenever I use the technique I am usually successful on the first try, since I have been using EFT for years and have total confidence of success. If you have a negative attitude towards something like this, then as with anything else I have suggested (prayer, meditation, repentance, etc), it will hinder your success.

Complete trust that Hashem has given us a body that can heal itself with very little effort on our part is essential to success of solving medical problems. It all starts with the mind being emotionally stable and happy. The rest is easy.

There is another very important aspect to good health that I have to include – proper diet. The chemical part of our wellbeing is enhanced greatly by what we eat. The biggest diet problems in the world today are the fast food (more appropriately called junk food) and processed food that has become the typical diet. Hashem gave us the gift of our body with instructions to take care of it. If we think that poisonous junk food is fulfilling the Torah request to take care of Hashem's gift, then we should not complain when medical problems arise. (I should mention that non-kosher food for the Jew is poisonous, mostly on a spiritual level, but will lead to health problems). Doing the right thing should always include common sense. This is not rocket science; it is simply using the intelligence that Hashem gave us in His handbook of life (the Torah) and applying it. The diet that nutritionists suggest may not be as enjoyable as a pizza, but it is much more enjoyable than medical problems.

I have mentioned several times that we become sick, measure for measure, as a way of giving our soul Tikun (rectification) which is one of our most important purposes of this life on Earth. The soul actually controls and gives us our sickness to achieve the Tikun. Why? To compensate for what we are not doing to accomplish our mission in this life, voluntarily.

There are many techniques that I have not discussed since I feel they are counterproductive to what we are supposed to be doing. As an example, the particular statement (a Pizmon) that I mentioned in Prayer Works, completely takes away pain. By talking to my soul and convincing it to not give me pain, I can completely avoid the discomfort, but also lose out on the Tikun that my soul needs and is trying to achieve. The soul has a way of robbing Oxygen from an area of the body which results in the pain. By tricking my soul into believing that it is not necessary, I can cause pain to be completely eliminated. I mentioned the man with a slipped disc, a woman with severe migraine headaches, a man with horrible knee pain and many others with chronic pain problems that used this technique and were totally relieved of their pain. This is how a placebo works.

There are many stories from times of war about injured soldiers that, when pain medication was not available, they were given placebos (basically fake pills) and told to go easy that this is strong medicine and they shouldn't overdo its application. The pain greatly subsides by tricking the mind (the soul) of the individual and actually causing the mind to remove the pain signals from flowing (it also causes chemicals to be released in the brain, endorphins, that act like an opiate to reduce the pain). By teaching this method of using words to control the soul's ability to not administer pain, the Tikun is not achieved; and, Tikun is more important than having to put up with the pain (most people would disagree with that statement, but life is too short to miss out on ways to make us more perfect – such as trying to achieve temporary relief). Of course, if we just involve ourselves in the voluntary methods previously mentioned, many medical problems will diminish or even disappear.

It is far more important and beneficial to remove the cause of the pain or sickness by doing everything to receive Tikun without the soul having to substitute for the lack of service to Hashem. I have mentioned that prayer works. That is a very good method of achieving Tikun and is, according to Torah, the way Hashem wants us to help ourselves and others. I have already discussed the research "why faith healing works." What these researchers concluded is a very important message from Hashem. Very positive words (even positive sounds such as pleasant music), the DNA of a person can be changed. That is physically why prayer (especially Psalms) works. I have experienced many, many people who were with severe medical situations (even being on their death beds) that are now out dancing and enjoying life. It works.

Wow, Hashem has really given us all the tools needed for our own wellbeing; all we have to do is use them. All the tools that I have mentioned so many times (prayer, repentance, charity, doing the mitzvot, Torah study, helping our fellow human being, etc) are more than just good ideas – they are life's success factor (this life and all eternity). They are all methods of achieving Tikun and absolutely promote good health. After all, if you are eliminating the reasons why we suffer with poor health, you are left with good health. Simple!!!!

I have used the techniques mentioned above and know beyond a shadow of a doubt of how tremendous they are. If you don't believe it, you are arguing with success. I am not telling you to not go to doctors anymore. I am suggesting that if you have a medical or even an emotional problem that doctors have not satisfied, try the more natural approach. Even better, as a preventative measure, follow Hashem's guidance and avoid the need for doctors.

I have not mentioned holistic medicines, exercise programs or another procedure called NAET that are also very enhancing to your medical wellbeing. My message is simple. Hashem gave us miraculous ways to solve life's problems; all we need to do is listen to Him, follow His instructions and, above all, thank Him every day for His help. The way to a happy, healthy life begins with Torah.

3.18 Religion

Judaism is not a religion, there is no such word in the Torah, because it is the 'Eternal Truth'. When the Messiah comes and those of the nations that remain will all know that there is ONLY Hashem and no other, Ein Od Milvado; for the knowledge of Hashem will fill the earth as the waters cover the sea beds.

Religion is **a belief system made up by people**. There are approximately 4200 religions in the world, but only one system that came from the Creator; therefore, it is not a religion.

Decades ago when I became a Torah Jew, people said to me "it looks like you discovered a new way of life." I used to answer: "No, I discovered life itself." When you start living the truth, the reality as it was created for the people of this Earth, you are not in a belief system, but a system of knowledge. I don't believe in Hashem – I know He exists. I don't believe that Judaism is life – I know it is; and, I have infinite proof to justify my knowledge.

The big difference between now and the time of the Messiah is that now we live in a physical, fantasy world of falsehood. The upside-down world (previously mentioned) described in the Talmud (Pesachim 50) is our daily existence. The time of The Messiah will be a time of truth, a spiritual existence and therefore all made up religions in the world will no longer exist. When the good, righteous people of the world (and that is all that will remain) do not believe but KNOW of the One Living G-d, everyone will KNOW and LIVE the Absolute Truth. They will not have to be taught such feelings – it will be as natural as our fantasy world is to us today. Hashem will no longer be hidden and everyone will know beyond a shadow of a doubt: "Ein Od Milvado!!!!!!! – There is only Hashem."

Those who develop the feeling now and start living the absolute truth even before The Messiah is announced, will be the happiest people of all. Jews and righteous non-Jews who abandon the fantasy world of today, the total nonsense that is happening in the world (it is obvious to see), will experience the total happiness and peace of mind NOW, and will not have to wait for the time that The Messiah will lead the world (actually Hashem leads everything, The Messiah will just be His servant on Earth). You and your loved ones can have "The world of truth – the world of total happiness, now." Why wait?

You will find out soon how sound this advice is, and how Hashem will change your life to total goodness and happiness. Just follow His instructions and it is yours – guaranteed (in writing). Of course, if by the time you are reading this book it already has occurred, MAZEL TOV!!!!!

3.19 For My Thoughts are not Your Thoughts

This simple quote from the prophet Isaiah (55:8) is a very profound message to the people of the world. Human thought and human logic is flawed. We do not live according to Hashem's reality, but our own evaluation of each situation. There are concepts in this life that we think we know exactly what the truth is and how we should react to a situation. But, we find that the Torah advises us in a completely opposite direction, and we are perplexed when our way fails. Hashem is running the show. His plans are the only system that works. Our thoughts, as logical as they may be, are incorrect and in many cases, dangerous.

One of the most glaring examples in history is assimilation. Throughout history, when we went into the non-Jewish countries, we often tried to blend in; act just like the local populous. But, we found them turning on us – discriminating against us and even killing us. Why? We were acting nice; we were friendly and in many ways contributing to their society. But, the Torah tells us to keep separated and do not do the ways of the nations. We are on this Earth "to be a light unto the nations," to teach the world Hashem's messages, but to stay separate and not blend in. Why? When we assimilate, we go away from Hashem. We go away from doing the mitzvot – not keeping Kosher, not observing the Shabbos, not dressing properly, not educating our children and ourselves properly, etc, etc. Yes, it doesn't seem logical but when Yaakov is studying Torah (and living Torah), Esav can't touch (or kill him) – so says Hashem in the Torah.

We also have a very distorted view of history believing the nonsensical interpretation of what the history books say. Many have argued that the Jews of Europe in the 1930's were very religious and yet they suffered greatly. The fact is in Germany over 90% of Jews were assimilated and completely away from their Jewish heritage. Many had even converted to Xtianity in an effort to blend in. They were shocked at how their so-called dear friends and neighbors turned against them when the Nazis came. In other words, it happened as the Torah said, not as the human logic dictated.

I grew up with Holocaust survivors who tried to stay Jewish in the face of danger. I remember one individual telling me that he knew exactly why he had spent four years in 13 different labor camps. He told me exactly where in the Torah it said so. But, he also told me stories about how he survived because he still had Hashem with him and how others didn't survive because they were angry at Hashem. It is ironic to be angry at the One Who gives you the information on how to survive, but you are angry because you ignore His advice.

The most profound story that I was told was by a very pleasant, observant Jew in Lakewood with whom I prayed. He was in Auschwitz and was actually led to the gas chamber along with about 200 other men. They were put in, and locked in as they awaited death. He started to chant the verse we say in Hallel: "The dead do not praise G-d, nor do those who go down into the silence of the grave." They all joined in and repeated it to Hashem over and over again. How can we serve Hashem if we are dead was all they had in mind. Nothing happened. They waited 5 minutes, ten minutes, twenty minutes (my friend described it as an eternity). All of a sudden the door opened and the guards said "we need a work detail, everyone out." My friend and all those who turned to Hashem that day survived as members of a labor camp to which they were taken. My friend had no doubt what had happened and spent the rest of his life in total service to Hashem.

Why am I telling you all this? We have received messages from Hashem recently through Rabbis and the Facilitated Communications individuals. Some of the information was not according to human logic; of course not, it was from Hashem. I have received an abundance of Emails and comments telling me how much these messages just don't make sense or are undoable or are impractical. My Thoughts are not Your Thoughts applies here. Do you want information from Hashem that will work, or is much more comfortable and will not work?

I always try to answer inquiries that I receive with the same question: What is Hashem's opinion about this? I ask people to be with an open mind and realize that it may not be the answer they want, but it is the only correct answer that will work and be beneficial. Don't argue with success; just thank Hashem for His guidance.

3.20 Let Gratitude Be Your Attitude

We are told many places in scriptures about the final testing that will occur in the end of days. Hashem is sorting it all out and giving us, measure for measure, what we need to finish our Tikun, our rectification. The great amount of suffering and hardship occurring in the world today is a very positive sign that we are very close to the end, since it is brought down that this chaos will occur before the Messiah is introduced. Each of us having a very positive attitude towards what is happening helps the redemption process.

As an example, I recently had a virus that has caused me pain and discomfort. I thank Hashem on a daily basis for paying attention to me and giving me what I need for a higher level of Tikun. With a very positive attitude I look at this discomfort as a blessing; and, I believe that this is my final sickness for eternity. But, the most important thing for me is to react to this message from Hashem. Such actions as adding on perhaps an additional 15 minutes a day of Torah study; giving a little bit more to charity; evaluating my mistakes and human fragilities and improving the way I perform every day in serving Hashem, praying with more concentration and inspiration (especially in the pronunciation of the names of Hashem), improving my performance of the 613 mitzvot (commandments) and thousands of other actions that I do that could be done better. I am constantly making changes in my life and never being satisfied with what I do – always looking to improve my relations with my Creator is the key to success. Hashem will heal me faster since He knows that I accept His will as always being for the good, and that I have a strong desire to react to the messages

He sends me in a very positive way. I do not want sickness, suffering, poverty, unemployment, hunger, etc for anyone (including me and my family). But, I very much encourage everyone to realize how much proper reaction to all the messages Hashem sends us can work to our benefit.

Problems should not be considered disappointment, but opportunity; and, we should all thank Hashem for what He does. Someday, very soon, we will fully understand and be so gracious for the help He bestows upon us as individuals and as a people. In other words: don't be disappointed but instead "Let gratitude be your attitude."

Continue to anticipate the redemption every day. If all the Jews would have a strong sense of anticipation, The Messiah would be here instantly. The good news is that since all Jews are not doing what they should, Hashem is helping us in many other ways and will bring the redemption soon – all signs are pointing to it. The only thought that each of us should have is "what do I as an individual still need to do?" Just remember: measure for measure we each get from Hashem in return what we do to serve Him and how we follow His ways. It's a simple system that results in a tremendous amount of happiness and joy for each one of us for eternity. Thank you, Hashem.

3.21 Flawed Human Logic

I have stated the verse from Isaiah 55:8: "For My thoughts are not your thoughts, neither are your ways My ways – the Word of Hashem." We cannot look at anything written in scriptures, especially in English and declare "I know exactly what Hashem is telling us." I have also stated that Torah is by far the most difficult subject in the world. It would be much easier to discuss Quantum Physics, Business Law, Brain Surgery, Differential Equations, etc, etc, etc. Why? Because most of these subjects can be explained by human logic – or can they? I thought I would take one example of a subject that everyone has heard about, even though very few people have studied. The topic is Einstein's Theory of Relativity.

In 1905 this nice little Jewish boy, Albert Einstein, theorized certain concepts of the physical world that were so radical, so different that he introduced his work over a couple of decades and published the final version in the 1920's. It wasn't just that it went against human logic; it also disagreed with the most prolific scientist in history, Sir Isaac Newton. Sir Isaac had set the standard for study of the physical world. Another conflict was that Newton, who was British, was being challenged by Einstein, who was German, even worse he was Jewish. The important message here is that Einstein made statements about the physical world that were not logical and not even comprehendible.

So, what did Einstein say that was so disturbing to the scientific community? He said that time was a variable. Time is dependent upon the gravitational field that you are experiencing, he called that General Relativity; and, time is dependent upon the velocity that you are traveling; he called that concept Special Relativity. Well, that could be upsetting even to us a century later. Of course he is talking about excessive gravity and speed that we human beings don't have a clue whether we are experiencing or not. As an example, let say that I was living on the Sun (I know, it is not possible to have enough air conditioning to be a resident there nor could I take the gravitational effect, but just play along). Because of the size of the Sun the gravitational effect means that the Sun, according to General Relativity, is 72 minutes shorter a year than life on Earth. I would not see any difference since all processes, cell division, thought processes, growth, etc would slow down. I wouldn't notice any change. I would experience a full year as the people on Earth, but I would return to Earth 72 minutes younger.

Let's get really involved. Don't try this at home; but, what would happen if I went into a space ship and travelled close to the speed of light (186,000 miles per second) for about a year. Of course, I would take along enough Cholent to cover the trip, but at that speed, I would return to Earth and find that the people on Earth lived maybe 10 years. I would not notice any difference because, once again, the Special Relativistic effects would slow down all processes around me making everything seem normal, but allowing me to travel 9 years into the future.

Einstein also said "space is curved." When you see a star in the sky, it is not in the direction that you are looking since the light coming from that star was bending as it went through space. If I could look into a telescope, looking out into the universe, and see infinity, I would see the back of my head. I would have made a complete trip through the curved universe and returned to me.

Why am I bringing up these things? Good question. When you get into the deepest secrets of this world and explore the scientific proof, you will see that many, if not most, subjects are beyond comprehension. It should be mentioned that Einstein's Theory has been proven beyond any doubt (using atomic clocks, particle colliders, spacecraft, satellites, etc) and is no longer called a theory – the scientific world calls it The Law of Relativity. The important message is that things are not what they seem and those who have studied science for many years may know all the facts, all the mathematics, but still have no comprehension of the reality. Variable time, curved space, teleportation (being one place and instantly being somewhere else), the computerized structure of DNA in every cell (the instructions of how that living organism will grow), the chemical makeup of everything (everything is made up of the exact same particles just in different numbers and configurations), no such thing as real matter, the mind, the metaphysical realm, etc, etc, etc are all concepts that we experience every day and have no comprehension of the reality.

Even something that may seem simple can be beyond our grasp, as an example (back to Einstein):

$$E=MC^2$$

A simple formula that is so complicated that I thought I would show you an analysis of the development of the simple formula (this is not for the faint of heart considering to this day they are still evaluating the formula). Go to web:

http://www.ptep-online.com/index_files/2006/PP-07-03.PDF

What subject can we talk about, that we can grasp the basic information of the text; but, the subjects are so deep that, it is beyond human comprehension? You guessed it: **Torah**. Hashem gave us the Torah on Mount Sinai as a string of letters, 304,805 letters to be exact. Moses put the spaces to give us the basic wording that we have used for 3327 years. Hashem also gave us all the information of the Oral Torah, the Talmud, to explain the deep concepts of the written Torah. Hashem also gave us all the prophecy of everything that would happen in this world. Hashem also gave us the Zohar information of every mystical concept of this world. But, Hashem, Who is of infinite intelligence (a concept beyond our grasp), gave us the Torah which has everything as a genetic code of the entire universe (everyone who ever lived, is alive and who will live, with infinite detail), every animal, every plant, every rock, every star, nebula, galaxy, planet, every word ever spoken, every meal ever eaten, every piece of clothing ever worn, every living establishment, every piece of furniture,

216

appliance, etc, etc, etc, etc, etc. That means that all of science and mathematics is in the Torah.

There is nothing missing; if something is, it doesn't exist. So if we have to study science for decades in order to grasp all these concepts that are beyond our flawed human comprehension, how is it that everyone knows the answers to Torah questions that are sometime infinitely further out of our grasp than any scientific principle? Let us analyze.

I already mentioned how most of us learned Bible stories when we were young children and as we got older they still remained child level stories (at the Peshat level). If I asked someone to tell me about Quantum Physics or corporate law or differential equations or brain surgery (that's enough – we get the point), most would answer "Oh, I've never studied those subjects." But, if I ask them questions about the Torah or the Bible, everyone would have an opinion. Even worse they would state: "I'm skeptical as to whether that really happened." To know that the Torah and even all of Jewish Scriptures are so deep and even beyond comprehension is not according to our flawed human logic – after all "I read it once and know all the 5 year level Bible stories."

I have mentioned that 10 lifetimes of Torah study would only scratch the surface of what the deeper meaning is. What is even worse is we study in English which is Peshat personified. The true, deeper meaning can only come from the mystical and miraculous letters of Hebrew. We are told in Talmud that we must study a subject 101 times before we can begin to understand its true meaning.

You may ask: How am I to learn what Hashem wants from me if I can't fully understand His instructions? He let us know in the Torah that throughout the ages the great Rabbis would give us the codification of His law and the interpretation that would bring us up to modern times. I word it that way since there are always those who ask: How do I know all my obligations pertaining to modern situations: electricity, telephones, cars, lights, etc. Obviously, the scriptures written thousands of years ago cannot be interpreted for today's world. Or could it? The answer is the bottom line of what I am discussing. The study of Torah is not to find out what we need to do to serve Hashem, it is to try to understand all that He has told us and to get a much better understanding of this world and the life on it. The instructions that we must follow have been codified in the Shulchan Aruch, the Mishnah Berurah, many volumes of Halacha-made-easy books from the Rabbis of today. I am not giving a class here on how to fulfill your obligations to Hashem – for that you need competent Torah scholars with which to study – best done one on one. My goal here is strictly to give you confidence that good information is available and that you need not study Torah to figure out what to do (nor are most of us capable of doing so). My overall point is that Torah is the most complicated subject in the world since it entails everything in this world. For us to try to interpret its message or even worse to try to force our opinion on others, is counter-productive and, in most cases, dangerous. You may ask: Isn't that what I am doing in this book? The answer is "no," I am encouraging everyone to study (in person) with a very competent source and to live Torah as we should. I have said: Don't believe anything that I say since discovery on your own is far more exciting and internalizing.

The overall message is if you don't believe that you must follow Hashem's ways, you are throwing it all away – happiness, success, goodness, prosperity, peace of mind, love for your family, everything for a tremendous future (forever and ever). This is all guaranteed in writing from the One Who created you and the world that you live in. Don't argue with success and don't throw it all away, because you used your flawed human logic and think that you know better. Hashem was not waiting for any of us to come along to figure out His Torah. We have thousands of years of brilliance to refer to and see exactly what Hashem wants from us. Study to learn but not to figure out the meaning – none of us are intuitive enough to do so; and, it is not necessary – it has already been done for us.

Hopefully, you read above about the simple subject of science, and can now compare it to the infinitely more complicated subject of Torah. Hopefully, you have more perspective to not stumble on the world's most difficult subject, Torah, by using flawed human logic. Instead, study it with great excitement and expectation and enjoy its enormous benefits.

3.22 The Receiving of the Torah

On Rosh Chodesh Sivan (literally the Head of the Month, or the 1st of the Hebrew month Sivan) 3327 years ago we arrived at Mount Sinai. We got settle in – getting ready for the most exciting day in history – the receiving of the Torah.

When we were in Egypt, Moses told Pharaoh that he wanted to take the Israelites into the desert for three days, per Hashem's instructions. Was Moses lying, trying to trick Pharaoh into letting his people go? Not at all. Hashem told Moses to take the Israelites into the desert where they will prepare for three days. Even though Pharaoh misunderstood these three days of being in the desert, Moses was aware that they were not told to which three days Hashem was referring. We became aware after arriving at Mount Sinai that Hashem was informing everyone that starting on the third of Sivan there would be three days of preparation leading up to the greatest event in history. These were days of purification, praying, repentance, soul searching, meditation, asking forgiveness, etc, etc, etc. We needed to become as spiritual as possible and find a way to suppress our physical presence. After all, we were getting ready to experience our Creator and receive His Word.

Every year we have the same ritual of preparing ourselves to receive the Torah. Wait a minute, didn't we already receive the Torah 3327 years ago and are only commemorating the anniversary on the sixth of Sivan, the holiday of Shavuot? Shavuot has more significance than remembering, it is a time that we prepare to receive the Torah all over again, every year. Our most important mission is learning Torah and living that which we have learned. We are excited about the fact that we are entering another year of learning Torah. In other words, the excitement of Shavuot is not just what happened in the past but what is about to happen. We are psyching ourselves up to receive all the new Torah that we will learn in the coming year.

A very important thing happened before we received the Torah. Collectively, we said as a nation "na'aseh v'nishma," "We will do and we will hear" (Exodus 24:8). Hashem wanted to verify that we truly were the people to bring His message to the world. The Torah was offered to other nations before the Jewish people. One nation questioned "What is in this Torah?" When told "don't steal," this people rejected the Torah stating that theft was necessary within their lives. When another group was offered the Torah, they questioned "What is in this Torah?" When told "don't kill," this people rejected the Torah stating that killing was needed for their survival (I am leaving out who these nations were on purpose – they still exist today). Only the Jews accepted the Torah stating that they will do as Hashem commanded and then after they will question what these commandments mean, as they study them. In other words, with complete faith in Hashem as their Father in Heaven, we will obey and learn. We are not without curiosity as to the deeper meaning of the mitzvot; and, Hashem wants us to satisfy our curiosity by looking at deeper meanings. The result of studying is always to show love to Hashem. We accomplish this by demonstrating more desire to serve Him and serve Him correctly. Our intensions have always had high merit, which is why Hashem chose us to be the bearer of His message.

Another very important message that we conveyed to Hashem with "na'aseh v'nishma," is that we talk in the plural. We did not say "I will do and I will hear." I have mentioned many times that Hashem wants us to help each other and even be responsible for each other. It is very easy, as an individual, to say "I'm in good shape, things are pretty good for me, let the other guy take care of himself." It is not the Jewish way and not the lesson of Torah. Even today if we don't help each other we are really sinning. Yes, we are judged as individuals, measure for measure; but, a big part of our test on Earth, which affords us a way to succeed in that test, is our desire to give, rather than receive.

As an American I used to take pride in the fact that I had rights. Under the constitution I had the right to life, liberty and the pursuit of happiness. I had the right to sing the blues and the right to wear blue suede shoes (I'm sorry I don't remember all my wonderful rights). When I became observant, I realized that I was put on this Earth not with rights but with obligations. There is a big difference between believing that I had the right to have my property protected versus I have the obligation to protect the property of others. When everyone in a society believes the world owes them a living, that society can't succeed. America succeeded not because of rights but because of its Biblical foundation, which did advocate people helping people. We see a big decline in the world morality these days since greed has become the rule of the day and everyone for himself the psyche of the people. The good news is this was meant to happen in the end of days. When the Messiah takes over and everyone turns to Hashem for leadership, all will be as it should be according to His Torah.

I have mentioned that one of the biggest changes that occurred in my life when I became observant was that I found that I was learning something new and exciting every day. I got up every morning wondering: what will it be today? What new Torah will I discover today that will change me, enlighten me, improve me and gladden me? The most interesting thing about this new positive approach to starting my day is after decades of being observant, it continues and hasn't diminished. It was not the just the excitement of being a new Ba'al

Teshuvah (one who has returned to Hashem's ways), but was the start of something that only gets better every day. I wake up about 2 to 3 AM every morning – not because I have to, but because I want to. There is not enough time to learn the amount of Torah that I want, since a lifetime of learning just scratches the surface. Making every day count and even wanting the day to be longer by starting earlier is actually a joy to me, not a burden. Most people have no idea what true happiness can be. I have to admit, if you told me 30 years ago that I would find happiness in getting up that early to discover something new and exciting about this world and this life, after I stopped laughing (you know the rest).

One of the most exciting things that happens to me every day is seeing what is occurring in the world and knowing that it is a message from Hashem and a further indication that the time of the redemption and the Messiah are upon us. It doesn't get much more exciting than that. One may say that my favorite hobby is comparing scriptures to our world of today. Hashem has let us know in advance what to look for, and I love finding it.

I know that this year's Shavuot, 5775, will be the most special Shavuot that we will ever experience since we were at Mount Sinai. Enjoy and do your best preparation for the occasion ever – not as an individual, but with others – you won't regret it.

3.23 Lashon Harah

One topic that I have mentioned but have not really emphasized is that of Lashon Harah, the evil tongue. I believe that Lashon Harah is one of the most misunderstood concepts in the Torah but one of the most important personality characteristics that Hashem wants us to work on. In simple English it is the idea of talking about people, sometimes called gossip, which always has a negative effect. It is an abomination to Hashem since he wants us to love and help each other and not hurt each other.

The Chofetz Chaim, who has written books on Lashon Harah, is considered one of the best sources of information on the subject. He teaches us that it is not just saying unfavorable statements about someone, but even praising the individual could have negative effects for that individual. We are not even concerned whether the Lashon Harah is true or false; it is just the idea of talking about someone and the damage it could do. One caveat is if the information that you are providing someone will save them suffering, then it is allowed. If someone stole money from me and is offering to loan money to a fellow Jew, I am obligated to help an honest Jew from being swindled or hurt in any way.

Let me give you an example of Lashon Harah that is more subtle in nature. You want to take a particular college course and a friend tells you "make sure you only take the course with Prof. Peloni." One would think what is wrong with suggesting Prof. Peloni that his friend had as his teacher. But it is actually Lashon Harah because now you have said favorable things about Prof. Pelosi and hinted to negativity about the other professors teaching that course. That may not have been intended, but yet the individual suggesting one particular professor probably doesn't know the others that available to teach the course. They may even be better at the subject than Prof. Peloni. The better way would be to just tell the individual "I had Prof. Peloni who I thought did a good job."

Something else that is subtle is to never disclose that a fellow Jew may be very wealthy. Information like that tends to cause people to bother the individual for more charity, loans, help with financing and who knows what else. A wealthy Jew is judged by Hashem on his own merit as to how he uses his money and not from the pestering of others (unless that is part of the test from Hashem). How other Jews treat a wealthy Jew is part of their test in life.

There are many who would tell you that the example I gave above is not Lashon Harah. One reason is that most people don't really know what Lashon Harah is. The fact is I got the example from a book by the Chofetz Chaim. Yet this could lead to a bigger problem. When one makes a statement and someone else disagrees, Hashem does not want us to promote sinat chinam, baseless hatred, but to open friendly dialogue about the disagreement; respectfully listening to the other side of the argument and resolving it the Torah way with love of our fellow Jew. All parties are being tested by Hashem as to how they handle the situation. When someone is misinformed about the truth and is hardheaded about his or her personal opinion, it should never result in anger and name-calling. That is some of the worst Lashon Harah. It is totally offensive to Hashem and is punishable.

Let us talk about a more severe situation and how it can cause someone permanent damage. When I was in the Army, there was a particular sergeant who was absolutely a delightful and pleasant individual. Everybody liked him. One day he was exiting a building and there were two policemen and a young woman standing at the exit. The young woman pointed to my friend and said "that's him; he is the one who raped me." My friend was handcuffed and imprisoned awaiting his trial. At the trial the young woman admitted that she had just had an argument with her boyfriend. Due to a dislike she developed for all men, she decided that she would accuse the first person who walked out of the building. Obviously, my friend was released from custody as he was completely innocent. However, never again did anyone look at him the same way. They always wondered whether he was really involved; and, that maybe she had just changed her mind. People never treated him the same after that incident. How sad to just have your entire life upset because of Lashon Harah.

I have had Lashon Harah said about me on the web – not everyone agrees with what I have written, especially if they don't ask my favorite question: "What is Hashem's opinion?" I didn't feel bad about some of the things that were said about me. I was more concerned about how Hashem is judging the perpetrator of the Lashon Harah, and what the individual has done to him or herself. My love of my fellow Jew means I am bothered when I see someone sinning needlessly and causing suffering and hardship to come upon him or herself. The other concern is: those who believe Lashon Harah are also in danger. Hashem lets us know that the severity of Lashon Harah can be diminished by everyone hearing it not listening or believing the nonsense. Yes you can be punished for believing Lashon Harah as well as saying it or writing it.

Let me give an example written of what a total lack of education can do to a person. I once received a comment warning me about statements that I make about the Messiah being close. The Rambam curses an individual who calculates the end. The comment I received called me a unfavorable name. What a big negative report went into the Hashem's book of the one who made such a comment.

Let us analyze what happened. First of all, one must know what the Rambam really said, since he even gave a possible calculation of the end. He gave two provisos, telling us under what conditions one can calculate. One: if the date is far away, it is very depressing to tell people such news and it should be avoided. If the date is very close, as it is now, many Rabbis say that you should disclose such information to give encouragement. If it results in people doing repentance, more mitzvot, more praying and more Torah study, what a blessing has occurred.

Hashem will even speed up the arrival due to the increased effort. That is what is meant by "if we are deserving."

The second suggestion from the Rambam is that you say that the calculated date is your opinion. What is interesting about this entire episode was that I never calculated a date. I only compiled a vast amount of information from very reliable sources, such Scriptures, and reproduced what was presented on many other blogs. I came up with none of the information, but only gathered it all into one place and offered it to my readers. The conclusion was obvious since it repeated itself over and over again in the compiled documentation. I compiled over 100 pages of evidence that we were getting very close to the happy ending. Most of the information actually came from messages from Hashem, which means it was meant to be disclosed.

The Jewish way to disagree with someone is to ask questions and get a clarification discussion started. How many times I have gotten E-mails from individuals who didn't agree with my postings. Sometimes they ask what references I used for the information (that is the Jewish way). Sometimes they just told me you are wrong or they stated this is not the absolute truth. What is interesting is how many times they completely misunderstood what I had written. Unfortunately, most comments are No Reply E-mails so I can't even get a discussion going. If people would send me a private E-mail to which I could respond, that would be the Jewish way and would prevent that individual from being negatively looked upon by Hashem.

I unfortunately cannot write everything that I wish about a subject, whether it be on my blog or this book. I already have stated that many subjects require a volume of details, especially since most subjects that I cover come from many volumes that I have personally studied. It's very difficult to summarize many subjects and cover every aspect as I would prefer. This unfortunately leaves room for questions and sometimes comments that show that the individual does not understand what was presented.

Of course, I also have a hidden motive and that is to get my reader to research the subject. I have stated that when you read new facts, never seen before, you have just seen information that may or may not register with you. If you research a subject and make your own discoveries, now you have internalized something new – hopefully something from Hashem that is very beneficial to your life.

This may come as a shock but "I am human." I have made some very minor mistakes and was blessed by someone intelligent enough to point them out allowing me to make a correction. I like to consider myself a nice guy, a friendly person who loves other people and wants to help them. All I ask is that you reciprocate in a kind manner by treating everyone with total respect. Bringing Lashon Harah into the picture is very counterproductive for one who does the bringing and anyone who believes the Lashon Harah.

I would like to disclose something about myself that has been misunderstood. I am not a Rabbi. I am called Rav by many of my readers and those who have heard me in public lectures. Wikipedia states: The term **Rav** is also a generic term for a teacher or a personal spiritual guide. For example, Pirkei Avot tells us that "Joshua ben Perachyah said: Provide for yourself a teacher (*Rav*). It doesn't diminish my level of scholarship, that fact that I never was ordained a Rabbi, even though I am referred to by friends, and even when I had coworkers, as Rabbi. In my environment, it is a very common title whether one has been ordained or not. It is based more on the level of scholarship and above all a tremendous desire to help people.

It was comical in my last employment environment, before I retired, I worked in an office with other engineers who called me their spiritual leader. I remember one day a woman from an adjoining office coming in to talk to me and asked me for guidance. When I asked her why she was asking me, she said "you are my spiritual adviser." When I said to her "but you are Catholic, why aren't you talking to your Priest?" she answered with Lashon Harah "he is useless." My desire to teach and help others is not out of arrogance, but strictly to perform Hashem's will. All I ask is that we work together, respect each other, learn together and do everything the way Hashem wants to see it done. It's the best thing for both of us.

One little caveat: as to major reason that I never became a Rabbi. My wife requested that I don't. She did not want to be called "Rebbetzin Robinson." I thought it was a catchy title; she disagreed. One other caveat. My ancestry is Lithuanian. I believe the name Robinson in Lithuania comes from Yiddish meaning the "son of the Rabbi," Rabban sohn. In America it seems to pertain to a basketball player – go figure.

3.24 Opinion

It is interesting that the less Torah learning an individual has, the more opinion they use. Opinion is based on life's experiences and not so much on knowledge. When I was doing Kiruv, outreach (helping fellow Jews find their way in life), in the states, I saw it all the time that you can teach Hashem's opinion on a subject and get as a response: "I always believed it was this way or that way." I find the more Torah that I learn, the less I know. When I discover the truth about a subject, I find I have a lot more to learn and that I have been running on my opinion for years on whatever the subject is at hand.

I am experiencing, almost every day, "the me of the past (the way I used to think when I had an opinion)" since most people, who are without Torah answers, think they know much more than Torah scholars – after all, they have an opinion. The biggest problem is, unlike when I was face-to-face with my Kiruv (outreach) students, the web is a cold hard place to correct and help people. In person, we provide instant help and a much friendlier atmosphere. People are much more brave and show much more belligerency when they deal long distance by writing. Since they can say any nonsense they want and even use the name Anonymous to spout their misgivings, they become as brazen as they want without consequence.

Or, is it without consequence? Anyone who has fear of heaven knows very well that everything one does, every word one says and even every thought one has is known and is recorded in heaven. Psychologist will tell you that people like to have a scapegoat. Jews have been the most famous scapegoats in history. It's very difficult for us to admit our own shortcomings. If we have a way to vent our frustrations, blame someone else in a way that we think is safe, we take advantage of it. The web has perpetuated much hatred, especially Jew-hatred, because it is a haven for cowards. It is so easy to blame someone else for one's problems; especially a stranger that I will probably never see or encounter in any way.

A few years ago there was a debate on another blog about whether my blog really was the Absolute Truth. Most of the 110 comments were positive and even complimentary. But, I saw within the comments, individuals with a great lack of Torah knowledge, screaming for help. It was a vent for personal problems and frustrations. The big problem was it hurt good people. It definitely included Lashon Harah, and the permanent damage it could cause. You can't take it back and can't fix the damage. I saw on my blog a decrease in comments and a decrease in page views. This indicates to me that many of my readers may have lost confidence in some of the material that I was presenting, because they were victim to believing Lashon Harah. I was getting more personal Emails from people who wanted to talk, but did not want the other readers to read their questions or concerns. The sad part is that I did not get challenged when points of disagreement were voiced.

Instead of somebody doing it the Torah way by saying to me "I disagree with something and here is my evidence to prove my point," I received anger and nonsensical accusations. Anger is always a sign of frustration and lack of knowledge on the part of the individual. I can see that they were not angry at me; but, they just could not admit it that the psychological failing is on their part. In other words, they were angry at themselves and were merely looking to vent their frustrations and using the safety of the internet was the perfect outlet.

Since I am aware of this, I am in no way concerned about myself, but I'm very concerned about those who are having this problem, since I cannot help Anonymous (the name that is almost always used by the one not able to cope). The biggest frustration of all is how many people listen to Lashon Harah and believe it. Both are grave sins in the eyes of Hashem – listening and/or believing. I know that I can control the comments on my blog. I can delete any comment that is inappropriate. But when it appears on somebody else's blog and as Lashon Harah, I have no control over the hurt it causes good people. What the moderator of another blog prints becomes that moderator's responsibility, even if it contains very sinful and damaging rhetoric. Printing Lashon Harah is a way of condoning Lashon Harah. That hurts everyone involved: the one being talked about, the one saying the Lashon Harah, the blogger allowing it and the readers who read it (even if they don't believe it). What is sad is that no topic that came from my blog was questioned or debated. I was just told I was wrong and end of story. In every case, I had excellent sources to prove my arguments. In some cases I had to do further research, since it was dealing with something that I had heard many years prior, but I was still able to vindicate my position.

I take very seriously the idea of presenting the absolute truth as I spend many hours a day researching and writing before I post. It's amazing how someone with a total lack of scholarship on the subject can, with a distorted opinion, voice dissension the way they do. I find almost no one will ever research the subject;

only that they comment based on what they have experienced themselves – an opinion based on flawed human logic. I know basically people are lazy; but, if they really know how much damage they are doing to themselves and others, they would become more ambitious. Don't forget: this is damage for all eternity.

I am with very little concern about myself. I know that everything in this world is for the good. I see this as testing for myself and for any blogger who faces the same situation. In other words, Hashem is providing me with challenge to help me grow, which gives me Tikun. I thank Hashem for the personal growth, but I still feel bad if any of my readers have been led astray and had their personal growth negatively affected. Also, I feel bad for the frustrated individual who comments in an incorrect way by not asking questions, but just voicing dissention. That person's entire future depends on it as well. I have mentioned that we are getting close to the Day of Judgment "the two late date." How much I wish everyone would take this seriously. It's not the anger that you are venting, it is the fact that you may be shooting yourself in the foot while doing it. Other bloggers should note that taking the Absolute Truth off of your favorites list has sent a very strong message to your readers and mine. It condones Lashon Harah and hatred. It says that judging a fellow Jew is not important. Judging is against Torah, especially if you state publically that Hashem's truth is not your opinion. That is a grave sin. Remember that one of the greatest traits for which Hashem is judging us is Ahavas Yisroel, love of one's fellow Jew.

When you read something on the web ask yourself: "Am I seeking the truth or just giving in to the loudest protesters to appease them? Fairness is the Torah way and is the best lesson for readers of all the nonsense on the web. Your eternity will be reviewed on Judgment Day; do the right thing.

I have a love for all people and those who can't control their own emotions, I wish to help. I am neither a hateful person nor a vengeful person, but only one who wants to do the will of Hashem and help everyone. If you lack knowledge on the subject that I am covering, then join me in learning. If you know more than I on any subject and wish to contribute, I'd like to consider myself as open-minded an individual as can be, and I am ready to learn from you. All I ask is if you frequent blogs, be nice to the other readers and any blogger to whom you provide comments. I am sure you will receive niceness in return, especially from Hashem. That's the Torah way; and, that's what makes Hashem happy.

One word of advice is **the best way to learn the Absolute Truth is through books that are based on Hashem's opinion, not the horrible web that is mostly the flawed human logic opinion of people.**

3.24.1 The Danger of Having an Opinion

I must include a very important aspect of living with opinion, instead of education – DANGER!!!! There are many, many topics that I have not covered in this book. Obviously, in an effort to keep this under a thousand volumes (that is actually a very low estimate, since Jewish scriptures includes everything in the Universe). This means if you wish to learn the truth about a subject, you will have to research yourself. The most important thing to keep in mind is until you know the absolute truth about a subject, don't, and I really mean don't go by your distorted flawed human logic opinion, rather than Hashem's correct infinite intelligence opinion.

I would like to give some examples of controversial subjects that have been in the public debate arena, and how opinion has totally devastated lives.

The *brit milah*, circumcision, is a physical symbol of the relationship between Hashem and the Jewish people. It is a constant reminder of what the Jewish mission entails. Hashem commanded the Jewish people (Leviticus 12:2), "On the eighth day, the flesh of his foreskin shall be circumcised." The act of circumcision, marking the completion of the body, is a human act. This teaches us that our spiritual, emotional, moral and ethical perfection requires human effort. Hashem does not do it for us, but requires our devotion to carry out this vital commandment.

The *brit milah,* ritual circumcision, is a symbol of our partnership with Hashem. This covenant with Hashem surpasses human comprehension. It is a bond that pledges unconditional devotion, no matter what may transpire between Hashem and an individual. It is a bond that is absolute and unchallengeable. For this reason a Jew is circumcised as an infant, when he has not yet developed his capacity for reasoning or making judgments, for the covenant of circumcision is not an intellectual or calculated partnership. The circumcision of an infant demonstrates that the connection between the Jews and Hashem is beyond rationale.

Since opinion can dictate a very negative attitude towards circumcision, we can see how ignorance can ruin this important covenant that lasts for eternity for this person. A lack of fulfilling this commandment does include eternal suffering. The spiritual loss is devastating and too complicated to discuss here. Just be aware that adult opinion has caused a very important covenant with Hashem to be lost forever. It is a very important benefit that should not be withheld from a Jewish baby, just because of a parent's ignorant opinion.

For thousands of years, even under persecution, Jews have circumcised their sons using the services of a *mohel*, ritual circumciser, who knows all the intricacies of performing the circumcision. By having your son ritually circumcised, you join their ranks in connecting your child with Hashem in an unbreakable covenant.

On a spiritual level, circumcision is absolutely vital for the future of the Jewish male. On a physical level, there is much research that has shown the great advantages to the health of a male, even a non-Jew. I am fascinated by the fact that blood coagulation in the human male reaches its highest level on the eighth day of life – what a coincidence.

Another sticky subject is animal sacrifice. There is no doubt that hunting is very cruel. It is as painful a death to an innocent animal, as a human being would experience being shot or any other tortuous method of slaughter. Yet we have already talked about Kosher ritual slaughter and how there is no pain involved. Hashem created the kosher animals with complete mercy for the animals.

So how about the sacrifice that occurred in the Temple? The system in this world, set up by the Owner of the world, is to allow substitution for the sins of human beings by sacrificing an animal. It could mean that by Jewish law, a person, who should be put to death, can repent his or her ways and avoid death with an animal sacrifice. Once again, the spiritual ramifications here are beyond human comprehension, but suffice it to say that it is very merciful to people.

But how about the mercy for the animal? Two aspects of this system to learn. One is that most animal sacrifice is given to the Kohain, the priest, for consumption. The Kohain and his family will have food to eat in the same way that we get kosher meat for our Shabbos table. The second hidden aspect is that the animal experiences great benefit. It is a great honor for an animal to be sacrificed in the holiest of services in the Temple. Since this is not the real world, this animal gets to go on to something far better than this life on Earth.

But, let us talk of an even greater benefit that very few people would even think about. Most human beings require several lives on Earth to reach Tikun. We are reincarnated as an opportunity to fix what we did not fix in a previous visit to Earth. There are people who come back as animals. It is more embarrassing than being a respected human being, especially since the soul of a human encased in the body of an animal knows its situation and its embarrassment. Why does this person have to come back as an animal? Hashem knows exactly what a person needs to reach Tikun. There is a possibility that the person was cruel to animals, which is against the Torah (possibly the hunter mentioned above), and the perfect rectification for this inhumane behavior towards animals is to become one himself. But, now the merciful part. When an animal is sacrificed in the Temple, or even for our Shabbos table, that sacrifice is the release of the person from this difficult incarnation, and the achieving of Tikun. This is a very happy benefit for the animal, and, more importantly, for the person reaching rectification. It puts a very different spin on animal sacrifice for the people who only had an opinion and no scholarship of the subject.

A man walks into a hospital and accidentally strays into an operating room. He arrived at the exact moment that the skilled brain surgeon is cutting open a patient's head, ready to remove a cancerous tumor. The man is totally grossed out and had the initial reaction to stop the procedure – after all, he was of the opinion that this doctor was killing the guy on the table. Of course, we know that the doctor is saving his life and should be greatly commended for his skills.

That may seem like a silly scenario – how can a guy be so ignorant, just because he didn't know the truth about the situation? Yet, how many of us do the exact same thing based on our opinion rather than educated decision making. How many people drive while intoxicated or even worse while texting a friend? The number of fatalities a year is alarming. Yet, anyone doing such acts would have given you their opinion: "I can handle it – accidents don't happen to me, they happen to the other guy." How many people speed down the highway with total disregard to the Laws of Physics that say the road was not designed for that speed and you can get killed if something goes wrong, such as two vehicles trying to occupy the same space at the same time.

These are all examples of people whose opinion is different from Hashem's opinion. But, human beings have that dangerous characteristic of thinking "nothing will happen to me," until it happens to him or her.

Hashem knows what is best for each of us; and, His commandments teach us exactly how to enhance our lives to the maximum. Our opinion decreases the benefits; after all, we know better. Only Hashem's opinion is correct. When you live the absolute truth, you are living His opinion and completely protected from your own.

3.25 Instructions from Hashem for our Time

From Rosh Chodesh Elul to Shemini Atzeres, we recite an extra prayer every day that is very appropriate for our times. In fact, if you read it carefully, it comes out as definite instructions that Hashem is giving us to carry us through this time of chaos and travail. The prayer is Psalm 27. The best way to understand the message is to state the prayer and do a cursory analysis of what Hashem is telling us. First read the Psalm:

Psalm 27 (from the Birnbaum Siddur)
> A Psalm of David. Hashem is my light and aid; whom shall I fear? Hashem is the stronghold of my life; of whom shall I be afraid? When evildoers press against me to eat up my flesh - my enemies and my foes - it is they who stumble and fall. Even though an army were arrayed against me, my heart would not fear; though war should arise against me, still would I be confident. One thing I ask from Hashem, one thing I desire - that I may dwell in the house of Hashem all the days of my life, to behold the pleasantness of Hashem, and to meditate in His sanctuary. Surely, He will hide me within His own tabernacle in the day of distress; He will conceal me in the shelter of his tent; He will set me safe upon a rock. Thus, my head shall be high above all my foes around me; I will offer sacrifices within His tabernacle to the sound of trumpets; I will sing and chant praises to Hashem. Hear, Hashem, my voice when I call; be gracious to me and answer me. In Your behalf my heart has said: "Seek you My presence;" Your presence, Hashem, I do seek. Hide not Your face from me; turn not Your servant away in anger; You have been my help; do not abandon me, forsake me not, 0 G-d my Savior. Though my father and mother have forsaken me, Hashem will take care of me. Teach me Your

way, Hashem, and guide me in a straight path, in spite of my enemies. Deliver me not to the will of my adversaries; for false witnesses have risen up against me, such as breathe forth violence. I do believe I shall yet see the goodness of Hashem in the land of the living. Hope in Hashem; be strong, and let your heart be brave; yes, hope in Hashem.

This is not rocket science. It is so simple to evaluate that when we are in times of peril, as we are now; in time of war, as it seems imminent now; in times of great danger from our enemies, as it is now, the only relief, the only protection that is available is from Hashem. This Psalm is read every year, but it has never seemed as urgent as this year.

I have mentioned that I believe war will come, but that Hashem will say: "Enough" and completely control the situation by what we like to call "natural disasters." There is so much instability on this Earth for potential earthquakes (with possible tsunamis), hurricanes, tornadoes, flooding, volcano eruptions, etc, etc, etc, that it may be another sign of the way Hashem will, measure for measure clean up the evil of the world. It says above that it is "they who stumble and fall" and Hashem knows each of us exactly where we stand in following Hashem's ways. Even atheists will have an opportunity to be scared enough from pending war to change their nonsensical ways – after all "there are no atheists in foxholes." Also, I believe "there are no atheists in storm cellars."

Time is running out. Be as skeptical and as stubborn as you want; but, when the time comes, know that "I do believe I shall yet see the goodness of Hashem in the land of the living. Hope in Hashem; be strong, and let your heart be brave; yes, hope in Hashem." It is the only instructions you will need to survive.

3.26 Happy Wednesday

Our daily Morning Prayer service (Shacharis) includes a particular Psalm designated for that day of the week. I have mentioned how Psalms give us guidance in solving many of life's problems and also are very prophetic. The Psalm we say on Yom Revi'i, Wednesday, Psalm 94:1 to 95:3 provide insight into the situation that plagues this world these days. Read the Psalm carefully (copied from the Artscroll daily Siddur) and understand the connection it has with our present situation. Hashem is talking to us and giving us more valuable guidance:

Today is the fourth day of the Sabbath, on which the Levites would recite in the Holy Temple:

O G-d of vengeance, Hashem; O G-d of vengeance, appear! Arise, O Judge of the earth, render recompense to the haughty. How long shall the wicked - O Hashem - how long shall the wicked exult? They speak freely, they utter malicious falsehood, they glorify themselves, all workers of iniquity. Your nation, Hashem, they crush, and they afflict Your heritage. The widow and the stranger they slay, and the orphans they murder. And they say, 'G-d will not see, nor will the G-d of Jacob understand.' Understand, you boors among the people; and you fools, when will you gain wisdom? He Who implants the ear, shall He not hear? He Who fashions the eye, shall He not see? He Who chastises nations, shall He not rebuke? - He Who teaches man knowledge. Hashem knows the thoughts of man, that they are futile. Praiseworthy is the man whom G-d disciplines, and whom You teach from Your Torah. To give him rest from the days of evil, until a pit is dug for the wicked. For Hashem will not cast off His people, nor will He forsake His heritage. For justice shall revert to righteousness, and following it will be all of upright heart. Who will rise up for me against evildoers? Who will stand up for me against the workers of iniquity? Had Hashem not been a help to me, my soul would soon have dwelt in silence. If I said, 'My foot falters,' Your kindness, Hashem, supported me. When my forebodings were abundant within me, Your comforts cheered my soul. Can the throne of destruction be associated with You? - those who fashion evil into a way of life. They join together against the soul of the righteous, and the blood of the innocent they condemn. Then Hashem became a stronghold for me, and my G-d, the Rock of my refuge. He turned upon them their own violence, and with their own evil He will cut them off, Hashem, our G-d, will cut them off. Come - let us sing to Hashem, let us call out to the Rock of our salvation. Let us greet Him with thanksgiving, with praiseful songs let us call out to Him. For a great G-d is Hashem, and a great King above all heavenly powers.

This reading of the day can basically be broken down into three parts. One is to establish that Hashem is everything. There is nothing in this world that isn't without Hashem's involvement. Everything that is heard, seen, every rebuke, every thought is all Hashem in partnership with us. When people ask "where is Hashem?" they are oblivious to Hashem's plan, how He lets us do things according to our own free will and how in the end Hashem's will is the final answer. And, it is all good news for us.

Second, is knowing that all is for the purpose of **Tikun HaOlam**, the correction, rectification, perfection of the world. We may question why all these evil events are happening in the world, and even the hint that the righteous are suffering and the wicked seem to be thriving. It is all for the purpose of helping us and guiding us towards Hashem. When things go well we tend to say arrogantly: "Me, me, me! I did it all," and tend to take Hashem out of the picture. When problem arise, we seem to turn to Hashem and ask for help. Now in the end of days, it is the "ask for help phase of history." A quote in the Siddur gives an interesting commentary on the words *"Praiseworthy is the man."* The wicked ask why the righteous suffer, if G-d truly controls everything. The psalmist answers that G-d afflicts the righteous only when it is to their benefit, to correct them, to make them realize the futility of physical pleasures, or to atone for their sins *(Radak;Meiri)*.

Third, is the reassurance that in the end 'Hashem will turn upon the evil ones their own violence, and with their own evil He will cut them off.' All that is going on today within many countries, terrorist groups, evil governments with evil leaders, etc all seem to be leading up to the final Tikun. A reminder of what Rav Nir Ben Artzi, Shlita, and the Facilitated Communications individuals have been telling us that the world is in chaos, but the craziness is continuing to increase. Hopefully by the time you are reading this, the Tikun has occurred and the world is at peace.

Finally, 'Come - let us sing to Hashem, let us call out to the Rock of our salvation. Let us greet Him with thanksgiving, with praiseful songs let us call out to Him. For a great G-d is Hashem, and a great King above all heavenly powers.' That is the happy ending to history of which I have talked. It will be shared by all the righteous of the world.

How close are we to that happy ending? There are many indications from Bible and the Rabbis that the final war, if it unfortunately happens, will be a very short one, since Hashem will take over with so-called "Acts of G-d." I have even seen predictions of Iran experiencing great earthquakes to solve the nuclear problem and end the conflict with them. As the Psalm says "He turned upon them their own violence, and with their own evil He will cut them off, Hashem, our G-d, will cut them off. Natural disasters are very effective in cutting off an evil force and even ending a war. Are we that close? Hopefully, this is the happy ending looming and the benefits that go along with it.

There is another Messiah. His name is Messiah son of Joseph. He will be the one responsible for the ingathering of the exile from the four corners of the world. Are we close? Have you packed yet?

I have to admit a personal agenda that I have in including this Psalm in this book. I have mentioned how reciting Psalms is so advantageous to the individual reciting them and for all the people of the world. Psalms can solve many of life's problem – they can heal the sick, help you with finding a marriage partner, help with financial problems, protect you in a dangerous situation, etc, etc, etc. Reciting the Psalm above is not just for information, but can help lessen the burden from the evil ones and the trauma they are putting on this world. And, it can bring our salvation faster.

My agenda? By discussing this very pertinent group of Psalm verses, I sneakily got you to recite a Psalm that they may not have done otherwise. If I did get you to say verses that you would not have said, then the only thing I can answer with is "You're welcome." One additional suggestion is not to just read the Psalm, but to internalize its message. Your soul needs it. It's good for you and it is good for everyone around you and I was glad to help. If you can get into a regular habit of saying Psalms and even praying every day, then I know you will someday say to me, maybe even in person when you come home to Israel, "Thank you." If I introduced several of you to some of the most powerful tools you have in life to succeed, I am happy, you will be happy and above all, Hashem will love it.

"You're welcome!!!!!"

3.27 Sometimes a Child's Insight is Better

I recently received a story on Email about a child's view of a thunderstorm (posted by Goanna2). When you read this, you will never think of thunderstorms the same way again.

A little girl walked to and from school daily. Though the weather that morning was questionable and clouds were forming, she made her daily

236

trek to school. As the afternoon progressed, the winds whipped up, along with lightning.

The mother of the little girl felt concerned that her daughter would be frightened as she walked home from school. She also feared the electrical storm might harm her child.

Full of concern, the mother got into her car and quickly drove along the route to her child's school. As she did, she saw her little girl walking along.

At each flash of lightning, the child would stop, look up, and smiled. More lightning followed quickly and with each, the little girl would look at the streak of light and smiled.

When the mother drove up beside the child, she lowered the window and called, "What are you doing?"

The child answered, "I am trying to look pretty because G-d keeps taking my picture."

I thought this was so cute; but then realized, wouldn't life be much simpler and less stressful if we could view it as a child? Instead of being uptight about everything, just have complete faith that Hashem is there, loves us and wants to help us through every situation, even take our picture.

When you have Hashem in your life, you feel His protection and do not fear the world. Scriptures tells us not to put ourselves in danger – it is like you are testing Hashem and you will fail. But, if you find yourself in a dangerous situation, and turn to Hashem for help, you will not come to harm.

Remember my friend who accidentally strayed into an Arab village. Simply turning to Hashem and an event that was a certain calamity becomes a miraculous happy ending.

There are so many stories like this including miraculous stories about 911 where people turned to Hashem and survived. I know several people who experienced such miracles.

There is one last word about putting oneself in danger that is a little more subtle. We were put on this physical world to serve Hashem by doing the mitzvot and perfecting ourselves. Hashem gave us a body to accomplish these physical tasks and told us to take care of this body. That means that we are obligated by Torah to eat properly, exercise, get proper sleep, etc. If we violate our own physical needs, we put ourselves in danger. The level of obesity in the US of A, as an example, is a great Torah violation. The overall life expectancy of Americans is down. It is about 78 to 79 years of age and ranks about 36 in the world (several organizations have done a review with variations). Israel, where the average Israeli is thin, eats better and more physically active, is ranked number about 14 with an average age of 82. I know it is due mostly to the fast food establishments in the US of A that are much more interested in profits for their stockholders than the welfare of their customers. Laziness is also involved. If you want something at a store one block away, why are you driving there? Couch potato is a very prevalent way of life (I haven't figured out whether the person is being compared to a potato or a couch).

Hashem watches everything we do. The protection that He gives us is measure for measure what we deserve. Subtle or not – danger is danger, and Hashem notes it all, and rewards or punishes it all. Part of doing repentance is evaluating every aspect of our lives, even the subtle events. But, repentance does include change – making corrections.

3.28 Summary of Part 3

In Part 3 of this book I tried to spell out "what the Absolute Truth means to us" and what we must do to reap its benefits.

They say the "Ignorance is bliss." I say that ignorance is dangerous. Learning the absolute truth is a start, but living the absolute truth is the only prudent way to thrive and reap the absolute best happy ending – coming soon, and continuing forever.

Part 4 - What is happening in the world and what is coming up?

4.1 Jew-Hatred

Although very misunderstood, a great increase in Jew-hatred around the world is actually an indication of the end of days. First of all, let me correct a misnomer seen every day in the world. The term anti-Semitism has become synonymous with Jew-hatred. The term was popularized in Germany in 1873 as a scientific-sounding term for *Judenhass* ("Jew-hatred"), although it had been used for at least two decades prior. The term started to tone down the harsh term Jew-hatred, after all we wouldn't want to offend such evil people.

From the scriptural genealogical record comes some of the most well-known terms relating to Israelite people: "Semite and Semitic" originate from Noah's son Shem. The Shemites are all the descendants of Shem, but a more modern term is Semite. The misnomer of Shem's descendants includes all Arabs and even other cultures. The Mayan culture, as an example, which made news in 2012 due to their calendar and prophecies, dwelled on the Yucatan Peninsula. Yucatan is an improper pronunciation of Yoktan who was a descendant of Shem. This gives us the possibility of the Mayan culture stemming from Shem making them decedents of Shemites.

Anyway, what really is Jew-hatred? There are facts that need to be clarified first. One is that the Jewish people were designated by Hashem as Am Segulah. Although the world translates Am Segulah as the Chosen People, it is more properly translated as the "nation of the remedy." When Hashem told the Jews through the prophet Isaiah (49:6) "To be a light unto the nations," He was tasking the Jews, who would be spread throughout the world, to bring the message of Hashem to the world. That message, the instructions from the Owner of the world, is the remedy for the world's problems. The message, however, has been greatly rejected by the people of the world – they are not interested in carrying out the will of Hashem, but doing their own thing, no matter how evil or dangerous it may be. It is the biggest reason the world is in so much trouble today. The problem is "if you can't kill the message, kill the messenger." Jew-hatred in essence is the world fighting Hashem and His word, but the Jews are the scapegoat since Hashem is not touchable.

This has gone on for thousands of years, but now it has increased greatly for another reason. The work of the Jewish nation is basically finished. It is time for the Jews to return to their ancestral homeland. Many Jews, however, are stubborn and think they will remain comfortable outside of Israel. Hashem is sending a strong message to the Jews worldwide. The economy, the political situation, the threat of war and, above all, the Jew-hatred is telling the world Jewry it is no longer possible to continue outside of Israel, come home. Israel is the only safe place in the world for a Jew (even with occasional conflict occurring in very isolated areas, it is far safer on the streets of Jerusalem than the streets of any other city in the world. Google statistics of homicides in major cities and see for yourself.

If you are worried about terrorism, Google that too and be amazed. If you think I shouldn't compare homicides to terrorist activity, then you are greatly mistaken – dead is dead, what difference does it make if it was a terrorist or a mugger? It is clearly stated in many places throughout scriptures that the Jews have the mission to be in every corner of the globe, spread the word of Torah and then return home after the mission is accomplished. Being the end of history as we know it, it is time to come home – the message has been spread, our job is done (whether the world wants it or not).

If the Jews have performed well in completing their mission to save the world and help the people, why has our history been so replete with suffering? Wouldn't one think that Hashem would make it easy to do His will? The answer is very complicated and well covered in scriptures, but was already covered when we discussed assimilation and secularism. Simply put, Hashem said "if you follow My ways, you will be protected." Just be aware that the greatest miracle of the history of this world is that the Jews are still here. As mentioned the Torah says "you will remain small in number, but will never disappear." That prophecy, told to Moses 3327 years ago. We have witnessed its fulfillment; and, it is a testimonial to the fact that the Torah truly is the word of Hashem.

We see every day that Jew-hatred is greatly increasing worldwide. I saw recently that many incidents of Jew-hatred are not even reported and very few make the news. Therefore, the numbers are much worse than we know. The way the conflict around Gaza is being depicted in the news has nothing to do with reality, but everything to do with Hashem's message: "It is time for the Jews to come home."

When the theme of the news is that the poor downtrodden people of Gaza were horribly invaded by Israel and responded with some rockets. That is beyond lies; it is pure Jew-hatred, pure evil. I sent the following answer to an article written about the horrors of Gaza and "the Israeli terrorism," as they like to call it.

The article forgot to mention that Hamas has sent over 750 missiles, rockets and mortar shells into Israel at civilians (that is non-military men, women and children), always before Israel started its defensive reaction. The world doesn't think Israel is allowed to defend itself. Gaza has fired over 15,000 rockets and mortar shells over the years and we are supposed to just take it and not retaliate? Israel is so careful to not hurt civilians; but, the barbaric Arab terrorists shoot off their deadly rockets from the middle of civilian populations. When you use children as shields, who are the bad guys here?

Gaza is lacking nothing except decent leadership. Their beautiful new shopping malls are well stocked; their beautiful water slide park did a great business last summer and their tremendous luxury hotels make it the perfect vacation spot (unless you are non-Muslim). Did you know that Gaza has about 600 millionaires? What, the Jew-hating media never mentioned that? People in all the other Arab countries don't have it as good as the Gazan Arabs. By the way, Arabs kill more Arabs than Jews ever did. The Islamists don't want the land of Israel, they have repeated over and over they only want all non-Islamists dead — "first the Saturday people, then the Sunday people," is the popular expression (but only in Arabic). Americans and Europeans don't have a clue as to how important it is to their safety that Israel wipes out terrorist groups. If you don't believe that, you will soon. They say that "Ignorance is bliss, but I say it is very dangerous.

Also, according to international law and Biblical law (you remember – G-D), all the land from the Jordan River to the Mediterranean Sea is Israel (including Gaza), which has existed for about 3700 years and does not belong to Arabs. The renaming it as Palestine was done by some evil Roman 2000 years ago but it was never a legitimate name – never a sovereign nation. Did you know that before 1948 all Palestinians were Jews? When the terrorist organization, the PLO, rewrote history in 1964

241

and decided that the Arabs were the Palestinians, it was all a lie, but the Jew-hating media loved it. The time of truth is coming soon.

This comment never showed up until after the news article was eliminated and archived. The article appeared on my computer with a statement "the comment will appear after moderator review." It is comical but, once again a very deep message. The world does not want Hashem's message and can only fight it by suppressing and hating the messenger. I say to you, my fellow messenger deliverers (as I ended my comment): "The time of truth is coming soon." Don't get wrapped up in the minutia of the world's lies – it is totally unimportant. The only reason I wrote the comment is that I knew there were Jews and righteous non-Jews who believe the filth that is in the news. The number of self-hating Jews in the world has greatly increased since they believe the lies and want to distance themselves from reality and, unfortunately, Hashem. I am always trying to reach the good people and give them the truth. I know with complete confidence that Hashem measure for measure will take care of the evil people of this world – I am not interested in helping them; but, I feel bad if they convince good people to believe their Lashon Harah and join their cause.

There is so much more that I could say about what is going on. I think my favorite article was that Israel sent 100 rockets into Gaza. Israel doesn't send rockets. So, what was the meaning of this article? There were about 100 rockets that were fired off by Hamas that went astray and landed in Gaza. They blamed Israel for it. Cute?

The most important message I wish to convey is that we all have some Jew-hatred in us. Since Jew-hatred is nothing more than rebellion against Hashem. If we are not doing all that Hashem wants from us to survive and thrive, we are lacking in serving Him and rebelling against His will. If we say that what I am doing is good enough, we are rebelling. If we go by our own flawed human logic instead of studying Hashem's logic, we are rebelling. None of this may look like Jew-hatred on the surface, but Hashem will answer our rebelliousness with people turning on us – both as a nation and as individuals. In the end we are still responsible measure for measure for ourselves. It is so important to read Hashem's messages and to react. If we, as individuals, experience Jew hatred, please, please, please, look in the mirror and evaluate who you see, based on the message received. When you catch on to the system, you will thank Hashem and realize how much He is trying to help you. Thank you Hashem.

One last message that I have already said, but I still get comments about. The turmoil that is happening in Israel now is so isolated, that Israel is still the safest place (the only safe place for a Jew) in the world. Somebody wrote to me and said that even Jerusalem is under attack. The fact is there was one rocket that went in the direction of Jerusalem but was nowhere near the city. The sirens went off, but it was a false alarm (literally).

Let me tell you something comical about Israel. Biblical Israel is basically Samaria and Judea with Jerusalem right in the middle. The terrorists renamed this area "the West Bank (the world loved the new name)." Actually it was Hashem that provided this scenario. Because there are Arab towns dispersed in the area, no terrorist group would ever send a rocket into this area. Hashem protects His most valuable land and people (this is where the most observant people live) by putting the enemy here out of harm's way. An example of this is that the Temple Mount is completely off limits to Jews. Why? Because Hashem told us that during this time of great impurity amongst our people, we cannot desecrate the holiest land in the universe by ascending to its ground. So Hashem provided us with enemy to keep us away and out of spiritual danger. When we receive the Third Temple, we will regain entrance and the Arabs will be gone.

In all the wars, there has never been a rocket or mortar attack in this area because the Arabs know that if they send something our way, Hashem will make sure it lands in an Arab town (or hit the mosque on the Temple Mount). It holds true even outside of this area. During the war with terrorist groups in southern Lebanon, many rockets were thrown at Israel's northern area where there are many Arab towns. There were more Arabs killed by these missiles than Jews.

The 39 Scud missiles that were thrown at Israel in the Gulf war were all in the Tel Aviv to Haifa area (miraculously only one death occurred – a Jew hater). There were no Scuds anywhere near Biblical Israel. Because the roads were all closed that week, the Gulf war is on record as the one week in modern Israel's history with the least amount of fatalities – one. Only in Israel does a war keep the people safe. Why do you think the secular left parties in Israel want to give away the so-called West Bank? Remember that Jew-hatred is fighting Hashem and His message. Get it?

4.2 Who Owns This land?

There is no more controversial land in the world than the land of Israel. Wars have been fought over it and, for some strange reason, this country, the size of the state of New Jersey, is in the news and on the agenda of many governments and the United Nations, more than any other country in the world (except, perhaps, for the US of A). Why?

The answer has a similar connotation to the topic of Jew-hatred. Who is the real owner of the land? HASHEM!!!!!!!!!!!! Of course, He owns the entire universe, so the Land of Israel is on the same deed. But, what did the Owner say about the land. Also, in all fairness to the world – especially those who don't go by the word of this Owner, what does international law say about this land?

Israel was the name given to Jacob after he fought the angel (Genesis 32:25-30). The country was named the Land of Israel meaning that Hashem told Jacob, or Israel, that this land belongs to his descendants.

Of course, this was the same message that was given to Jacob's father, Isaac and his grandfather, Abraham. Later it was told to Moses and all the Israelites (called as such since they were the descendants of Israel). The Jews or as they were referred to in the time of Abraham, the Hebrews, have dwelled in this land for over 3700 years. Even with two exiles, which were accompanied by the destruction of the Temples, there has always been a Jewish presence in the land of Israel. There is no doubt that biblically, the Land of Israel belongs to the Jews.

We are told in the Bible that when the Jews return to their homeland, the land will miraculously start to produce. This land had remained desolate for close to 2000 years. After 1948 this totally useless land that many cultures unsuccessfully tried to cultivate, became some of the most fertile producing farmland in the world. Hundreds of millions of trees have been planted since 1948 and Israel in present time exports produce in great quantity. They even designated the area where the Jews live "the green line" since the areas where non-Jews live is still not fertile and still remains desert. This is a strong message from Hashem that His people are returning and this is the end of history, as we know it.

This is a miraculous proof from Hashem that the Green Line, where the Jews presently live, matches the area told to Moses 3327 years ago. The satellite picture on the left shows where the Jews live, and the map on the right, from the

Artscroll Stone Edition of the Chumash (The Five Books of Moses), is the area designated by Hashem for the Israelites. There is an area to the north that is not presently inhabited by Jews, but will be in the near future:

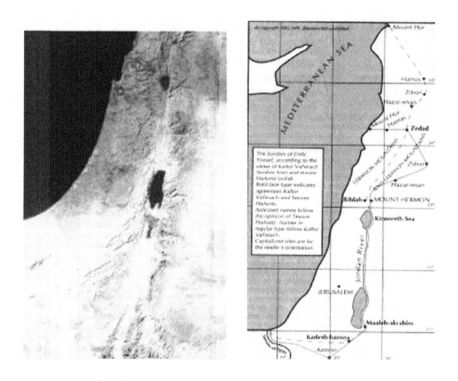

Let's talk international law.

With the second exile in the year 68, some crazy Roman renamed the country Palestine (mostly because he couldn't pronoun Philistine). Even in the almost two thousand years, that the country was called Palestine, there was still a presence by its designated owner, the Jews. Before 1948, the Palestinians were the Jews. I have neighbors who were born here before 1948 who joke about the fact that they were the real Palestinians. They became Israeli's when the country was once again named Israel. In 1964, with the forming of the Palestine Liberation Organization (a terrorist group), they started a very well organized propaganda campaign and pretended that the Arabs who live in Israel were the real Palestinians.

The British Mandate (in effect, British rule) of Palestine, including the Balfour Declaration, was confirmed by the League of Nations in 1922 at the San Remo conference. It came into effect by treaty in 1923. The boundaries of Palestine were drawn by the British and included modern Jordan, which was called Trans-Jordanian Palestine (you mean there is a Palestine that exists today that is much bigger than Israel?). The declaration included the wording "His Majesty's government view with favor the establishment in Palestine of a national home for the Jewish people.

This eventually led to the establishment of the State of Israel in 1948 by the newly formed United Nations. The problem was that the UN took away 82% of the land designated for the Jews including most of the area that was biblical Israel. It was well known that the United States State Department advised the then President Harry Truman to sign in favor of the Jewish state, but only because the US was convinced that 4 mighty Arab armies would obliterate this new nation. How noble of the US and many other Jew-hating countries who thought they had the next final solution. Hashem had other plans. To this day the US military will never teach the tactics of the Israeli army used in the 1948 war since miracles aren't part of military tactical training. Israel had no usable effective army, no armament with which to fight and only One top General to lead them – Hashem. I guarantee that Israel in every conflict that followed (1956, 1967, 1973, 1982, 1991, 2006, and all the terrorist attacks in between) was not as mighty as they thought and had to rely on great miracles to experience the success they enjoyed.

So what does it mean when you see in the news how Israel is constantly trying to occupy Arab land? It is the most effective propaganda from terrorist groups and has the complete support of the Jew-hating media and Jew hating-nations of the world. All of the land from the Jordan River to the Mediterranean Sea is Israel. The only way that land can be given to someone else is by a legal treaty such as the treaty that resulted from the San Remo Conference, 1920. That treaty officially by international law gave the Land of Palestine back to its owners, the Jews. The UN resolution of 1947, the Oslo Accord of 1993 and any other bogus agreements to give the land away are not legal by international law – it can only be accomplished with a treaty. Another consideration is that any country that is attacked and wins territory in that war, keeps it. Why does Israel have to give back land to Arab terrorist organizations after Israel won the war – land that belongs to the Jews in the first place?

The Arabs of the Middle East have about 650 times the amount of land that the Jews have. If we talk about Islamic countries, we increase to over 1000 times the land area that the Jews have. The Jews are in great shortage of land, the Arabs are not. What is even worse is that the Arabs don't even want the land. When we hear speeches in English they talk of the horrors of the Jews stealing their land. When they talk in Arabic (in their mosques, for instance) they tell their true agenda – we want all the Jews dead. What is even sadder is they say "first the Saturday people, then the Sunday people." In other words the bottom line is to kill all the infidels and make the entire planet Islamic. They are making great strides since the Jew-hating world supports their efforts even though it would mean the demise of all non-Jewish nations. I wish Israel's propaganda was that good!!!!!

All this is prophesied in the Torah. In the book of Deuteronomy 32:21:

> "They have moved Me to jealousy with that which is not G-d, they have provoked Me to anger with their vanities; and I will move them to jealousy with those which are a non-people; I will provoke them to anger with a foolish, senseless nation."

Hashem is telling us that when we are not doing His will (since Israel is being run by a secular government that does a lot of improper things), He will provoke us with a vile people who are not represented by a sovereign nation, but, as in this case a bunch of terrorists pretending to be a government.

There is an organization that wrote an article in their magazine several years ago. They said "We know the land belongs to you, but as long as you fear people more than you fear G-d, you do not deserve the land." Who said such a truism? It appeared in the first addition of the new Al Qaeda magazine. Our enemy knows more about our mistakes than we do, since Hashem uses them to bring us around to what we are supposed to be doing in this world.

It is interesting to note that Jerusalem, the so-called third holiest city to Islam, is not even mentioned in the Koran – that's right, zero times you will find Jerusalem. However, it does say in the Koran that the land promised to Moses is for the Jews – all of it.

Mohammed was honest and acknowledged the special relationship of the Jewish people with G-d and the land He gave them. It says in the Koran:

[Sura 5:20] Recall that Moses said to his people (the Jews), "O my people, remember G-D's blessings upon you: He appointed prophets from among you, made you kings, and granted you what He never granted any other people."

[Sura 5:21] "O my people, enter the holy land (Israel) that G-D has decreed for you, and do not rebel, lest you become losers."

Later in the Koran, in order to make it clear and leave no doubts that the Jewish G-d had given ownership of the land to the Jews, Mohammed took additional time to repeat the writing of the Torah in Sura 7 about the Jews and Moses:

[Sura 7:137] "We let the oppressed people inherit the land, east and west, and we blessed it. The blessed commands of your L-rd were thus fulfilled for the Children of Israel, to reward them for their steadfastness, and we annihilated the works of Pharaoh and his people and everything they harvested."

[Sura 7:144] He said, "O Moses, I have chosen you (the Jews), out of all the people, with My messages and by speaking to you. Therefore, take what I have given you and be appreciative."

Wouldn't it be nice if the world knew the Absolute Truth, including all the Jews?

4.3 So, When is Moshiach Going to be Announced?

Note: From here on we will use the term Moshiach for the Messiah. Additionally, hopefully by the time you read this section the Moshiach will already have been introduced to the world and you can skip this section.

First, I have two questions.

1. Don't most people, Jews and non-Jews alike, believe that we are close?

2. Is he going to be a little baby or an adult?

248

If you answered yes to number one and adult to number two, then you have just admitted that the Moshiach is already here and just hasn't been introduced, yet. The fact is *"The Moshiach is alive and well and is living in Jerusalem."* What is my proof, you ask? The list of signs and proofs are longer than I could cover in this book, but I will give you my sources and you decide.

I could write books on each subject, or I can just point you to hundreds of books that I have already devoured that prove that we are there. Each of the sources deserves its own book, but hopefully I will touch upon many of them briefly. The best that I can do is to tell you some of the most compelling facts (some of my personal favorites that give me the most chills) and let you check out the rest.

We have lists of events that will happen before Moshiach comes. The sources that I am talking about include the Torah (prophecies fulfilled), the remainder of the Bible (prophecies fulfilled), the Talmud (prophecies fulfilled), the Zohar (prophecies fulfilled), commentary by many great righteous people throughout history (prophecies fulfilled), the Autistics and others using Facilitated Communication (prophecies fulfilled), the mystical Rabbis (prophecies fulfilled), scientific discoveries (that's a good one), hidden codes, numerology, secrets of the Hebrew letters, the 600,000 ways that facts are encoded in everything, hints in our daily prayers, everything happening in the world (especially the weather and natural disasters), people's attitudes (much more important than one would think), everything occurring in the news and much more (I think this is a run-on sentence, but you get the point). So what? If I have all these sources and happenings, what does it mean? The exciting answer is "all of them already have occurred or are happening as we NOW!!!

One of the first impressive indications that I received was from the Elder Kabbalist Rav Yitzhak Kaduri ZTVK"L. The Rav received blessings from his Rabbi, the *Ben Ish Chai* (Rabbi Yosef Chaim of Baghdad) in 1908, who told him three predictions. 1. You will live to a very old age – Rav Kaduri lived to about 113 (exact age not known), 2. You will never wear glasses – the Rav never wore glasses, and 3. That he would meet the Moshiach – on 9 Cheshvan 5764, 4 November 2003, Rav Kaduri met and interviewed Moshiach ben David. In 1990 the Lubavitcher Rebbe (Rabbi Menachem Mendel Schneerson) also told Rav Kaduri he would meet the Moshiach.

After his death in 2006, it was disclosed that Rav Kaduri left a note with his son that had the name of the Moshiach encoded in its letters. A few years hence, the note was shown to the public. The name was of a high level of encryption that only certain Tzadikim would be able to decipher the name. What was comical was that someone made changes to the note and came up with proof that JC was the name. The changes were not legit, since it changed the Hebrew to words that don't make any sense, and added a letter that was totally different from the hand writing of Rav Kaduri (the letter appears 6 times in the note). An obvious deception, but it convinced many uneducated people of the fraudulent attempt.

The next verification that I personally had, of the meeting between Rav Kaduri and the Moshiach, came from a neighbor of mine who happened to be a student of Rav Kaduri for 15 years and heard from the Rav directly of the event. Of course, it also made the news in Israel at the time.

4.4 Prophecy Being Fulfilled

I have mentioned that being in the end of days (the end of history before the Moshiach is announced) means that we know that all prophecies have either been fulfilled or in the process of being fulfilled. One such prophecy that is happening in an obvious manner is found in the last of the prophets, Malachi. It is spooky when the prophet tells us what we will be our complaints in the end of days and then we see it happening.

First I will state the verses from Malachi Chapter 3, with my commentary on the meaning of each verse in brackets. The fulfilment is alluded to in my commentary.

13. "Still harder did your words strike Me," says the L-rd, but you say, "What have we spoken against You?" [Hashem is stating that we are complaining]
14. You have said, "It is futile to serve G-d, and what profit do we get for keeping His charge and for going about in anxious worry because of the L-rd of Hosts?" [Why should we serve Hashem and keep the commandments?]
15. And now we praise the bold transgressors. Yea, those who work wickedness are built up. Yea, they tempt G-d, and they have, nevertheless, escaped. [Especially when we see the wicked people going against Hashem, thriving and getting away with it]

250

16. Then the G-d-fearing men spoke to one another, and the L-rd hearkened and heard it. And a book of remembrance was written before Him for those who feared the L-rd and for those who valued His name highly. [Hashem is totally aware of the complaint of the righteous people who are trying to do His will. This is so much happening now – kvetch, kvetch, kvetch]

17. And they shall be Mine, says the L-rd of Hosts, for that day when I make a treasure. And I will have compassion on them as a man has compassion on his son who serves him. [We are receiving the final, difficult testing before the end. But the time of Hashem helping us and ending our difficulties is here]

18. And you shall return and discern between the righteous and the wicked, between him who serves G-d and him who has not served Him. [For Hashem is noting that even though it looks very unfair, who amongst us will still have faith and trust in Hashem and still will continue to serve Him. He truly knows His faithful followers and will take care of them]

19. For lo, the sun comes, glowing like a furnace, and all the audacious sinners and all the perpetrators of wickedness will be stubble. And the sun that comes shall burn them up so that it will leave them neither root nor branch, says the L-rd of Hosts. [When the test is over in the near future, justice will prevail and the situation will completely reverse. Those who defied Hashem will be destroyed before our very eyes (I'm talking to you good people who follow Hashem).]

20. And the sun of mercy shall rise with healing in its wings for you who fear My Name. Then will you go forth and be fat as fatted calves. [Then all the righteous will thrive and be in want of nothing]

21. And you shall crush the wicked, for they will be as ash under the soles of your feet on the day that I will prepare, says the L-rd of Hosts. [The wicked with be like dust under our feet instead of the present situation that the wicked are subjugating the righteous – it will be our turn]

22. Keep in remembrance the teaching of Moses, My servant - the laws and ordinances which I commanded him in Horeb for all Israel. [We are being told not to waver from the commandments]

23. Lo, I will send you Elijah the prophet before the coming of the great and awesome day of the L-rd, [the Moshiach will be introduced by Elijah the prophet before the "too late date"]

24. that he may turn the heart of the fathers back through the children, and the heart of the children back through their fathers - lest I come and smite

the earth with utter destruction. [All will be corrected and great for the righteous but there will be (or should we say that there is now) great upheaval on the Earth that will be dangerous to the evil ones]

A fascinating yet not so obvious phenomenon that is happening these days is that the sun is with much higher activity that is causing increased radiation levels on Earth. It says in scriptures that in the end of days Hashem will unsheathe the sun to cause such a phenomenon. But, the effect to the people on Earth is that some people will suffer from this, while others will receive benefit and increased energy levels (that is already happening today).

One of the events demonstrating an increased energy level was brought to our attention by a very unusual source. The Mayans said that at the end of their calendar, 21 December 2012, the Earth will be in direct alignment with the center of the Milky Way galaxy causing maximum energy levels to be experienced on Earth. The Mayans mention that this will have an effect on the people on Earth (in the same way that scriptures predicted). The Mayan prophecies were completely misunderstood, since the news constantly said that the Mayans predicted the end of the world, which they never did. They gave us very scientific changes that would happen and they were correct. The event was also the beginning of the change in energy level brought down in scriptures.

Measure for measure the wicked will suffer greatly and be destroyed and the righteous will survive and even thrive. Concepts to be gleaned from scriptures are that at the end of history as we know it: the testing will be finished, war and suffering will end, sickness will be no more and even death will be no more. The energy level increase will have the effect of healing the sick and actually changing our ability to avoid death. These events are beginning and will continue due to other scientific changes that are occurring with the Earth. The magnetic poles seem to be reversing – the axis seems to be changing. There are major events in land shifting causing a great increase in earthquakes and volcanoes. I have only given these big changes a cursory look and do not have all the details. The more important thought is that the prophecies of scriptures are happening.

We have already seen an example of this type of change on Earth causing energy levels to change. Before the great flood that happened in the year 1656 (2104 BCE), we are told that the Earth was not on the axis we experience today but was perpendicular to the direction of the sun. This means there were no seasons since the sun was always over the equator. Seasons came about after the flood (Genesis 8:22 alludes to the fact that there were no seasons during the flood and that it was established when the flood ended). Since all the people of the Earth lived in the central region not too far off of the equator, the sun's high energy level was experienced by everyone. That is why they lived 8 and 9 hundred years and never got sick. People died when a sneeze would occur (which is why to this day we say "bless you" since we sneeze and live to talk about it).

There was no aging process until Abraham requested it about 350 years later. Abraham complained to Hashem that he and his son Isaac looked the same age. People couldn't tell who the father was and who the son was. Hashem obliged. And, gray hair and wrinkles (and some other things) came to be. Adam who lived 930 years probably looked like a man of 20 or 30.

After we have the redemption and the Moshiach is introduced, these things will return along with the resurrection of the dead. We don't know how immediately this will occur, but it will occur. We are told that the miracles in the end of days will be greater than when we left Egypt. When we see scientific phenomena that could bring it about, we get a very confident feeling about the prophecies in scriptures. More so, we should feel that Hashem's instructions of our obligations to ourselves and loved ones should not be taken lightly. I have been saying all along it is our future and our eternal happiness that is at issue here. Don't gamble – the evidence is so overwhelming. At one time I used to present the idea of an observant life style to individuals or audiences and tell them to check it out and decide if this is for you. Now I tell people we have no choice. It is "do or die" (and die means with much suffering forever and ever). I don't see the idea of following the ways of Hashem as a choice anymore, but as a staunch requirement for survival.

4.5 The Obvious Signs of Moshiach

We have seen quite a lot of convincing bits of information that scream the obvious announcement of Moshiach being immanent. I thought I would give you a short list from one source in the Talmud (Tractate Sotah 49b). What follows is the actual translation from Artscroll of the Mishnah that states what to look for just prior to the coming of Moshiach and the notes that discuss sources and commentary of the event. I present this for your review and evaluation of the obvious signs that we have already experienced. I need not say any more – just read and decide for yourself what it means.

Mishnah

In the period which will precede the coming of *Moshiach,* [2] insolence will increase, and costs will soar. [3] The vine will yield its fruit yet wine will be dear [4] and the government will turn to heresy, [5] and there shall be no rebuke [6]. The erstwhile meeting place of sages will be [used] for harlotry [7] and the Galilee will be destroyed and the Galvan [8] desolated, and the people who dwell on the borders will wander about from town to town [9] but they will not be succored (Assisted in time of distress; provided with relief). And the wisdom of scribes [10] will decay [11] and those who dread sin will be despised [12] and **truth will be absent**. [13] Youths will blanch the faces of elders; [14] elders will stand in the presence of minors. [15] *The son derides his father; a daughter rises against her mother [and] a daughter-in-law against her mother-in-law; a man's enemies are the people* of *his household.* [16] The face of the generation is like the face of a dog; [17] a son is not abashed [in the presence] of his father. [18 pertains to the Hebrew not the English] Upon what, then, can we lean? Upon our Father in Heaven! [19]

NOTES:

2. Literally: with the heels of *Moshiach,* an expression borrowed from *Psalms* 89:52. The simile refers to the final period of Exile (Rashi), when *Moshiach* will not yet have come but signs of **his imminent arrival** will be discerned, as though his approaching footsteps were already audible.

Alternatively: *a heel,* the lowest extremity of the human body, may be used as a synonym for *end* (see *Ramban* to *Deuteronomy 7:12),* so that the wording used simply denotes *the end of* [the period which will usher in] *Moshiach* (see *Rashi* to *Sanhedrin* 97a and to *Psalms* ibid.).

According to *Radak* to *Psalms* (ibid.), the wording used may mean: *while Moshiach delays.*

3. *Taanis* 7b lists insolence and desistance from Torah study among those sins which cause droughts [and resultant high prices]. The curse of inflation is therefore a direct consequence of two conditions enumerated earlier: the decline of scholarship until *scholars [are] like - schoolteachers,* and an *increase of insolence (lyun Yaakov).*

A parallel passage cited in *Sanhedrin* 97a *honor will be contorted;* people will not respect each other *(Rashi* ibid., first explanation).

4. For all will be engaged in drinking parties *(Rashi)*, so that even a plentiful supply of grapes will not suffice to fill the demand for wine (cf. *Rashi* to *Sanhedrin* ibid, first explanation).

5. The world's dominant power *(Meleches Shlomo)* will aid the spread of non-belief *(Tiferes Yisrael)*.

6. No man will be able to reproach another, because all men will be iniquitous. When a sinner is admonished, he will simply retort, "You are no better than I!" *(Rashi)* Alternatively: *and there shall be no proof* The bearers of truth will be unable to demonstrate the falsity of heretical views *(Zekukin D'Nura* to *Seder Eliyahu Zuta* Ch. 16).

7. In Tannaic times, *batei midrash* (study halls) were generally built outside the towns. With the decline of Torah study they fall into disuse, and their isolation makes them favored locations for illicit trysts *(Rashi)*. Alternatively: *There will be meeting places for harlotry.* Sinners will be so brazen that they will openly designate places of immorality *(Yad Ramah* to *Sanhedrin* ibid.).

8. The name of a place *(Rashi* to *Sanhedrin* ibid.). *Psalms* 83:8 mentions *Geval* among the lands that border Eretz Yisroel to the south. *Targum Yonasan* to *Genesis* 32:4 renders *the land of Seir* (Idumea, the northwest tip of Arabia, just southeast of Eretz Yisroel) as *Gavla;* similarly, *Targum Yonasan* to *Deuteronomy* 33:2; compare *Targum Yerushalmi* ibid. *Tosofos* to *Avodah Zarah* 59a, see also *Knrlxm HaEdah.*

9. [The borders will be attacked intermittently at various points, so that the inhabitants of border towns will be driven from town to town.] *Maharsha* to *Sanhedrin* ibid. suggests an alternative translation for: *the people of the provinces.* The term used is often applied to Eretz Yisroel outside of Jerusalem. [Thus, the northern and southern environs of Eretz Yisroel will be utterly barren, while the inhabitants remaining in the inland area will wander as exiles in their own Land.]

(I have heard Rabbis of today describing the devastation of the Galilee as the results of the many rockets that decimated the area during the 2006 war with Southern Lebanon and the discussion about the people of the border as everything that has transpired with Gaza – the disengagement of the people of Gush Katif, who to this day many still have not received help in relocating or compensation that was promised, and the continued firing of over 15,000 rockets and mortars on the border towns of Israel.)

10. A common designation for Torah scholars. See above, 15a; see *Kiddushin.* 30a.

11. From *Jeremiah* 49:7: *Counsel has been lost from the children; their wisdom has decayed.* Or: *will melt away* (see *Psalms* 58:8). A paraphrase of *Isaiah* 59:15: *And truth was absent.* As rendered by the *Targum* there: *Those who follow truth shall [be forced to] conceal themselves.* Truthful men will be compelled to flee the towns and subsist in small secluded groups *(Maharsha)*. They will shame them [publicly] *(Rashi* to *Sanhedrin* ibid.). Youths will demand honor from elders, a manifestation of the *increase of insolence (Rashi* ibid.). (I rest my case – it is difficult these days to tell the truth – not too many people want to hear it.)

16. The entire sentence is a verse in *Micah* (7:6), except that the verse begins with the preposition meaning *For the son...*

17. They will be shameless *(Rashi* to *Sanhedrin.* ibid., second explanation); *and the dogs are audacious (Isaiah* 56:11). Alternatively, *the face of the generation* refers to the affluent (see *Rashi* to *Genesis* 41:56), who will lack compassion and will refuse their destitute brethren charity, like dogs that refuse to share the meat they have scavenged *(Eitz Yosef)*.

Rabbi Elchanan Wasserman in *Kuntres Ikvos Meshicha* quotes an explanation heard from the *Chafetz Chaim. The face of the generation* are the leaders (see *Bereishis Rabbah* 79:6). A leader must guide his people authoritatively and teach them right from wrong. But in the period before *Moshiach*, the ostensible leaders will first check to see if their views will be popularly received, like a dog that looks back to see if his master follows. (You mean that they get elected by telling you whatever you want to hear and then forget their promises and do whatever they want? Their own hidden agenda for personal advantage.)

18. Some variants read *whom* instead of *what;* see *Dikduhei Soferim HaShalem.* (Strictly talking the Hebrew interpretation)

19. Following immediately upon the previously quoted verse from *Micah*, verse 8 reads: *But I put my hope in Hashem [and] await the G-d of my salvation; G-d shall hear me!*

As suggested by *Malbim's* explanation of *Psalms* 89:52, the Tanna's depiction of the final stage of Exile should be viewed not as a litany of woe, but rather as a consolation. When the ruin foretold befalls, and the triumph of iniquity appears assured, that shall signal the advent of the Moshiach.

This was only on small list of events from one source that will happen just before the Moshiach is introduced. It is a small sample from thousands of events that we have been told from the Bible, the Talmud, the Zohar, the Midrash, commentary from many, many Rabbis for thousands of years, etc, etc, etc. I presented this for your review since you should come away with the feeling that all of the above has happened (past tense).

Are there events that we have heard about that have not happened? Let me tell you just a couple, even though there are more (of course, by the time you read this, I may be describing history). One can see that even though these events were prophesied a long, long time ago, there are obvious signs that they are developing in the world and are imminent. Two examples:

From Link--- http://yahadoot.net/videoitem.asp?id=585
The Zohar says: that when the king of Damascus falls, Moshiach will come. The numerical value of the words: Melech Shel Damesek (the King of Damascus) = Bashar Assad

Plus the Yalkut Shemoni said: "Rabbi Yitzchak said: 'In the year in which the Moshiach-King appears, all the nations of the world are provoking each other. The King of Persia (Iran) provokes an Arab king and the Arab king turns to Edom (the US and Europe) for advice. And the King of Persia goes back and destroys the entire world. And all the nations of the world are in panic and distress and they fall upon their faces and are seized with pains like those of a woman giving birth, and Israel is in panic and distress and asking 'where shall we go? Where shall we go?' and Hashem says to them: "my sons do not fear; all that I have done, I have done only for you. Why are you afraid? Do not fear, your time of redemption has come, and the final redemption is not like the first redemption, because the first redemption was followed by sorrow and servitude under other kingdoms, but the final redemption is not followed by sorrow and servitude under other kingdoms."

There is the discussion in the Talmud (Yoma 10), where it talks about Edom (the US and its coalition) attacking Iran. The additional commentaries that we have seen recently hint to a possible war with Iran. Both these events: The fall of Assad in Syria and the attack on Iran are in the news every day and are even believed possibly to be imminent (or history).

In decades of reviewing scriptures to what is happening in the world, I have never seen such an obvious comparison and vast list of signs that we are there. Get ready and, of course, continue to prepare. I repeat myself but I am becoming more emphatic every day; the need to repent, pray, give charity, study Torah, help others, do mitzvot and completely turn to Hashem is of a great necessity for you and your loved ones. Time is running out.

4.6 A Very Interesting Quick Story (or Two)

A friend of the family called with some very interesting news. This person (no name allowed to avoid possible Lashon Harah) has been seeing a particular Rabbi, who is a Mystic, for advice (also, no name is permitted). The Rabbi has helped many people for years, by prescribing appropriate Psalms.

The Rabbi told our friend to continue just one chapter till the Moshiach comes. He said that since our friend was saying it to advance the process of Moshiach, he could share something about that topic. That's when he told this person that he had a conversation with Moshiach the day before. The Rabbi shared the info in order to be encouraging.

That is as much detail as I am permitted to say. I just wanted to pass this on. I was very excited to hear the tale, and can state that it came from a very good source (we have known this person for about twelve years – a very righteous and honest person).

Hearing this in conjunction with all the messages that we have been receiving from Rabbis, Mekubalim (Kabbalistic Rabbis) and the Facilitated Communications individuals, has made me feel very encouraged that we are there – the happy ending is imminent for those who want it, and also for those who are advancing the Geula process, B"H.

One last thought about children saying prophetic words (Bava Basra 12b). I have a granddaughter who when she was 4 year old she lived in Tzvat and went to school every day by a particular root that includes a particular set of steps. She told my daughter on several occasions "The Moshiach walked here," when they walk on those steps. I once saw a message from a great Rabbi who said he knows who the Moshiach is and even talked about the fact that he lives in Jerusalem. He also mentioned that Moshiach had traveled to Tzvat (for reasons more involved than required here). Out of the mouths of babes.

4.7 The Folding of History

What is the timing of events that are yet to happen? First, we must know that the entire time for all to happen – the length of history for this world is 6000 years. Not including the six days of creation, which took 15.34 billion years (already covered in The Age of the Universe). The 6000 years are broken up as 2000 years of chaos, 2000 years of Torah and 2000 years of Moshiach. The first 2K years took us up to the time when Abraham at age 52 started his outreach work to teach the world about monotheism – One G-d. He discovered that Hashem existed at age 3, but didn't really start his quest to bring the world to the same realization until later. This started the second 2000 years where the Torah would be studied and handed down to a newly formed nation at Mount Sinai in the year 2448. The Torah was actually conceived by Hashem 2000 years before the creation. That means the Torah is about 15,340,007,775 years old (my rough calculation). Any question as to what is the oldest text in the world?

The Oral Torah, the Talmud, which is a very detailed and complete explanation of the laws in the Torah, was passed down orally until the time of the Roman siege. The writing of the laws, or the Mishnah, was finished around the year 3950 (190 CE). The extensive discussion by the sages codifying the law, or as it is known the Gemara, was completed around the year 4260 (500 CE). The timing is very significant for a couple of reasons. There is a Gemara (Tractate Sanhedrin) that tells that the earliest time that the Moshiach can appear is the year 4250 (490 CE) about 500 years after you-know-who. We also are told that the information in the Talmud was only for the Jews, considering that it gets extensively into the 613 commandments that only Jews are obligated to fulfill. There is no coincidence that the information was handed down orally until after the time that the Christian religion and the church doctrine were established (after The First Council of Nicaea of 325). It was not for the world but only for the Jews. We see why the third 2000 years became the time of the Moshiach, from about the year 4000 to the end at 6000.

Anyway, getting back to the timeline. Now we are in the year 5775 which means that everything has to be completed in the next 225 years which is called the Messianic age. The return to Israel, the land producing, the final stages of Gog and Magog, the ingathering of the exile (including the 10 lost tribes), the coming of the Moshiach, the Third Temple, Judgment day (the too late date) and the Resurrection of the Dead all will occur by the year 6000.

We have one other bit of information that really makes all this exiting and gives us much better detail of our schedule of events. The holy Zohar tells us that history is folded (in case you were wondering why this section is called the folding of history) and that the 210 years that we were in Egypt followed by 40 years in the desert is prophecy for the end of time. The folding of the calendar means that the last 210 years will be the time of the Resurrection of the Dead and that the other events will occur within the 40 years before that. Translated into actual years, 210 years before the year 6000 is 5790 (2030). The 40 years before that, means that the events already have started in the year 5750 (1990).

Scorecard:

- Return to Israel – completed

- Land producing – completed

- Gog and Magog – The Chafetz Chaim said the final battle will be a spiritual war that obviously is already ongoing. Will there be further war? We have many indications from world events that there will be a war; however, many Rabbis have said it will be a very short war at which time Hashem will take over with so-called natural disasters to, measure for measure, rid the world of the wicked with only the righteous remaining. This final stage of Gog and Magog commenced with the Oslo accords in the early 1990's and will probably be completed this year, falling into our timeline. The Talmud (Sanhedrin 97) tells us of the events that will happen in the seven year Shemitah cycle prior to Moshiach that will conclude with Moshiach ben David being introduced to the world. The event of the seventh year, in which we are presently, is "war."

- Ingathering of the exile (including the 10 lost tribes, which already are showing up) – ongoing with the biggest boost starting in 1990, the demise of the Soviet Union, Operation Solomon – the Jews leaving Ethiopia, the exile of Jews from many of the Arab countries, the increase of Aliyah from the rest of the world, including the great surge of Aliyah from France recently, etc. All the Jews of the world should be here this year considering the next paragraph. It is brought down that the Jews will return in two stages – a remnant before the coming of the Moshiach and the remainder shortly thereafter. I'm not going to get into the details but there are two

Moshiachs. One is a descendent of David (that's the popular one that we all know about) the other is the Moshiach, descendent of Joseph. Moshiach ben Yosef, as he is known, will be the one to take us through the final battle of Gog and Magog and gather in the remainder of the Jews. The final group to come over will fly on the wings of Eagles. It will be very miraculous since there is an estimate that the trip will take about 5 minutes (no time for meals or movies).

- The coming of the Moshiach – he is already here with great expectations that he will be introduced to the world shortly (this year, 5775).

- The Third Temple – hopefully this year, 5775.

- Judgment day (the too late date – it is coming fast enough to take it seriously).

- The Resurrection of the Dead – will probably occur over many years considering that is should be completed by the year 6000. First the righteous will be resurrected (that could start this year, or already has started – we have some possibilities of which we are aware) – then the remainder of Jews from history.

There are many changes that we will see in this period of the Moshiach (from now to the year 6000). Very soon should be the end of war, evil, hatred, greed, death and sickness since that phase of the rectification of us and the world should be relatively complete with the introduction of the Moshiach. Many other wonderful changes will happen during this timeframe approaching 6000.

What happens after the year 6000? The next 1000 years, 6000 to 7000 are called the years of Shabbat (we are going to need a really big cholent pot). This period is not totally understood because we will not be on Earth but in Heaven. Since time as we know it will be over, the 1000 years may be a single day in Heaven, the World of Souls (Psalms 90:4: 1000 years is but one day in Your eyes). At the year 7000 the body and soul will be reunited and brought back to what is called the World-to-Come. A final judgment will occur at that time to determine the eternity of each of us. As with Heaven, the World-to-Come will be many levels of holiness – with those more deserving being closer to Hashem. There are also stages of the World-to-Come that are beyond the scope of this discussion. The years 7000 to 8000 will be followed by additional rectification in the years 8000 to 9000 and even further happenings 9000 to 10000. Once again, just know that all is for the good. Those who are worthy will be experiencing a future that is so tremendous it is beyond our human comprehension. Hashem takes good care of those who follow His ways.

I highly recommend the book "Talking About the End of Days" by Rabbi Pinchas Winston which covers this subject in much greater detail.

4.8 Another Mystery Solved

Something that I have heard for decades is that we don't really know what the order of events is in the Redemption process. Is the Redemption first, then Moshiach, the return of the Jews to Israel, the Temple, etc? What will be the mysterious chain of events that we will experience? Well, it turns out that we do know. Hashem has given us extensive detail in scriptures and even information on where we are now and to what we should look forward next. An even bigger surprise is we say the order five times a day in our prayers.

The Talmud, tractate Megillah 17b, states that the order of blessings and requests of the Shemoneh Esrei (some call it the Amidah or silent prayer) is the order of the redemption process. We say the Shemoneh Esrei three times a day silently and then twice we have the repetition, totaling five times.

This is perhaps one of the most difficult topics that I can cover. The information is extensive (volumes have been written), and is very deep. To try to describe the deepest meaning of the order is close to impossible, as related to this physical world when most of it is very spiritual in meaning. But, I feel it is very important for me to try, since it answers many questions that I have had, as well as what the readers of my blog have posed.

I have explained several times that the Torah is the most difficult subject in the world. The text at its deepest level is beyond human comprehension considering that it was created by an Infinite Intelligence. Enough said. Let's get started.

I've organized this in several parts. The first is to briefly (not completely) tell you what the Talmud says. Then I will attempt to explain most of the parts. This also will be a very abridged discussion since, as already stated, there are volumes written on the subject. Then, with Hashem's help, I will attempt to explain where we are in the process. The last part will be the most difficult part to understand and will probably be the most controversial answer I have ever attempted. The bigger problem is that where we are today at the time of this writing, and where we will be at the time you read this, could be two different stories.

4.9 Babylonian Talmud - Megillah 17b

'To the 'Amidah prayer.' Where is this derived? — As it has been taught: 'Simeon the Pakulite[5] formulated eighteen blessings in the presence of Rabban Gamaliel in the proper[6] order in Yavneh.[7] R. Johanan said (others report, it was stated in a Baraita): A hundred and twenty elders, among whom were many prophets, drew up eighteen blessings in a fixed order.'

Our Rabbis taught: Where do we derive that the blessing of the Patriarchs[8] should be said? Because it says, *Ascribe unto Hashem, you sons of might.*[9] And where that we say the blessing of mighty deeds?[10] Because it says, *Ascribe unto Hashem glory and strength.*[11] And where that we say sanctifications?[12] Because it says, *Ascribe unto Hashem the glory due unto His name, worship Hashem in the beauty of holiness.*[13] What reason had they for mentioning understanding[14] after holiness? Because it says, *They shall sanctify the Holy One of Yaakov and shall stand in awe of the G-d of Yisrael,*[15] and next to this, *They also that err in spirit shall come to understanding.* What reason had they for mentioning repentance[16] after understanding? Because it is written, *Lest they, understanding with their heart, return and be healed.*[17] If that is the reason, healing should be mentioned next to repentance?[18] — Do not imagine such a thing, since it is written, *And let him return unto Hashem and He will have compassion upon him, and to our G-d, for he will abundantly pardon.*[19] But why should you rely upon this verse? Rely rather on the other! — There is written another verse, *Who forgives all your iniquity, who heals all your diseases, who redeems your life from the pit,*[20] which implies that redemption and healing come after forgiveness. But it is written, 'Lest they return and be healed'? That refers not to the healing of sickness but to the healing [power] of forgiveness. What was their reason for mentioning redemption in the seventh blessing?[21] Raba replied: Because they [Yisra'el] are destined to be redeemed in the seventh year [of the coming of the Mashiach],[22] therefore the mention of redemption was placed in the seventh blessing. But a Master has said, 'In the sixth year will be thunderings, in the seventh wars, at the end of the seventh the son of David will come'? — War is also the beginning of redemption. What was their reason for mentioning healing in the eighth blessing? — R. Aha said: Because circumcision which requires healing is appointed for the

263

eighth day, therefore it was placed in the eighth blessing. What was their reason for placing the [prayer for the] blessing of the years ninth? R. Alexandri said: This was directed against those who raise the market price [of foodstuffs], as it is written, *Break You the arm of the wicked*; and when David said this, he said it in the ninth Psalm.₂₃ What was their reason for mentioning the gathering of the exiles after the blessing of the years? — Because it is written, *But you, O mountains of Yisrael, you shall shoot forth your branches and yield your fruit to your people Yisrael, for they are at hand to come.*₂₄ And when the exiles are assembled, judgment will be visited on the wicked, as it says, *And I will turn my hand upon you and purge away your dross as with lye,*₂₅ and it is written further, *And I will restore thy judges as at the first.*₂₆ And when judgment is visited on the wicked, transgressors cease,₂₇ and presumptuous sinners₂₈ are included with them, as it is written, *But the destruction of the transgressors and of the sinners shall be together, and they that forsake Hashem shall be consumed.*₂₉ And when the transgressors have disappeared, the horn of the righteous is exalted,₃₀ as it is written, *All the horns of the wicked also will I cut off, but the horns of the righteous shall be lifted up.*₃₁ And 'proselytes of righteousness'₃₂ are included with the righteous, as it says, *you shall rise up before the hoary head and honor the face of the old man,*₃₃ and the text goes on, *And if a stranger sojourn with you.* And where is the horn of the righteous exalted? In Yerushalayim,₃₄ as it says, *Pray for the peace of Yerushalayim, may they prosper that love you.*₃₅ And when Yerushalayim is built, David(₃₆) will come, as it says.

5) Possibly this means 'cotton dealer' (Rashi).

6) I.e. one based on Scriptural texts, as explained infra.

7) V. Ber. 28b.

8) The first blessing, containing the words, the El of Avraham, the El of Yitzchak, and the El of Yaakov'. For the 'Amidah prayer v. P.B. pp. 44ff.

9) Tehillim 29:1. 'Sons of might' is taken as a description of the Patriarchs. The Talmud renders: 'Mention before Hashem the sons of might', i.e., the Patriarchs.

10) The second blessing, mentioning the 'mighty deed' of the resurrection.

11) Tehillim 29:1. (12) The third blessing beginning, 'You are holy'.

13) Ibid. 2. (14) In the fourth blessing, beginning, 'You grant to man understanding'.

15) Yeshayahu 29:23f.

16) In the fifth blessing, commencing, 'Bring us back, O Father'.

17) Ibid. 6:10.

18) Whereas in fact it comes in the next blessing but one, 'redemption' being interposed.

19) Ibid. LV, 7.

20) Tehillim 103:3f.

21) Concluding, 'Blessed are You, O Hashem, who redeems Yisrael'.

22) V. Sanh. 97a.

23) In our books it is the tenth (v. 15), but the Talmud apparently reckoned the first and second Psalms as one.

24) Yechezkel 36:8.

25) Yeshayahu 1:25.

26) Ibid. 26. The next blessing proceeds, 'Restore our judges'. etc.

27) MS. M. minim (plur. of min v. Glos.).

28) Mentioned in the next blessing. This, however, was not one of the original eighteen, v. Ber. 28b.

29) Ibid. 28.

30) The next blessing concludes, 'the support and trust of the righteous'.

31) Tehillim 75:2.

32) Mentioned in the same blessing. 'Proselytes of Righteousness' are converts who completely accept the Jewish creed and life.

33) VaYikra 19:32.

34) Mentioned in the next blessing.

35) Tehillim 122:6.

36) Mentioned in the next blessing, which commences, 'Cause to sprout quickly the shoot of David'.

The blessings of the Shemoneh Esrei, in their correct order, are:

1. *Patriarchs.*
2. *G-d's Might.*
3. *G-d's Holiness.*
4. *Insight.*
5. *Repentance.*
6. *Forgiveness.*
7. *Redemption.*
8. *Healing.*
9. *Blessing of the Years* (prosperity).
10. *Ingathering of Exiles.*
11. *Restoration of Justice.*

12.*Downfall of the Heretics.*
13.*Support of the Righteous.*
14.*Rebuilding Jerusalem.*
15.*Reinstatement of the Davidic Kingdom.*
16.*Acceptance of Prayer.*
17.*Temple Service.*
18.*Thanksgiving.*
19.*Peace.*

That was the easy part. Now to try to explain the parts without writing a book.

1, 2 & 3 make us realize before we can make our requests in life that we must know to Whom we are talking, and to have complete confidence that He is the Only Source of Salvation. As our forefathers discovered, it is only with the Might and Holiness of Hashem can we succeed. The first three blessings should be said with great feeling – clearly pronouncing the names of Hashem and understanding their meanings.

4. Insight
You graciously endow man with wisdom. [This blessing begins the middle section of the *Shemoneh Esrei,* in which we make our requests of Hashem. The first plea is for *wisdom* and *insight,* because a person's intelligence is his or her primary characteristic, the one that sets us apart from animals.] We ask for *wisdom* and for *insight,* so that we can draw proper conclusions and achieve intellectual *discernment (Vilna Gaon).* This request is fulfilled by our study of Torah, so we are asking Hashem for all that is needed to strive and succeed in our efforts.

5. Repentance
Our Father. Only in this prayer for repentance, and in the next one, for forgiveness, do we refer to Hashem as *our Father.* A father has the responsibility to teach his son the proper way to live, but even if a son has rebelled and become estranged, the father's compassion will assert itself if his son repents and seeks forgiveness *(Eitz Yosef). And influence* us *to return. Hashem* never compels anyone to repent, but if a person makes a sincere beginning, Hashem will make his way easier. The most important aspect of repentance is not admitting to your mistakes, but the action taken as a follow-up to correct the mistake. No trickery, no shortcuts – just good honest effort to make positive changes. Hashem knows our intensions better than we do. If we do what we are supposed to, our

repentance isn't needed. If we make mistakes and repent properly, with actual correction, our repentance will be successful.

6. Forgiveness
Forgive ... pardon, Forgiveness, means not even harboring resentment or ill will, while *pardon,* means only giving up the right to punish for a wrong, *(Abudraham).*

7. Redemption
See *our suffering.* Though Israel's suffering results from its own sins, our enemies cannot rightfully claim that they merely do Hashem's work, since Israel suffers much more than necessary at their hands. Similarly, many commentators explain that the Egyptians were punished for oppressing and enslaving the Jews, even though Hashem had decreed the suffering and slavery, because the Egyptians, in their wickedness, greatly exceeded Hashem's decree *(Eitz Yosef). And redeem us,* from the trials and agonies of everyday life *(Rashi; Megillah* 17b). *For Your Name's sake.* Israel's suffering is a reflection on our G-d, and therefore, a desecration of His Name *(Eitz Yosef).*

8. Health and Healing
Heal us, HASHEM; then we *will be healed.* Sometimes human beings or angels are Hashem's agents to heal illness, but in that case, the cure may only be partial or temporary. [Or the pain or other symptoms may be relieved, while the illness itself remains uncured *(Siach Yitzchak).* But if Hashem Himself undertakes to cure the patient, we are confident that it will not be a temporary or a partial measure: *then* we will *be healed (Eitz Yoseffrom Zohar).]* A very important concept is that this blessing provides spiritual healing. As I have said, the Soul causes physical pain and illness as a way of helping us reach Tikun. If we have spiritual healing, physical healing results as well. This is a prime example of a very deep concept being made simple – it would take much more to truly explain all the details.

9. Year of Prosperity
Bless on our behalf. We request a blessing on our general business activities and then proceed to ask for abundant crops. Even in bad times some people prosper, and even in good times some farms and businesses fail. We ask not only for general prosperity, but that we be allowed to share in it *(R'S.R. Hirsch).*

Dew and rain. The mention of rain in the second blessing of the Shemoneh Esrei is an expression of praise only. There we praise Hashem the Life-giver, Who controls the elements and provides wind and moisture as needed in the seasons when they generally occur. Here we make the request that He give us rain; therefore it is recited only when rain is actually beneficial for the agricultural cycle. Since rain is needed in early fall in Israel, the recitation begins on 7 Cheshvan, much earlier than elsewhere. From Your bounty. Food acquired in a morally corrupt manner lacks the holiness to nourish the soul. Therefore, we ask that Hashem to satisfy us from His bounty, not from earnings to which we are not entitled (Yaaros D'vash).

10. Ingathering of Exiles

Sound the great shofar: There are three differences between this prayer for redemption and the earlier one of #7 *Redemption:* (a) The earlier blessing refers to Hashem's *daily* help in all sorts of crises and suffering, while this one refers to the *future* Redemption from exile; (b) the earlier blessing refers only to *physical* salvation, while this one is a plea for *spiritual* deliverance; (c) this one specifies not only freedom from oppression, but the ingathering of all exiles to *Eretz Yisroel.* What this means to us is that Geula can come to an individual before the ingathering and the final Geula. Many of us living in Israel already feel the effects of the redemption, and will not see great differences when it occurs worldwide.

11. Restoration of Justice

Restore our judges. When Elijah heralds Moshiach's coming, he will first re-establish the Sanhedrin (the ancient Jewish court system), and then the Redemption will begin. A secondary theme of this prayer is the wish that Hashem help all Jewish judges rule wisely and justly *(Yaaros D'vash). - And* our *advisers,* i.e., the prophets who gave wise advice in both spiritual and temporal affairs *(Olas Tamid). Sorrow and groan: sorrow,* results from actual want or pain, such as hunger or destruction; *groan,* refers to inner turmoil, such as worry, depression, or fear (Vilna *Gaon)*

12. Against Heretics

And for slanderers. This blessing was not part of the original eighteen blessings; it was instituted in Yavneh, during the tenure of Rabban Gamliel ll as Nasi of Israel, sometime after the destruction of the Second Temple. The blessing was composed in response to the threats of heretical Jewish sects such as the

Sadducees, Boethusians, Essenes, and the early Xtians, who tried to lead Jews astray through example and persuasion, and used their political power to oppress observant Jews and to slander them to the Jew-hating Roman government.

13. The Righteous

The remnant of their scholars. The term Sofer refers to those who transmit the Oral Torah from generation to generation (Auodas Yisrael*)*. These four categories of people - righteous, devout, elders, scholars are the leaders of the nation. Because the nation needs them, the Sages instituted a special prayer for their welfare *(R' Yehudah ben Yakar)*, *And we will not feel* ashamed. One who puts his faith in people feels ashamed, for he has been shown to be helpless on his own. But he is not ashamed to have trusted in Hashem as no one can succeed without His help *(Dover Shalom)*.

14. Rebuilding Jerusalem

And to Jerusalem. Having sought Hashem's blessing on Israel's leaders and the righteous; we seek His blessing for the Holy City. No blessing is complete until the seat of holiness, Jerusalem, is rebuilt in all its grandeur *(Iyun Tefillah)*. *The throne of David.* Jerusalem cannot be considered rebuilt unless a worthy descendant of David is seated on the throne *(R' Yitzchak Zev Soloveitchik)*.

15. Davidic Reign

The offspring of ... David. Zechariah (6:12) teaches that Moshiach's name will be *Tzemach,* literally, the *sprouting* or *flourishing* of a plant. This indicates that the normal process of redemption is like the barely perceptible daily growth of a plant *(Iyun Tefillah)*.

In the previous blessing the mention of David indicates that the realization of Jerusalem depends on the Davidic heir. Here we are taught that the ultimate salvation of the Jewish people is possible only through the Davidic Moshiach.

16. Acceptance of Prayer

[In the middle section of *Shemoneh Esrei* we have asked Hashem to grant our specific needs. We now close the section with a general plea that He take note of our call and grant our requests. *Pity and be compassionate. Pity* refers to an artisan's special regard for the product of his hands; while *compassion* is the emotion aroused upon seeing a totally helpless person. 0 Hashem, *pity* us because we are Your handiwork, and *be compassionate* because we are nothing without You! *(Vilna Gaon)*.

Prayers and entreaties. Rashi (Deut. 3:23) explains that an entreaty is a request for *an unearned gift.* This expression is used by the most righteous people, because they are aware that no human being can claim that Hashem "owes" him something. *Gur Aryeh* explains that the righteous use the term entreaty only when praying for themselves, but when praying for the community they use Prayer, because Israel as a *community* deserves Hashem's help,

17. Temple Service

Be favorable. This begins the final section of *Shemoneh Esrei.* Like a servant who is grateful for having had the opportunity to express himself before his master, we thank Hashem for having been attentive to our prayers.

The service. As we conclude *Shemoneh Esrei,* our substitute for the Temple's sacrificial service, we ask that the *true* service be restored to the Temple *(Eitz Yosef).*

The fire-offerings of Israel. Since the Temple is not standing, this phrase is allegorical. It refers to: the souls and deeds of the righteous, which are as pleasing as sacrifices; Jewish prayers that are like offerings; or the altar fires and sacrifices of the Messianic era. Some punctuate the blessing to read: ... *restore the service...and the fire offerings of Israel. Their prayer with love accept favorably.*

18. Thanksgiving [Modim]

Rock of our lives. Our parents are the "rocks" from whom our bodies are hewn, but from You we receive life itself *(Eitz Yosef). We shall thank You.* Having begun the blessing by describing Hashem's greatness and our relationship to Him, we now specify those things for which we thank Him. *For our lives.* Lest anyone think that he is master over his own life, we acknowledge that every breath and heartbeat is a direct result of Hashem's mercy *(Olas Tamid). Our souls that are entrusted to You.* The word *neshamah* refers to the higher soul that provides man his holiness, as opposed to the lower soul that merely sustains him. During slumber, the *neshamah* leaves the body and is, so to speak, entrusted to Hashem's safekeeping, to be returned to man in the morning *(Derech Hashem).*

Your miracles ... Your wonders. Miracles are the extraordinary events acknowledged by everyone to be the results of Hashem's intervention. *Wonders* are the familiar things that we do not regard as miracles because we have grown accustomed to them, such as breathing, raining, and growing. We thank Hashem for both *miracles* and *wonders,* because we recognize that He is their Creator *(Eitz Yosef).*

19. Peace
Establish peace, is recited only times when the Priestly Blessing is given (O.C. 127 :2). At other times, Abundant peace is recited instead. The six forms of good listed here - peace, goodness, blessing, graciousness, kindness, and compassion - allude to the six blessings of Bircas Kohanim, the priestly blessings (Eitz Yoseg).

Graciousness, kindness and compassion. Man goes through stages of development in life. When he is growing and improving, he is the recipient of Hashem's graciousness. In his period of maturity, when an individual may not improve, but continues the accomplishments of his more fruitful period, then Hashem grants him kindness. Sometimes he declines or does not deserve Hashem's help, but even then Hashem shows compassion (lkkarim),

The above description of the 19 prayers of the Shemonah Esrei came from the commentary of the Artscroll daily player book, Ashkenaz. Although the order of the prayers are as described in the Talmud, there was much information in the Artscroll commentary that would enhance the statements that I am about to make concerning the process of the Geula and the time within which it will happen. First of all, you can see that the process is not instantaneously accomplished. From start to finish the goal of the process is very involved and could take time. What determines the amount of time is you the individual. It is obvious that not every one of us is at the same stage of the redemption process. For example the most prominent Rabbis of today are not waiting for insight, looking to start their repentance, waiting for forgiveness and, for that matter, waiting for redemption. As you saw above number 7 and number 10 both talk of redemption. Number seven was more of an individual redemption, while number 10 after the in gathering of the exile is alluding to the final redemption. Yet, one might ask if an individual has received all the stages of redemption up to number 10 and has already made Aliyah in Israel, has he or she already completed the in-gathering of the exile on an individual basis? If an individual is up to step 14 the rebuilding of Jerusalem, one might argue that the Jews have returned to Jerusalem and the city is very much built up. I personally have gone to Jerusalem hundreds of times, and am in awe at how beautiful and built-up the city Jerusalem is.

Then we get to the coming of Moshiach ben Dovid. Rabbi Kaduri, and many other sources, said that the Moshiach is already here. The problem with most of us is we don't understand this statement. Rabbi Kaduri never said that he would be announced on the international news including a videotape showing him coming in on a donkey. He never said that he was coming to my house to knock on my door and shake my hand. All he said was he met and interviewed the man that would be crowned Moshiach, we know the individual that is to be anointed Moshiach lives in Jerusalem; he is, nevertheless, here.

I even question what does it mean that the Geula will be upon us? By the Rambam's definition, redemption will be "business as usual but there will be no enemies or evil around us." I have mentioned that I personally live in the city that doesn't even have a police force. In 12 years that I have been here, I have not seen any evil around me. Nobody in this city has television. Very few people listen to radio since we are in a mountainous area, there are very few stations available to make it even worthwhile to have a radio. Very few people have computers other than those who need them for business purposes. The schools in the city frown upon children being around computers, and even have been known to turn down children who come from homes with computers. What does all this mean? Most of the people in this city don't have a clue as to what is going on in the world. They are not aware of the evil, suffering and, in many cases, even the financial hardships. If there were such a thing as the redemption being announced to the world, most people around me including myself would see no daily change in our activities. In other words, I, and most of my neighbors have already received our personal redemption (bli ayin harah).

Am I personally waiting for the Moshiach with the changes that the Moshiach will bring about? Even that is a misnomer since everything that will happened as a result of the Moshiach and the Geula will come from Hashem, not a person. So it is not Moshiach that I'm waiting for, but Hashem's changes. Did Moses cause plagues, split the sea, bring Manna from heaven and water to come from rocks? There are many other changes that are expected that I am already living on a daily basis – all from Hashem. I experience miracles all the time that wouldn't have been known to me in New Jersey, my former residence.

Yes, I am waiting for Moshiach to be introduced. Why, when I have everything that I want? A very important commandment in the Torah, which I take very seriously, is to love my fellow Jew. It is worded several different ways, but the most famous is in Leviticus 19:18 "Love your fellow as yourself." This has become known at the golden rule (mostly by the non-Jewish world, which means they also believe it) and is worded "One should treat others as one would like others to treat oneself." The point is that I am commanded to do so; however, I personally feel the pain of my fellow Jew and every righteous non-Jew. I was never a person to say: I am in good shape why should I worry about others?" When I feel the pain of others, I am acting as a Torah Jew and living Hashem's will. So yes, I am waiting for Moshiach; yes, I am waiting for the redemption and yes, I want every good person on this planet to have the best Tikun possible! Enough said.

It says in Scriptures that Hashem created many worlds. One of the connotations of that statement is that each one of us is a separate world. No two individuals in this world experience the same thing. The design that Hashem provides for each of us is for the good and merciful treatment that each of us needs. I have been asked why certain things that the Rabbis have been predicting have not come to fruition. I believe that all is happening as they had said, but it is being experienced on an individual basis according to where you stand with Hashem. If you are skeptical about things, then in essence you must be lacking faith and trust in Hashem.

I believe you may be waiting much longer for redemption or not experiencing it at all. What are my statements based on? Prophecy from the Torah. We are told that the events of the first redemption would repeat themselves in the end of days. Interestingly enough only 20% of the Israelites had enough faith in Hashem to follow Moses into the desert. 80% of the Israelites perished in the plague of darkness. There seems to be similar numbers and percentages of Jews today that may fall into the same categories of having faith or not having faith. In other words, one might ask are most of the Jews of today not going to experience redemption? Even the 20% that went into the desert were still measure for measure happy or unhappy depending upon how much they were serving Hashem and having faith in Him.

It all comes down to measure for measure (how many times have I said that) when we ask what each of us individually should be experiencing in the end of days. If we are following the ways of Hashem, I believe we are either already there, or soon to be. If you are a skeptic, a complainer or, even worse, a heretic, don't expect Hashem to shower you with blessings. We really need to do the best repentance we have ever done. Whatever you do measure for measure you will receive in return. We are individuals and are treated as individuals. There is no such thing as blending into the crowd or assimilating into society. Throughout history the Jews have painfully experienced that lesson. Hashem keeps tabs on each one of us – what we think, what we say and what we do. If it is a positive act according to His ways, we receive measure for measure a positive response. It is an exact science. Hashem is consistent and totally to be trusted. He doesn't play practical jokes and He doesn't change His mind. The design of this world and the life we live are constant. Hashem makes the world look random just to facilitate our free will; but, it is not random, it is, by design, for each of us. Your deeds, good or bad, will repay you in kind.

4.10 Acceptance of Moshiach

The acceptance of Moses as the Deliver was on an individual level. Many totally rejected him and even caused him to flee and return at a later time. According to scriptures, the Moshiach will not be accepted by many and, in some cases, there will be those who would never accept him.

The story of the first Geula is repeating itself. Moshiach is here and many know him and accept him even though he has not been anointment as King Moshiach yet. Likewise, King David was alive and well for many years before he became king. Many knew him and even were aware before it happened that he was to be anointed. Hashem is totally consistent, and so is history. Even with Moses one might ask was it Moses they wanted, or just an Individual that Hashem sent to remove them from bondage? People then and now are always concerned about what does this mean to me and my loved ones.

Are you feeling the redemption already, while most people aren't? I was asking that question since we have a comprehensive list of the events that will occur prior to the redemption; and, it seems obvious that the Rabbis of today and even many observant Jews that I know (such as my neighbors) are further along in the list of events than most people in the world. It was very tempting to evaluate where I believe I am personally and I thought it would be interesting for you to do likewise. Since the Talmud talks about two different types of redemption, personal – blessing #7 and national – blessing #10, it very much supports that we,

274

as individuals, are at different levels. Where I am personally is not important – where each of you are is my point of emphasis. Not just nice to know information, but a self-examination of what you need to do.

Do I believe that Moshiach will be knocking on my door to introduce himself? Perhaps a metaphorical knock, since he would have way too many people to visit. The more important thought is how would I react and what would it mean to me if he would knock on my door. My entire purpose of this book is to convey the tremendous possibility that is available to each of us, and to get everyone to make the correct choice – to be ready to meet the Moshiach when he is introduced.

Let me give you an analogy. Let say, an individual bought a lottery ticket, and picked the correct combination of numbers. Mazel Tov, he won 100 million dollars and was the only winner – no sharing (except maybe 90% to the government). This individual decided he was too busy to go collect. He was swamped at work, many things he had to fix in the house, kids to drive to school, etc, etc, etc. Everyone looked at him and questioned: "Are you crazy? You can retire for life, hire people to fix your house (or buy a new one that isn't broken), hire someone to drive the kids anywhere they want to go (hopefully to Yeshivah), a payoff for all eternity, etc, etc, etc. He answers: "I'm not sure if I want such a change in my life." He gets advice: "Why don't you try it; and, if it isn't for you, just give it to me."

I know this analogy sounds silly. But, you are each holding a lottery ticket worth much, much, much (and a whole bunch more muches) more than 100 million (tax-free) and answering "well, I'm not sure if this is what I want." In this case you don't have to give it to me; I already have cashed in my ticket and am enjoying the luxurious life of true happiness. I wish to share my winning life with you, however.

One additional thing on a personal level. Even though Moshiach is only a person, it is the Kingdom of Hashem that I crave. If you read again my chapter entitled: "He is Hiding Behind Nature," you will understand for what I am waiting. In a word: "Hashem." In the future when Hashem is no longer allusive to us and we are totally aware of Him, then we will truly be living in paradise with joy and happiness beyond comprehension. Moshiach is the agent that will help usher in this time of utopia, and is the major reason that I crave Moshiach. Now, you see where my heart is, and what I truly crave for me, my family and the entire world.

Most people in the world today would say "Moshiach is not here – don't try to fool me." Why? Because they don't have a clue as to what the Messianic era entails and how wonderful it will be. People reject change if they are unfamiliar with it. That is why no matter how much of a warning I give, and no matter how much proof I provide, there will still be a majority of people who don't want to give up their secular ways and follow Hashem. They argue with success, instead of realizing what truly "the way to success" is. They see an observant life as strange and possibly even scary. I believe atheists are not convinced that there is no Deity running the show, but that they are afraid of the concept. Being a coward provides limited options in life. But, it is like the child that you tell "this is a new food – taste it you are going to like it." His response: "I DON'T LIKE IT." How do you know if you didn't taste it? "I DON'T LIKE IT." Most parents have had this conversation (sound familiar?).

In years of doing Kiruv (outreach), the most honest Jew that I ever worked with was a fellow that I was wowing with hidden codes in the Torah, prophecies that have come true, science in the Torah (he was also an engineer with a very extensive science background); I poured on all my fancy footwork. He, after a short while, stuck his fingers in his ears. I asked "what is the matter?" He replied: "I think you are showing me truth about life for which I may not be ready." I was speechless. I complimented him on being the most honest person I have ever dealt with; considering, most people who can't cope with the truth just change the subject or pretend they have to leave or some other lame excuse. People do not know what is best for them and I fully understand that – I could spend hours telling you the mistakes I've made (but I won't). One thing I know is that every mistake I made in life was for my own good. We are taught "one does not really know good, unless one knows evil" or "one does not know right unless one knows wrong." The idea is to learn from ones mistakes and improve. This crash course that I have attempted to give was a way to cut to the chase, since time is very short in getting it right. My advice is to go collect on your winning lottery ticket – Mazel Tov!

4.11 Another Profound Message from Hashem

There is such a devastating episode going on in the US with the National Security Agency (NSA) spying on the citizens of the US. The whistleblower who disclosed this information is in hiding and fearful of his life. The extent of the surveillance and secret gathering on the part of the US Government makes the idea of 1984 look like a picnic. The biggest question in the minds of Americans is what this Orwellian fiasco is doing to the very fabric of the US. It is definitely unconstitutional and even very dangerous to those who are suspected of covert activity to the US. The government doesn't seem to care about its citizens since this is leading up to the very dangerous New World Order that has been planned by the elite for over a century (probably more than two centuries since it stemmed from the nonsense of the Illuminati, which was created in 1776). The debate about what is going on is not my concern here. It is the attitude, even the fear of Americans, since this is culminating in a system of no "liberty and justice for all." People of the US of A have great trepidations about their future and the future of their loved ones.

How can I tie this to a message from Hashem? Since everything is from Hashem, let's figure out the message. The system of this world is that Hashem gave us a Handbook (the Torah) to guide us completely through life and beyond; He gave us a free-will to take advantage of the instructions, or to go on our own wayward direction; and, here's the kicker: He set up a surveillance network to monitor every word and action we do – every free-will decision we make. Hashem has in His infinite database: the thoughts, words and actions of every person that every lived (His database makes the NSA information look like a Non-Sufficient Accumulation – maybe that really is what NSA stands for). What is the gigantic difference between the government collection of information and Hashem's infinite database? The government is doing everything with evil intent and Hashem only has love and mercy as His purpose. Hashem wants us to do the right thing and to discover what true happiness and success is for this life and forever.

The big question that comes from all of this is why are we so afraid of what the government is doing to hurt us, but so nonchalant to the real system from Hashem? Although Hashem's system is there to help us and provide us with everything, it is also a fair system, measure for measure, including correction (or punishment) for violators. The biggest difference is that the government is not a fair system and could result in unfair punishment; where Hashem's system is always fair. It is such a shame that we have available a way to achieve total happiness for us and our loved ones and we give it very little heed. I'm curious, if the government started monitoring who keeps Kosher and who observes Shabbos, would more Jews start to do the right thing – especially if we knew that mitzvah violators could wind up in a FEMA camp and never be heard from again (if you're not familiar with the FEMA concentration camp system in the US, Google it and be shocked – there are 800 such camps in operation)?

I'm going to tell you a very big secret (as I have always said this is Secret so make sure you tell everyone): whoever gets monitored and receives trepidations or even punishment from the government is receiving it from Hashem. Everything is from Hashem. If you are following the ways of Hashem (Yaakov studying Torah), the government will not bother you (Esav having his way). Hashem works in mysterious ways and uses everything of this world to do His Will. There is nothing random in this world – no coincidence, no accident, nothing by chance, nothing by luck. If you don't believe this, you will suffer by its consequences. In other words, things will happen in your life that will seem like coincidence, accident, chance, luck, random occurrences, etc and you will start playing with the Ouija board, reading the daily horoscope and all kinds of other crazy fortune telling nonsense. Turn to the real system, as Hashem has given us, and not paying attention to the falseness of the world. Pay attention if you are living in the upside-down fantasy world instead of taking advantage of the real kindness and love that is available.

What is the actual wording of Hashem's instruction?

Vayikra 26:23-24: "If despite this you will not heed Me, and you behave toward Me with casualness, I will behave toward you with a fury of casualness.."

The following is commentary on the Torah in Parshas Bechukosai. There are 5 series of admonitions that will happen – actually they would be a repeat of events that already have happened – when you don't take Hashem's guidance seriously.

What does it mean "with casualness?

Verse 24 (above) . ... with casualness. If you persist in thinking that all of My carefully calibrated punishments were merely coincidental - so that My message is wasted - I will punish you measure for measure by making it more difficult for you to perceive the Divine hand. The next series of punishments will seem haphazard, for their correspondence to your sins will not be as obvious as in the case of the earlier punishments (Or HaChaim). This follows the principle that if people refuse to "see" G-d, He withdraws His Presence [Hiddenness of the Countenance], and makes it harder for them to recognize the truth.

Well, I guess this makes me a whistleblower for Hashem's monitoring system (I consider myself more of a Shofar blower than a whistleblower). The good news is I don't have to go into hiding, but instead, I can be totally happy about my whistling. All I ask is: come whistle with me; you will be happy you did.

4.12 Pay Attention -- Messages from Hashem

It is both exciting and encouraging that there has been a great increase in the number of messages that we are receiving from Hashem. The individuals who inspire us through Facilitated Communications have been very silent for a while. It was an indication that we still had more waiting for the Geula and the time of Moshiach. But, recently messages have come from Ben Golden, Moishela, Daniel and Menachem, along with messages from Rav Nir Ben Artzi, Rav Fish, Rav Shternbach, Rav Amnon Yitzchok, Rav Yosef Mizrachi, Rav Matisyahu Glazerson. (especially showing us Torah codes) and many others.

I am not going to repeat any of these vital messages here, since they have been very timely and will not mean as much when you are reading this book. By now there are probably new messages. Once again, hopefully the Moshiach has been introduced to the world be the time you are reading this; the messages are not needed any more. Either way, you can do a web search and read these messages.

There is so much happening in the world, alluding to this being the time before the happy ending of history as we know it, and the immanent time of Geula. I am not a prophet who can interpret all these messages and give you a definite date. I consider myself a dot-connector. You know, the pictures you used to do as a child where you would connect the dots and a picture would appear (I am probably showing my age since most dot connecting is probably done with computers these days). What I am saying is that the information from the many messages is giving us a picture that we are getting close to the time of Geula. The messages are consistent from the different sources giving us confidence that the only Source that could be behind this is Hashem.

The other encouraging thought is that we are hearing from sources that have been very quiet for a while, and that it is coming at a time when the world is in such turmoil. Are these the final birth pangs of Moshiach that we would expect right

279

before the delivery? If you look into scriptures (many places), the dots are coming together in a very favorable way. What is prophesied to happen in the end of time, just before Moshiach, is actually happening or is already completed. It is exiting and encouraging. The only question to be asked is (I know, I repeat myself) have I as an individual brought myself closer to Hashem? What these messages mean to each of us is completely dependent upon where we stand in following Hashem's ways.

I do believe there could be very tough times ahead (possible war, further financial problems, more severe Jew-hatred around the world, possible severe weather, etc), but I know that the protection of each individual on Earth will be measure for measure according to his or her relationship with the Creator of everything. I also believe it will become more obvious as we go along, since each one of us is experiencing the Tikun that we need to survive and thrive, forever. Pay attention since the messages from Hashem are very much personal messages for each one of us. Consider it a heavenly gift that the personal and worldly messages are telling us what we need to do to arrive at the happy ending. It should be as happy and successful as possible.

Thank you Hashem for Your guidance – may each one of us make the most of Your merciful ways.

4.13 Don't Expect What You Expect, but Expect the Unexpected

Hashem works in mysterious ways. Trying to interpret the news and what it means and where it will take us is an impossible task. I think Hashem will make sure that we can't figure it out, since He wants us just to trust Him and have faith in Him, and all will work out for the best. There is no truth in the news, so what is really happening, only Hashem knows for sure. Just take care of yourself by doing repentance, prayer, giving charity, doing the mitzvot, helping your fellow Jews and studying Torah. The rest will work itself out – Hashem knows what He is doing; His plan is infallible. The much more dangerous time that is coming up will be from natural disasters, not war. That is when Hashem will measure for measure take care of everyone on Earth – goodness for the righteous who follow His ways, and suffering for the wicked who do what they want without regard for their Creator.

I have mentioned the too-late-date. The concept which I have been talking about didn't come from me, but from our Sages. They are referring to Yom Hadin,

Judgment Day, and with a very likely day of Hoshanah Rabah being brought down. I'm the one who changed the name to the "too-late-date" to impress upon everyone the urgency of preparing for the day.

We are all judged at that time of the year – that is what Rosh Hashanah and Yom Kippur are all about. We, however, are told that our final judgment can be extended to Hoshanah Rabah. Do we get the immediate report card from Hashem? Never, but the judgment is entered based on how well we followed Hashem's ways in the previous year.

This year seems very different in the sense that our judgment may be determining the path of our entire eternity and not just the coming year. All this is known by Hashem. I feel His mercy will work in the favor of every Jew and even every righteous non-Jew. We will someday (I do believe not too far away) know all and receive our report cards. Most will be pleased since it will be after the suffering and, in some cases, punishment, is completed; in other words, after our complete rectification (Tikun) has been reached.

All I have been saying is make sure you don't violate the system Hashem has set up, but to use it to your great advantage. The world situation is pointing to the final judgment and redemption; we may be a lot closer than we think. Is it today? I don't know; but, I do believe that every day is a possibility and should be treated as a very significant day for everyone on Earth, spiritually. When the final results are known for each of us, all will be made totally clear. Hashem is merciful and loves us; we are in Good Hands. All we need to do is keep up the good work as we have been instructed in the Torah and all will turn out amazingly well. Just never forget the system is measure for measure – what you put into it, is what you will get out of it – in this case possibly for all eternity.

Is today judgment day? Yes, every day is judgment day. Is today more significant than days before? Probably, but we will not know until we get our final redemption and we know for sure that we did the right thing, or we were stubborn enough to defy the truth about this world. Can we still continue to grow in our ways by making changes and following the truth of the Torah (our handbook of life and in this case our survival kit)? Absolutely, as long as we are still alive on this Earth, we still have the opportunity to get it right. How much longer do we have to get our act together? That is completely up to Hashem and what He has planned for the near future.

If a war starts today, follow immediately by the devastation of earthquakes, floods, hurricanes, tsunamis, tornadoes, etc, you have your answer as to how much time you still have. Please, please, please take all this seriously. I have thousands of years of history that has been accurately told to us in prophecy to back up my plea. I am not speculating, but totally knowing and trusting the word that Hashem has given us. It is the Absolute Truth. Anyone who wants to gamble that this is not our destiny is a fool. It is so obvious what is happening in the world and where it is going. The specifics we won't understand until it happens. After all, "don't expect what you expect, but expect the unexpected." Just be completely reassured that we know exactly how to make it all come out favorably for each of us – don't fight the system but use it to your advantage. It is your eternity and the eternity of your loved ones at stake. Do the right thing and thank Hashem for His merciful guidance – you will be extremely happy about it and, probably, very soon.

4.14 Additional Note of Interest

I have pages that I wrote for my blog on the subject of who is Gog and where is Magog? I decided not to include it in this book for a few reasons. One is that even though I have references from scriptures supporting my thesis, most of the information came from extensive research that I have performed over thousands of hours. I feel very confident that I have disclosed correct information, but can I call it the absolute truth? If it is based on my connecting the dots, then there is a degree of speculation involved, and a question of its place in this book.

The second reason is, after a very extensive analysis, I didn't really know how much credibility the research would add to my basic theme – trying to convince you of the only way to achieve total happiness and success in life.

A third reason was: I asked Hashem for advice and through a very unlikely source I got my answer. Who the source was is unimportant; the fact that every time I ask Hashem for help, He responds – sometimes in the most mysterious way (like the episode I told of going to sleep with a question and having my father come from Heaven to give me the answer).

I can't leave the subject without giving you an answer as to whom I believe Gog is and where is Magog. The post on my blog also includes information about 911, the New World Order, the Illuminati, FEME camps and other favorite subjects.

Go to my blog and read these two posts for the answer (I suggest you read the two posts in order):

http://absolutetruth613.blogspot.co.il/2012/04/who-is-gog-and-magog.html

http://absolutetruth613.blogspot.co.il/2014/09/the-absolute-truth-that-nobody-believes.html

Of course, there is always the possibility that by the time you are reading this, Moshiach will be here, Gog and Magog will be known and of no consequence.

4.15 An Answer to an Important Comment

I received this comment on my blog reflecting a concern that many of my readers have. Here is the comment:

I'm deeply concerned for Israel, should these so-called leaders agree to a false peace? How can Yidden be so ignorant and weak? Unless the Moshiach takes charge, who knows what else the Israeli leaders will do? Our enemies don't worry me, but Jewish leaders currently have me scared stiff.

My reply:

You are absolutely correct that the people of Israel, especially the leaders, are the worst enemy that we have – after all they are the Erev Rav. The Erev Rav were the mixed multitude of corrupt individuals who left Egypt with us and were destined to return in the end of days. Need you be deeply concerned? No, since it is more appropriate to review what is happening and why.

The most important statement that I can make is: "Hashem is completely in charge and running the show." Hashem wants us to turn to him for everything, and to show that we know He is in control. We are in a time when the last thing Hashem needs is effective leaders. Why would we need Hashem if Netanyahu or Obama or any other leader is giving us what we need? It is brought down that when all the Jews do Teshuvah (repentance), the redemption and Moshiach will happen instantly. You may ask: "how is it possible for all the Jews to repent?

The answer is Hashem is making the world so scary, that we will get to a point when all the Jews will look up and say one word of Teshuvah "HELP!!!!!"

The point is that everyone in the world is realizing that there is no solution to the problems we are facing, such as financial, social, political, military, terrorist, crime, hatred, WEATHER, etc, etc, etc. No leader is helping; in fact, Hashem is making sure they are causing the problems as the Erev Rav did in the desert. Conclusion: there are no atheists in foxholes and since everyone (outside of Israel) is preparing to go in the foxhole, or the bunker, the end must be near – the time when all the Jews will turn to Hashem and say "HELP."

That explains the world; but, how can I say that we shouldn't worry about Israel and all the nonsense that is happening here? Good question! Hashem pays more attention to Israel than any other country in the Universe. One way we can see it is when we pay close attention to what is happening here, it is very different than the way things happen in any other country. We have seen so many miracles; it is hard for anyone, who pays attention, to not see the Hand of Hashem in everything. But Hashem still needs horrible leaders in Israel to get us to do Teshuvah. Let me give you some examples of what happens in this country when problems arise.

War

Israel has fought more wars since 1948 than any other country except possibly the US (but they fight wars to make money – lots of money). All the wars that Israel has been forced into were miraculous. 1948 was impossible. We had no army, no armament, no real strategy against 4 mighty, well organized Arabs Armies (who also had reinforcements from other Arab countries). And we won?

I have talked to military buddies of mine who went to West Point to become an US Army Officer. They have classes in history, reviewing the greatest battles that have occurred, to study the strategies and tactics that were used to win the war. Good idea – learn from history. West Point refuses to discuss the 1948 war since they know the top General for Israel was Hashem. I have mentioned that 1948 was so impossible to win that the Secretary of State under President Harry Truman advised him to vote in favor of the establishment of Israel at the UN. The Secretary said to Truman before the vote: "don't worry there are mighty Arab armies that will wipe out Israel after it is established." Hashem let him down.

The Gulf War was a very dramatic event since Israel was not even involved. Yet, Saddam Insane (whoops, I spelled Hussein incorrectly) wanted to wipe out Israel, similar to what every other nation in the world wants now. He sent us 39 scuds that did tremendous damage (actually part of the damage came from the wonderful Patriot Missiles that the US provided). There were thousands of building damaged including many homes that were completely demolished. With all the devastation, there was one death that occurred (and he was a known Jew-hater). Outside of Israel the Scud story was different. As an example: there was one Scud that hit a US military installation in Riyadh, Saudi Arabia that killed 29 soldiers.

There are books written on this miraculous Israeli experience, but I thought I would show you one of my favorite pictures:

A house was hit by a Scud and completely demolished it. The family was home. When the house fell on them, the structure enclosed them in such a way that they all walked out without a scratch. Impossible? Not when Hashem is there to protect you. There was another story about a man who was in his dining room and decided to go to his living room. As soon as he left the dining room, a Scud completely demolished the room. The living room was not damaged.

I previously mentioned the funniest thing about the Gulf War. The week of the war was statistically the best week in Israel since 1948 for fatalities – the lowest number. There was the one fatality, mentioned above, but all the roads were closed, so nobody got killed in a vehicle accident that week. Only in Israel would a war save so many lives, and send so many messages from Hashem.

The war with Southern Lebanon saw many missiles fired at Israel. Many of the missiles including many fatalities occurred in Arab towns. Hashem even steers the missiles.

There are books written about the tremendous number of miraculous events that happen in Israel even on a daily basis without war, so I am not going to continue on the subject. Well, maybe one more. There have been about 15,000 rockets, missiles and mortars that have been fired from Gaza into civilian populations in Israel. Many of which caused no injury or even damage. Why such a small amount of injury and damage over the ten or so years against Israel's civilians? We can only say: "this is Israel, and Hashem is our Protector." In fact, there have been numerous rockets that didn't make it out of Gaza and hurt Arabs instead. OK! I'm finished with that subject. Some day when we meet, I have hours of stories to tell you.

How about the inefficient leadership? Let's start by mentioning Ehud Barak offering Arafat 97% of Yesha (Yehudah and Shomron – what the world incorrectly calls the West Bank – more Jew-hatred). Arafat stormed out of the meeting and rejected the offer. Just as Abbas is now not cooperating with any peace overture being made, Hashem will continue to control our so-called enemies, so they can cover the deficiencies of our Israeli leaders, you know, the Erev Rav.

We have seen it throughout history where the enemy was controlled by Hashem to make the results match His will. The most famous example is when Hashem hardened the heart of Pharaoh by making him not give in until all 10 plagues were complete. Even then, Pharaoh chases after us only to be devastated at the Sea of Reeds. Was Pharaoh crazy and not paying attention? No, Hashem made him do what He wanted to get the results He wanted.

We are seeing the exact same actions of the leaders of today. Our leaders are making the worse decisions causing us turn to Hashem; and, our enemies are helping us after our leaders try to sell us out. All the turmoil in the world, especially in the neighboring Arab countries, is all part of Hashem's plan and is working perfectly.

You may ask, but I see Jews getting hurt, killed, etc. To answer that, we must go back to what I have been saying repeatedly in this book. We are here on Earth to perfect ourselves and to get as close to Hashem as possible – to reap a tremendous eternal future. **This is not the real life, but only a temporary testing ground where we have the opportunity to get it right and prepare for ourselves and our loved ones a very happy and tremendous eternity.**

But, we are still helped measure for measure according to what we do. If we turn to Hashem and follow his ways, we survive and thrive. If we turn to our own devices, in other words we think we know better, we fail and suffer. Hashem gives us help both voluntarily and involuntarily. When we don't do Hashem's ways, we have sickness, accidents, premature death, financial problems, weather problems, etc, etc, etc. Either way we will get our Tikun and go on to the Geula, the redemption, the happy ending. How good a Geula we get, is up to what we do **NOW**. I know I have said this numerous times; but, I still get many comments from my readers telling me of great problems in their lives and asking me "what should I do?"

One last thought about suffering, hardship and testing in today's world. We see tzadikim, great righteous people, get sick and have problems in the same manner as those who are not tzadikim. Avraham was given ten severe tests that many of us couldn't pass (I include myself in that group). When someone is at a very high spiritual level, he or she is given the opportunity to go much higher – after all this is the life that will shape our eternity. We are not to compare ourselves with anyone else, but we must evaluate where we are as individuals and what we must do for ourselves and our loved ones to maximize our eternity. I didn't want to bring in my Army training. but we must "Be all that we can be" and "we can do it in Hashem's Army."

Israel these days is completely different from the rest of the world. The financial situation is great, the weather is spring-like in the middle of Winter, crime is very minimal (where I am it doesn't even exist – remember, we don't even have a police force in our city). I could go on, but you have to be here to experience the good life. Also, stop reading the lies of the Jew-hating press – it is all false propaganda provided almost completely by the Arabs and the Erev Rav.

Everything that is happening in the world to every country and to each one of us as individuals is exactly according to Hashem's plan. Everything is for the good to help us. We may not be able to see it; and, even if we do, we probably can't understand it, but we must have complete faith that Hashem is running the show and loves us a trillion times more than we could ever love Him. Follow His ways and it will become obvious. All the messages of the great Rabbis, the Facilitated Communications individuals, scriptures, etc are from Hashem to help us. Read them and use the information wisely and all will be wonderful. The future looks extremely bright for those who want it so.

4.16 Now what?

So, I hear you saying:

OK. You convinced me that there are tough times ahead (we ain't seen nothing yet – what bad English). We are at the end of history as we know it, and it is time for action. You convinced me that we live in a system of measure for measure and that I must do things voluntarily to help myself and family or face involuntary hardship and suffering that will still be for the purpose of helping me (I just did a search to see how many times in this book I have wrote "measure for measure", including "m for m." The total was 51 times! Did you catch on yet?). I just prefer the easy and much more pleasurable method of help. I may not agree with everything that you wrote in this book (or anything that you wrote); but, I agree that I do not want to find out the hard way what the absolute truth is. I never was much of a gambler and, as you are saying, this is a sure thing, I like the odds.

I apologize for putting words in your mouth, but I am trying to read your mind; I truly want to help. The question that you must have is "what do I do?" You told me why but you didn't tell me how.

Obviously, we are talking about turning to Hashem for help. We see that world leaders are horribly inefficient (a better word is evil) and seem to be on their own greedy agenda not looking out for the good of the people they claim to serve. It seems overwhelming to jump in full force when I don't know how to swim in the vast sea of Hashem's will.

Let us take it one step at a time. I wish to give you an easy plan that will allow you to make very positive changes in your life without you even noticing. We are creatures of habit. If you decide you want to jump in full force and do everything immediately, you will fail and be disappointed. If on the other hand you and, hopefully, family take your time, you will see great progress and very

288

satisfying results. I've mentioned several times "Hashem does not judge us by what we know, He judges us by how we grow." Hashem knows exactly where you are going, what you are trying to accomplish and how sincere your intensions are towards serving Him and doing His will. He knows us much better than we know ourselves.

Even though I have believed in Hashem all my life, I tell people that I was raised Conformodox (I'm getting a spell check suggestion on that one). The first 14 years of my life I lived near three Orthodox synagogues. My Jewish education started at about age 3 (at a Jewish folkshul) and continued at a Hebrew school after regular public school, six days a week. At age 14 we moved and I found myself attending a Conservative synagogue, but I still continued my Jewish education and even continued to pray 3 times a day. When I started college, it all went downhill, but I still had a yearning for Jewish education. I belonged to a Hillel organization at college which opened up new areas of Jewish education that I didn't experience before. When I was in the military (drafted in 1966 for Viet Nam) I found that wherever I was stationed, there was something available of which I took advantage.

A little side note is that twice I actually had orders to go to war, Viet Nam and the Gulf War, but both times something came up and I was redirected to other duty (I was stationed with our fighting boys in New Jersey). I realized in later years Who was watching out for me (thank you Hashem, I don't like war).

There is no such thing as coincidence. I even spent 6 years attending Reform Temples, since that was all that was available at two of my duty stations. It was still part of my learning curve. When I finally settled down in an observant community, about 20 years ago, my family and I became Torah Jews and started to do outreach work helping non-observant Jews. At this point in my life, I had a very good appreciation for all Jews and all lifestyles. I am no longer Conformodox; but, I can relate to most people, since I've been there and done that (so to speak).

One thing that I must add is that all along the way the Jews that I met and even many righteous non-Jews were absolutely the nicest people in my life. I found that anyone who had strong feelings for Hashem, even if they weren't observant, were pleasant, beautiful people who I felt very privileged to know. When I became observant and realized the tremendous advantage I had, I felt very bad for these good people who could have had it all in life, but didn't know or even live the absolute truth.

Enough about me. Let's get you started on the road to happiness and success.

I obviously am talking to all levels of readers from totally non-observant to very observant people – Jews and non-Jews. I have three different sets of suggestions that I believe will cover all.

1. For Jews that are totally new to all this and even those who are further along the way (adjust this information to your level and needs):

Start talking to Hashem every day. I like to tell Him when I wake up and when I go to sleep that I love Him. He likes to hear that, but it is important to work on believing it. The important thing is to know that He is there to help us, and that we confidently want to have complete faith and trust in Him. Also, don't forget to thank Him for all He does. Being human, I guarantee when you start to see results, it becomes easier and even a very good feeling. You won't even feel like you are making any changes in your life if you take it slowly. That allows you and family to comfortably succeed.

Don't start to pray everything in the prayer book. Get yourself a good kosher prayer book, siddur (in Hebrew), and start to pray a couple of minutes a day (or more depending upon your level). I highly recommend a prayer book from Artscroll,

http://www.artscroll.com

Artscroll give commentary and instructions on praying that is invaluable to the newbie. Pray in whatever language you understand; but, if you read Hebrew, go for it. Artscroll has thousands of books on an abundance of subjects. Also, there are many, many other excellent publishers that have a world of knowledge waiting for you – there is no shortage of learning material. Even the web has great possibilities, but beware since the web can also bring you very evil deception. Definitely try to stay with books, if possible.

2. Start learning. Education is the key. The most important part of learning is enjoying it. If you are not enjoying what you are doing, you are doing it

incorrectly. Hashem wants this to be a very joyous experience. The key to picking out books to read is made easy after you ask "what is my interest?" Whatever subjects you enjoy, make time for those subjects, it helps avoid boredom. However, the absolute best way to learn is from someone else. An orthodox Rabbi, for men or a Rebbitzin (the Rabbi's wife) for women is usually the best. If you live in an area that is totally secular or even non-Jewish, there is a wonderful program called Partners in Torah (in the United States) that you sign up and spend about one hour a week, by phone with a learning partner. The program is free and totally flexible – you decide with your partner when and how long.

http://www.partnersintorah.org/

I am a user of Skype and have used Yahoo messenger. These systems and others allow you to learn with someone anywhere in the world. This means if you contact someone in the country that you live, an arrangement can be made for learning on the web. It is important that you deal with another human being. Learning on your own is not as enjoyable and makes asking questions difficult. Of course, there are many books that you will enjoy reading during your personal leisure time and should still be part of your learning program. Welcome to the 21st century. Geographical location is not an excuse anymore. An organization that is all over the world is Chabad.

http://www.chabad.org

I have personally learned with Chabad instructors and enjoyed the experience. You may find that no matter where you are, there is a Chabad organization nearby or even close enough by electronic media. Whatever you do, the important thing is start learning. Since I recommend individual or even group learning with real people, it makes is easy to learn at your present level. Tailoring your learning to your needs makes it much more enjoyable and productive.

Learn the mitzvot, commandments, and try as much as possible to start living the mitzvot, especially the most pertinent ones that you need immediately. This education should include learning about the laws of keeping Kosher and even paying attention to labels when you do your normal shopping. There are plenty of products on the market that have some type of kosher symbol which makes it easy to find.

A little side story to emphasize taking your time is that my wife and I were Kosher one full year before we were Kosher. We took our regular dishes and split them into dairy and meat (pretend) and started to buy only kosher products. We continued to eat in non-Kosher restaurants but only ordered things that were in accordance with the laws of Kosher (no dairy with meat as an example). In other words, we became very comfortably informed and we practiced for a whole year before we brought a Rabbi into our home to officially kosher the kitchen. Of course, my wife was happy she got new sets of dishes out of this. Items of glass and metal (such as pots, pans and silverware) can be made kosher even though it was used for years on non-kosher products). Once again education is the key and should be done enjoyably. Include the children. My son and daughter were more involved than we ever expected. Once again, I know Who helped us with that.

3. That is more than enough to help the non-informed and partially informed to have something to work on. What do I suggest for the totally observant individual who already is in an education program and knows the importance of improvement? Reach out and help your fellow Jew. If you work with a non-observant or even partially observant Jew, offer to study with that individual and further his or her Jewish education. Invite individuals and families to your home for Shabbos. It says in scriptures the best way to teach is over food. It works.

4. What do I have to offer to the non-Jew who sees the merit in all this and wants to do more? First of all, know that scriptures say very emphatically that all religions will disappear once the real Moshiach comes and the time of the worldwide redemption is upon us. Judaism is not a religion! Religion by its very nature is a belief system that was created by people. Judaism is completely from the King of Kings, the Owner of the universe. It provides the instructions from the One and Only living G-d. In Judaism, there is none else, only Him. We do not pray to someone else or through someone. Our scriptures are from Him and not man-made. Deviating from His instructions is foolhardy and very dangerous.

I have talked about the love of Hashem, but there is also the concept of the fear of Hashem. That does not mean that I am afraid of Him. It means that I am totally in awe of His infinite power and control and that I fear the mistakes that I may make in serving Him. After all, we are under a system of reward and punishment, measure for measure for what we do. The system is totally to our advantage if we live it correctly, and something to fear if we violate its instructions.

So what am I suggesting for non-Jews? There is a belief system from Hashem that comes from the book of Noah in the Torah. It is called the Children of Noah or B'Nai Noach (in Hebrew). It is the way for a righteous non-Jew to follow Hashem and honor Him and only consists of 7 commandments. There are websites that give good information about it. One possibility is:

http://www.noachide.org.uk

However, beware of websites that will give you misinformation with Jew hatred tactics to deceive you. Once again, it is your eternity and that of your loved ones that is my concern. You owe it to yourself to investigate.

You will notice that I never mentioned conversion to Judaism. Jews, by the word of Torah are tolerant of other faith systems, but have never advocated conversion to Judaism. If a non-Jew ever talked to a good Rabbi about converting, he would try to talk the individual out of it. To me, it is truly a personal thing. If a non-Jew has a tremendous love for Hashem and has a burning desire to serve Him in a much more spiritual way, I welcome that individual. If a man is in love with a woman who will only marry him is he is Jewish, that is the wrong reason to become Jewish. I have worked with dozens of converts including helping certain non-Jews make the change. Each one had such a strong desire to serve Hashem and learn Torah, that I was greatly inspired by their effort. We are told in scriptures that the person who was secular and became observant is at a very high level for making such a wonderful change in his or her life. But, the convert is even at a higher level since the change is even more drastic.

One last word on the subject. We are seeing another sign that we are getting close to the time of the Moshiach since the number of converts to Judaism is at an all-time high. There were thousands of new Jews in Israel just last year. Something is happening.

I have a request to all my readers. Since a very important part of serving Hashem is helping others, please tell family members, friends, neighbors and even your enemies about all that has been covered in this book. I feel that what Hashem has to offer could benefit about 7.3 billion people on Earth (the rest are on their own). It is an important part of serving Hashem – helping others.

4.17 Summary and a Decision to be Made

In Part 3 of this book I tried to spell out "what the Absolute Truth means to us" and what we must do to reap its benefit. Based on all this information, we are left with a choice of what it means to each one of us, and a decision about what to do about it. The choice is: do we continue with our fantasy life in this upside-down world and hope for the best? Or, are the scary events of the world making us realize we need to do something to protect ourselves and our loved ones, especially since it seems to be getting worse?

Nobody really knows what Judaism is. Whether you believe the absolute truth or not, it doesn't go away, so why not live it and discover that it is the key to everything that you want for yourself and your loved ones. Stop living the fantasy of this upside-down world. The true reality is your spiritual existence, not The Matrix you experience on Earth. In the near future the real world will emerge – a world of truth, of pure goodness, love, happiness and, above all, Hashem.

Let us look into the Torah for advice – good idea, since the Torah has the answer to everything. One of the worst, scariest events talked about in the Torah was when we were at the Sea of Reeds (or if you like the uneducated version, the Red Sea). We were on the beach, had the sea to one side, the mountains to the other side with only one escape exit that happened to have the Egyptian Army blocking it – ready to wipe us out (of course, they were being held at bay by a pillar of fire). The Torah alludes to the fact that there were four groups of Israelites with four different solutions. The first group asked Moses: "did you take us out of Egypt to die in the desert?" Their solution was: "let us go back to Egypt" – the Pharaoh has us trapped, he won. The second group said: "we outnumber them, let us organize and fight." The third group said: "let us pray and maybe Hashem will help us." The fourth group with complete faith and trust in Hashem "Jumped into the sea; it split and they walked through on the dry land." Of course the other groups followed after they reconsidered their decisions; and, they all watched, including Pharaoh, as Hashem destroyed the Egyptians and provided safe passage for the good guys (and gals).

How is this event the answer for us today? I'm glad you asked. The same four groups exist today. We have the first group that says: "let us just give the terrorists the land and maybe we will have peace. That of course has already failed in the Sinai, Southern Lebanon, Gaza and parts of Judea, Samaria and Jerusalem. The famous two state solution is ludicrous and suicidal. The second group says: let's fight, we are stronger than them and can defeat them. That has been tried many times, but with a loss of life for the good guys (and gals). The third group, the knitted skullcaps, say let us pray and hopefully Hashem will help us. That has been effective but with concessions to the enemy, including making concessions to the other countries in the world, and it has not completely solved our problem. The fourth group, the black hatters, the Torah scholars, is ready to jump into the sea. They (actually, we since I am in that group), completely turn to Hashem with faith and trust.

How do we turn to Hashem? By doing exactly what He has told us, which is the solution to the world situation. We pray, we do repentance, we live the mitzvot, we give charity, we study Torah, we help each other with total love and respect, etc. We do everything Hashem told us to do, and what will be the results? Hashem will bring the happy ending. The redemption of the world, new leadership with Moshiach as the servant of Hashem, the King of Kings, elimination of all evil in the world, happiness, prosperity, security, love for all with no more testing, no more sickness and even no more death. All the Jews and the lost tribes will return and will live in total peace in the land "Flowing with Mild and Honey," and even our departed will return in total happiness. What we have coming in the future is a level of joy and happiness beyond human comprehension.

Now your decision. Do you wish the happy ending of the fourth group or are you in one of the other groups who will enjoy the future but to a much lesser extent. Our eternal reward is measure for measure what we set up in this world NOW. Seven point three billion people on planet Earth have seven point three billion different levels of future according to the decision they make NOW. Are you a gambler that you know better than the Creator of the Universe, or are you catching on to the only choice that you have to succeed – both you and your loved ones? You may want to gamble with your future if you are that stubborn and that ignorant to the Absolute Truth, but would you be willing to shoot you loved ones on that gamble? That is a rhetorical question, yet there will be many who read this book and make the wrong decision.

As I said, don't do anything on my advice; but, investigate, do research to answer my favorite question: "What is Hashem's opinion?" It is your life and the lives of those who depend on you for help and direction. As it says in the Torah "Choose life," – it is your eternity in question.

In part 4, I wanted to give you a flavor of what really is happening in the world today – not the lies of the money making media, but the Absolute Truth according to thousands of hours of research that I have done for about the last 24 years. I also have observed tens of thousands of people to see the results of remaining secular and doing everything without Hashem's advice or following the only prudent way to total happiness and success.

It is not rocket science to see that the world is exactly as Hashem told us thousands of years ago, exactly how the world would be in the end of days. It is not rocket science to understand that everything that is happening in the world today is for our benefit to help us make the correct decision. I am telling you the obvious and only a fool would say "we'll see."

I have mentioned that very few people have any idea what Judaism really is. If you could forget the nonsense with which you have been indoctrinated and take a good hard look, you will see a very different picture. Judaism is not a religion, it is not even a way of life; "it is life itself."

One point that I have tried to impress upon you is that Judaism is not a spectator sport. We are the team on the field and the only winners in this game of life are the ones who do their part with great enthusiasm and effort. The result of all this is an eternity of great joy and happiness – yours for the taking. Get in the game and be a winner. With thousands of years of obvious proof we already have lived, the only choice is to join the winning team and reap a winning life. There is no doubt whatsoever that the world is very scary and getting worse. Don't wait until it is too late, start doing what you must do as soon as you close this book. It is your life forever and ever that is at stake.

I close with an unusual bit of philosophy from, of all sources, a Chinese philosopher named Laozi. He wasn't even Jewish, but what he said probably was given to him by Hashem.

Watch your thoughts;

They become words.

Watch your words;

They become actions.

Watch your actions;

They become habits.

Watch your habits;

They become character.

Watch your character;

It becomes your destiny.

If your thoughts are thoughts of Hashem, then your destiny and the destiny of your loved ones will be tremendous. If you live the Absolute Truth, you have found the true secret to everything, and it is good and wonderful. Guaranteed in writing!

May Hashem grant you and your loved ones goodness and happiness forever!